Praise for Unparalleled Catastrophe

The Arms Control Association Book of Note for October 2023

Winner of the 2025 Science, Technology and Art in International Relations (STAIR) Book Award from the International Studies Association

'This is a timely and excellent book as President Putin lifts a ban on the testing of nuclear weapons and is facing pressure to develop Russia's nuclear arsenal. This is one of the first books on the Third Nuclear Age and there will be many more. It has additional merit that it is short and rightly concludes that it is not enough to say "a nuclear war cannot be won and must never be fought". Unless we return to meaningful nuclear negotiations between nuclear weapon states, there will be a war in which nuclear weapons are used.'
Lord David Owen, Former British Foreign Secretary

'Rhys Crilley has provided a highly innovative and highly readable examination of what the move into a Third Nuclear Age means for us as humans. By weaving together worrying military and political developments with personal, cultural and theoretical insights, this landmark work sets the benchmark for the burgeoning field of critical nuclear studies.'
Professor Andrew Futter, author of *The Politics of Nuclear Weapons*

'The multidisciplinary approach of this book makes it an essential read for everyone seeking to understand and comprehend the contemporary nuclear politics.'
Aleena Saeed, in *Modern Diplomacy*, online, 2024

'What is fresh in Crilley's writing is a critical approach that recognizes the ways in which nuclear weapons, the climate crisis, the Covid pandemic, institutional racism, the injustices built into the global economy, and the dangerous rise of authoritarianism are interconnected.'
John Loretz, in *Medicine, Conflict and Survival*, 44:1, 2024

'This book is a valuable tool for students interested in nuclear weapons … it is also a useful tool for policy-makers and academics, to locate the study of nuclear weapons politics within the global politics of intersecting crises … The book serves both to give an urgent warning of the imminent 'unparalleled catastrophe' and to provide meaningful recommendations for how this endpoint can be avoided.'
Laura Rose Brown, in *International Affairs*, 100:2, 2024

Unparalleled catastrophe

Manchester University Press

Unparalleled catastrophe

Life and death in the Third Nuclear Age

Rhys Crilley

MANCHESTER UNIVERSITY PRESS

Copyright © Rhys Crilley 2023

The right of Rhys Crilley to be identified as the author of this work has been asserted in accordance with the Copyright, Designs and Patents Act 1988.

Published by Manchester University Press
Oxford Road, Manchester M13 9PL

www.manchesteruniversitypress.co.uk

British Library Cataloguing-in-Publication Data
A catalogue record for this book is available from the British Library

ISBN   978 1 5261 7044 6   hardback
ISBN   978 1 5261 9129 8   paperback

First published 2023
Paperback published 2025

The publisher has no responsibility for the persistence or accuracy of URLs for any external or third-party internet websites referred to in this book, and does not guarantee that any content on such websites is, or will remain, accurate or appropriate.

EU authorised representative for GPSR:
Easy Access System Europe – Mustamäe tee 50,
10621 Tallinn, Estonia
gpsr.requests@easproject.com

Typeset
by New Best-set Typesetters Ltd

This book is dedicated to my Mum, Dad, Rhiannon, Vida, and Evelyn. Thank you, for everything.

Contents

Preface	*page* viii
Acknowledgements	xii
List of abbreviations	xv
Introduction	1
1 'We thus drift toward unparalleled catastrophe': a brief history of nuclear weapons	19
2 'Fire and fury like the world has never seen': understanding the Third Nuclear Age	39
3 'I got it. I got it. Why don't we nuke them?': August to October 2019	58
4 'This is a high time for hypersonic missiles': November 2019 to January 2020	74
5 'The world of post-apocalypse movies': February to April 2020	87
6 'I can't breathe': May to July 2020	100
7 'Money meant for face masks': August to October 2020	115
8 'A force that would shatter our nation rather than share it': November 2020 to January 2021	131
Conclusion: It's not enough to say 'a nuclear war cannot be won and must never be fought': February 2021 to the present	144
References	161
Index	188

Preface

We live in an age of unprecedented nuclear danger. This claim is not just my own fear mongering and doomsaying, but increasingly apparent in the words, policies, and actions of the nine countries that possess nuclear weapons. Every nuclear weapon state is currently modernising or increasing their nuclear arsenals. At the same time, relations between these nuclear armed states are deteriorating, and prospects for peace and cooperation feel ever slimmer. As this book documents in detail, we have entered the Third Nuclear Age.

This new era of global nuclear politics seems grim. Longstanding nuclear arms control treaties that limited the number of certain types of weapons, and facilitated cooperation between the likes of Russia and the United States have fallen apart. Russia's brutal invasion of Ukraine grinds on. Donald Trump is once again President of the USA with the sole authority to launch his country's nuclear weapons. China's nuclear build up continues apace. North Korea now has approximately 90 nuclear warheads, has tested missiles that can reach the US mainland, and has sent its troops to fight for Russia against Ukraine. Dialogue between India and Pakistan is breaking down as both states develop new nuclear weapons systems. France and the United Kingdom were two of only three states at the United Nations to recently vote against an independent scientific study into the effects of nuclear war (the other state was Russia). And following the horrific events of October 7th 2023, Israel, a country that has nuclear weapons but keeps all information about its nuclear program top secret, has killed over 46,000 Palestinians (of whom over 13,000 are children) in military action that is consistent with a genocide.

Whilst much of the world faces economic hardship and a cost-of-living crisis, nuclear weapon states are spending billions more on nuclear weapons every year. In 2025 it is estimated that the nine states that possess nuclear weapons will spend more than $100 billion on nuclear weapons (to put that into perspective, the United Nations estimates that it would cost $70 billion a year to end extreme poverty). As I write these words, the prospect of nuclear weapons being used seems likelier than it has in decades, as the threat of nuclear war looms over us once more.

This book is one of the first books to outline how and why the world has entered a Third Nuclear Age. Our current nuclear moment follows the First and Second Nuclear Ages, where the central concerns of nuclear policy were bipolar superpower competition during the Cold War and the risk of nuclear proliferation to rogue states and terrorist actors respectively. What makes the Third Nuclear Age so concerning is that the world is increasingly one of multipolarity with three nuclear armed superpowers (the USA, Russia, and China), where relations between these and other nuclear armed states are increasingly adversarial as they engage in conflict with each other. Simultaneously, the rise of 'new' nuclear weapon states such as North Korea pose challenges, as do the increasing risks of nuclear proliferation to other states such as Iran. This era is also shaped by the unpredictable and unknowable effects of new nuclear weapons technologies and the integration of Artificial Intelligence in nuclear systems. The situation is further exacerbated by recurrent threats from government officials to use nuclear weapons, whether that be Donald Trump's threats of 'fire and fury' against North Korea, Putin's threats against Ukraine and its supporters, or the statements made by Israeli cabinet officials and US senators that Israel should drop nuclear weapons on Gaza and Iran.

These events occur as the arms control treaties that have helped nuclear weapon states cooperate and limit their nuclear arsenals for decades are now unravelling and collapsing in front of us. Treaties such as the Intermediate Nuclear Forces Treaty and the Open Skies Treaty have been consigned to the graveyard of history by Russia and the USA. New START – the major treaty that caps Russian and the American strategic nuclear warheads and bombs at 1550 each – is in critical condition after Russia suspended its participation in it, and the clock ticks down to its expiry date in January 2026. Russia's 2023 withdrawal from the Comprehensive Test Ban Treat (alongside the USA's failure to ever ratify it) also signal that limits on nuclear testing need a lifeline. The Nuclear Non-Proliferation Treaty (NPT) is also in bad health, as each recent annual meeting fails to deliver any sort of meaningful agreement, and nuclear weapon states fail to deliver on their disarmament obligations.

These aspects of the Third Nuclear Age – multipolarity, adversarial relationships and increasing conflict, new nuclear weapons technologies, unpredictable changes in nuclear policies, and threats from state leaders to use nuclear weapons – are significant but they are not the whole story. As I argue in further detail throughout this book, a focus only on these aspects of 'high politics' limits both how we understand, and how we can effectively respond to, the challenges of our current moment.

By way of illustration, government officials in nuclear weapon states such as the USA and UK are increasingly referring to the concept of the Third

Nuclear Age themselves, and are using it to justify their policies of developing new weapon systems and increasing their arsenals of nuclear weapons (arsenals that already have the ability to destroy the planet many times over). One senior American official in the Biden Administration recently declared that 'a new nuclear age' meant that the US was moving away from a nuclear policy that balanced nuclear deterrence and arms control and shifting towards 'a more competitive approach'. In the UK, the Chief of Defence Staff outlined in a speech at the end of 2024 how 'the dawn of the third nuclear age' and the 'disruptive threats' that constitute this new era 'demand a disruptive response' of increasing military spending and nuclear modernisation.

Analysts from the foreign policy establishment who are close to the Trump administration affirm this view that the age of arms control and dialogue between nuclear weapon states is over. They argue that the US and its allies need to increase their arsenals of long range nuclear weapons, deploy more tactical nuclear weapons in places like Europe, and convince the public that nuclear arms control and disarmament is 'unrealistic and even dangerous for the foreseeable future'. Some even insist that the US needs to resume explosive nuclear testing, as others suggest that 'arms racing towards arms control' may be one of the best options right now, and this seems to be the adopted policy for policymakers in many nuclear weapon states.

Such accounts of the Third Nuclear Age serve to foreclose disarmament, arms control, dialogue, and cooperation as policy options, whilst also playing down the humanitarian and environmental harms caused by nuclear weapons. This understanding of the Third Nuclear Age also stakes out a claim that the current security environment is one of inevitable conflict and that the only way to ensure peace is to prepare for war.

This representation of the Third Nuclear Age and how to deal with it through developing more nuclear weapons is problematic. Whilst arms races may have ended in arms control during the Cold War, they do not always end this way. History tells us that periods of intense armament often lead to war, and in the 20th Century, arms races were central causes of both World Wars. In the 21st Century, the fact is that the planet will likely not survive a nuclear arms race that breaks out into nuclear war. Science tells us that even a 'small scale' nuclear war involving the detonation of 100 'low-yield' nuclear weapons with the explosive power of 15 kilotons of TNT each, could lead to 27 million direct deaths and 2.5 billion people starving to death within two years due to the effects of nuclear winter. To put this into perspective, the atomic bomb dropped on Hiroshima had a yield of about 15 kilotons, but most nuclear weapons deployed by nuclear weapon states have a much higher yield of at least 100 kilotons.

Arms races in the Third Nuclear Age may not result in arms control but in the utter destruction of everything we hold dear. We were lucky to make it out of the Cold War without a nuclear confrontation, but luck is no thing to base the stakes of our future on.

Since the hardback edition of this book was first published, events have proven that there is still salience to my argument. Exterminism – a concept that underpins my analysis and alludes to the organisation of politics, society, and economics in a way that thrusts them towards violence that could exterminate states, peoples, and the planet itself – seems ever more apparent in the world around us; whether that be in Russia's continued war on Ukraine, America's withdrawal from the World Health Organisation, Israel's genocide of Palestinians, or our collective failure to address the climate crisis.

At the same time, popular culture's role in shaping how we think about the Third Nuclear Age is now clear following the global success of Christopher Nolan's award-winning *Oppenheimer* film, Annie Jacobsen's *Nuclear War: A Scenario* book, and the *Fallout* TV show. Resistance to the nuclear status quo has also recently gained global prominence as Nihon Hidankyo – a collective of Japanese atomic bomb survivors – won the 2024 Nobel Peace Prize, the Treaty on the Prohibition of Nuclear Weapons has gained more signatories, and the majority of UN member states (bar the UK, France, and Russia) voted to support an independent scientific study into the effects of nuclear war.

The Third Nuclear Age is therefore characterised by increasing nuclear risks and grim exterminist actions, but it also contains glimmers of hope for a better world. As nuclear weapons return to the fore of foreign policy discussions and once again dominate headlines, there is a renaissance of nuclear pop culture and a growing public awareness about the dangers of nuclear weapons.

Can we turn public awareness about nuclear danger into a mass movement and political action to promote peace, cooperation, arms control and disarmament? Can we as a species and planet navigate the crises of the Third Nuclear Age? Can we develop better ways of addressing contemporary challenges in nuclear politics beyond building bigger nuclear weapons and more of them? I hope so, and I hope that this book helps you understand how we got to where we are today and what we might be able to do to break out from our current malaise. I am writing these words on the day of Donald Trump's second inauguration, and it seems like the Third Nuclear Age is here to stay. It doesn't have to end with a bang. As I explain in what follows, we can view the Third Nuclear Age in more critical, pluralistic terms, where war and conflict is not immutable, and innovation, positive change, and cooperation is possible.

Acknowledgements

I wrote this book between 2020 and 2022, but it is built upon the education, support and encouragement I received in the decades prior. So thank you, from the bottom of my heart, to everyone who has helped make this possible.

In 2008, after the first month of my undergraduate studies, I returned home to see my parents. I told them that whilst I was enjoying university, I was very much looking forward to getting my degree and then moving to the Alps to live out the rest of my days snowboarding in the mountains. As a first-generation student I never imagined that I could study for a Master's, let alone get a PhD, teach students, and write a book. But here we are. I'm not in the mountains, and you're holding my first book in your hands. So how did we get here?

As an undergraduate I was blessed to have Laura Shepherd as my first-year teacher for Introduction to International Relations. It was Laura's outstanding teaching and encouragement that helped me understand that we can think about, and do, world politics differently. Thank you, Laura, for providing the foundations for my career in research and teaching.

I would have left university after three years if it had not been for the support of Cerwyn Moore, who first supervised my undergraduate dissertation, and was then stuck with me for postgraduate study after he helped me to find funding. Thank you Ces – I owe you big time! Nick Wheeler agreed to come on board as a second supervisor for my PhD, and I couldn't have asked for a more supportive supervisory team. Cheers Nick – your expertise on nuclear weapons rubbed off even when I was working on a completely different topic.

I was also very lucky to be taught by Linda Åhäll and Andrew Futter, whose influence can clearly be seen in this book – a critical security studies take on nukes! Thanks also to Marco Vieira and Ben O'Loughlin for constructively examining my PhD.

I was fortunate to make an incredible set of friends whilst studying for my PhD, and fellow PhD students and colleagues at the University of Birmingham deserve thanks: shout out to Ana Alecsandru, Josh Baker, Lindsay Clark, Laurence Cooley, Lance Davies, Jamie Johnson, Max Lempriere, Cherry

Acknowledgements

Miller, Dave Norman, Jonna Nyman, Liam Stanley, Dan Rio Tinto, and Sam Warner for all the good times in the Muirhead Tower and in the pubs of Harborne.

I owe thanks to colleagues and students too numerous to mention who have supported me as an early career academic in jobs at the University of Warwick, the Open University, and the University of Glasgow. What a privilege it has been to have such fantastic colleagues.

An amazing cast of collaborators and co-authors have helped me learn and write about the world, and I owe special thanks to Raquel da Silva, Ilan Manor, Precious Chatterje-Doody, Marie Gillespie, Robert Saunders, Corneliu Bjola, Susan Jackson, Deena Dajani, Vera Tolz, Stephen Hutchings, Alister Willis, Bertie Vidgen, Vitaly Kazakov, Louise Pears, Richard Johnson, Victoria Basham, and Owen Thomas.

The research that this book is based on would not have been possible if not for the generous support of the Leverhulme Trust and their Early Career Fellowship. I would never have received that fellowship if not for guidance from Naomi Head, Jonna Nyman, Georg Löfflman, Julia Welland, Liam Stanley, Andrew Futter, and Marie Gillespie.

Starting a fellowship at the University of Glasgow in the middle of the first COVID-19 lockdown was weird, so thank you to the friends and colleagues who were so welcoming. In particular, Katherine Allison, Maha Rafi Atal, Ammon Cheskin, Sophia Dingli, Alan Gillies, Naomi Head, Beatrice Heuser, Mo Hume, Andrew Judge, Georgios Karyotis, Ana Langer, Rhys Machold, Aykut Öztürk, Ian Paterson, Jayita Sarkar, Ty Solomon, Ali Wedderburn, and the IR Research Cluster at large, deserve thanks for shaping what would become this book. Thanks also to Blair Biggar and Samantha Ellis who provided valuable assistance along the way. Cian O'Driscoll deserves his own mention for spending the past few years asking 'how's the book going?' Here it is Cian, it's done.

This book marks my first foray into writing about nuclear weapons, and I have learnt so much from reading the work of so many scholars and activists, some of whom I've had the pleasure to meet online and in person whilst writing this book. Big thanks to Alicia Sanders-Zakre at ICAN for showing interest in the project from the start, the Third Nuclear Age team for inviting me to the University of Leicester to talk about the book proposal, participants at the 2020 BISA Global Nuclear Order Workshop, the 2020 NATO Defence College Early Career Nuclear Strategists Workshop, everyone who attended my online workshop on Nuclear Disarmament in 2021, and the crowd at the Prague Peace Research Centre's Annual Conference in 2022, as well as the academics at the TPNW 1MSP in Vienna.

I owe particular thanks to Beatrice Fihn, Laura Considine, Vincent Intondi, Becky Alexis-Martin, Kjølv Egeland, Catherine Eschle, Shampa Biswas, Ray

Acheson, Olamide Samuel, Rens van Munster, Nick Ritchie, Michal Smetana, Carmen Wunderlich, Neil Renic, Lauren Sukin, Stephen Herzog, Michal Onderco, Maren Vieluf, Ulrich Kühn, Fabian Hoffman, Rebecca Davis Gibbons, Sascha Hach, Moritz Kütt, Jannis Kappelmann, and Jamie Kwong. You all know way more about nuclear weapons than I do, and it has been a pleasure to meet and learn from you all.

Thank you to Rob Byron and the team at Manchester University Press for taking on this project, and to the anonymous reviewers whose insightful feedback helped improve the manuscript. Thank you too to Benoît Pelopidas for also reading a draft and encouraging me to tighten up the argument in a few key places. Thanks to Caroline Richards for copyediting the manuscript.

In an age of unparalleled catastrophe where global pandemics, climate change and the threat of nuclear war are now part of our everyday lives, I am grateful to friends and family who make life worth living and a better world worth fighting for. Friends from home, Birmingham friends, Glasgow friends, mountainboard friends, the BFC, spookfest survivors – thank you. I owe special thanks to Rickie and Rhona, Cortney and Stuart, Miriam and Callum, Nathan and Mel, Ali and Elly, Katie and William, Eilidh, Josh, and Ali for being so kind as to regularly ask how the book is going. Stevie McKenna also lends an ear and ensures that I still get to live the dream of snowboarding in the mountains every year – cheers, mate!

Is it weird to thank a dog in your acknowledgements? Either way, thanks to Priscilla, the daftest dog in all of Scotland, for the walks where parts of this book were thought through.

I couldn't have asked for a more supportive family. My Grandad and Grumpy both saw conflict first hand, in the Second World War and Suez respectively, and their reluctance to speak about their experiences spoke volumes to me about the horrors of war. Nana was the family matriarch, who taught me the value of family and hospitality. I hope that they would be proud of their grandson writing a book. Thanks too, to the Liggitt clan, and to Maggie and Mike for taking me in as a son-in-law and for being so supportive over the years.

Finally, thanks are due to the people to whom this book is dedicated. Mum and Dad have been the most loving, caring, supportive parents anyone could ever ask for. Without them I would not be who I am today.

Rhiannon, you are the world to me. You inspire me to be a better person every day, and I love you more than you will ever know.

Vida and Evelyn, I'm sure you will think that this book has far too many words and far too few pictures. You are probably right. Your cuddles and wonder at the world keep me going.

Thank you, all of you, for everything.

Abbreviations

CBRN	chemical, biological, radiological, and nuclear
CDC	Centers for Disease Control and prevention
CND	Campaign for Nuclear Disarmament
CTBT	Comprehensive Nuclear Test Ban Treaty
EU	European Union
ICBMs	intercontinental ballistic missiles
INF Treaty	Intermediate-Range Nuclear Forces Treaty
IR	International Relations
JCPOA	Joint Comprehensive Plan of Action (Iran deal)
MAD	mutually assured destruction
MIRVs	multiple independently targetable re-entry vehicles
NAACP	National Association for the Advancement of Colored People
NATO	North Atlantic Treaty Organization
New START	New Strategic Arms Reduction Talks
NHS	National Health Service
NPR	Nuclear Posture Review
NPT	Non-Proliferation Treaty
NWFZ	nuclear-weapon-free zones
PPE	personal protective equipment
SALT I	Strategic Arms Limitation Talks, 1969 to 1972
SALT II	Strategic Arms Limitation Talks, 1972 to 1979
SLBMs	submarine-launched ballistic missiles
SORT	Strategic Offensive Reductions Treaty
START	Strategic Arms Reduction Talks
TPNW	Treaty on the Prohibition of Nuclear Weapons
UN	United Nations
USSR	Union of Soviet Socialist Republics (Soviet Union)
WMDs	weapons of mass destruction

Introduction

On 2 August 2019 the world entered a dangerous new nuclear age. Michael Pompeo, the United States Secretary of State under the presidency of Donald Trump, officially withdrew his country from the Intermediate-Range Nuclear Forces (INF) Treaty: a bilateral agreement that prevented the USA and Russia from deploying nuclear and non-nuclear ground-launched missiles with a range of 500–5,500 kilometres. Originally signed by Ronald Reagan and Mikhail Gorbachev in 1987, the INF Treaty was a cornerstone of nuclear arms control, and helped to reduce the American and Soviet nuclear arsenals during the final years of the Cold War. In 1986 the United States and the Soviet Union had a combined total of over 68,000 nuclear weapons. After the INF Treaty came into force in 1988, this fell to 64,000. As the Cold War ended and as further arms control treaties were negotiated and implemented, the number of nuclear weapons deployed by the USA and Russia drastically declined. By the time the INF Treaty came to an end in the summer of 2019 both states had a combined total of 12,175 nuclear weapons either deployed, in storage, or retired and awaiting dismantling (Kristensen 2020, 326). Despite the success of the INF Treaty in reducing the number of nuclear weapons in existence, the United States and Russia allowed the INF to collapse, and in doing so brought about the dawn of what many experts are referring to as a 'new' or 'Third Nuclear Age' that heralds unprecedented challenges and risks to international security (Hersman 2020; Legvold and Chyba 2020; Futter and Zala 2021). In this era of 'growing catastrophic threats' (Cirincione 2020) this book chronicles the dawn of the Third Nuclear Age, analyses the impact that recent developments are having on global security, and warns that we are racing towards unparalleled catastrophe faster than ever before.

Thinking about nuclear weapons in distinct 'nuclear ages' may suggest that we can neatly fit events, ideas, and policies into distinct and separate time periods. This is not the case. Rather, throughout history, nuclear policy making, technological development, strategy, public opinion and academic analysis 'evolve and bleed into each other rather than neatly shifting at an easily identifiable moment' (Futter and Zala 2021, 3). Even so, the concept of a Third Nuclear Age provides a useful means by which to understand the contemporary nuclear politics of our time. In speaking of a Third Nuclear Age, we can recognise the continuities and changes with previous nuclear ages, and capture, in essence, the nuclear zeitgeist of our current moment. Much policy and scholarly work on nuclear weapons, particularly in the 'West', identifies a First Nuclear Age beginning in 1945 and ending with the end of the Cold War. This era was subsequently followed by a Second Nuclear Age that spanned from the early 1990s to the late 2010s (Gray 1999; Bracken 2003; Narang 2014). As we shall see in the next chapter, these nuclear ages were characterised by different developments, concerns, and challenges, yet some of the issues overlap and are still important today.

The First Nuclear Age was defined by concerns of nuclear war in an era of bipolar superpower competition between the USA and the Soviet Union. In contrast, the Second Nuclear Age was marked by fears of nuclear armed rogue states and terrorists in the context of the post-Cold War world and the global 'War on Terror' (Bracken 2003). The Third Nuclear Age, which is now well under way, is characterised by a multipolar world of potentially confrontational nuclear relationships, trilateral superpower competition involving the USA, Russia, and China, as well as the development of new nuclear weapons technologies, and dangerous developments in states' nuclear weapons policies (Legvold and Chyba 2020; Futter and Zala 2021). Nowhere have the dangers of this new nuclear age been more apparent than immediately after Russia's invasion of Ukraine in February 2022. Vladimir Putin's brutal invasion of foreign territory was accompanied by threats to use nuclear weapons to cause 'consequences never seen in history' to anyone who opposed him. Subsequently, strategic dialogue between the world's two nuclear superpowers has come to an end, and Russia has now 'suspended' its participation in the New Strategic Arms Reduction Treaty (New START) that limits the number of nuclear weapons that the United States and Russia can deploy. As the Secretary-General of the United Nations recently stated, we are now living in 'a time of nuclear danger not seen since the height of the Cold War' (Guterres 2022).

While there are continuities between different nuclear ages (Hecht 2002), and while there is also 'nothing natural or predetermined' about distinct nuclear ages, they are socially constructed concepts that have real-world effects as 'actors think and act them into existence' (Futter and Zala 2021, 3). Ideas about nuclear weapons and the perceived threats that underpin the contexts of particular nuclear ages become 'common sense' and shape how political actors make policy, whether that be through states building up nuclear arsenals and causing arms races in the First Nuclear Age; or through states cooperating on nuclear arms control treaties in the Second

Nuclear Age; or through states investing in new nuclear weapons technologies and withdrawing from earlier arms control agreements in the Third Nuclear Age.

These nuclear ages are not simply apparent in the realm of state nuclear policies, but they also manifest themselves in the popular culture of the time. From 1960s films like *Dr Strangelove* and *Fail Safe* that brought fears of nuclear superpower confrontation to the fore of popular consciousness, via television shows in the noughties like *24* that depicted terrorists detonating nukes on US soil, through to recent popular songs about hypersonic missiles, as well as a long-awaited sequel to *Top Gun*, each nuclear age manifests in – and is made meaningful through – sites outside of the traditional focus in our studies of nuclear politics. Research on the First and Second Nuclear Ages, as well as burgeoning studies of the Third Nuclear Age, are often focused on the realm of 'high politics' where the central issues are understood to be at the elite level of state competition, military security, diplomacy, and the development of new weapons technologies (Weldes 2014). Here, the sources of insight used to understand nuclear politics are official policy documents, elite statements, and reports about diplomatic interactions or military doctrines. These 'serious' sources and issues are undoubtedly important because, for example, documents such as the US Nuclear Posture Review set out the official American nuclear weapons strategy, and what state leaders like Vladimir Putin, Xi Jinping, Narendra Modi, Rishi Sunak, and Joe Biden say about nuclear weapons matters because they are the people who have the authority to launch their states' nuclear weapons. Even so, a focus only on elite, state-level issues and sources provides a partial account of what shapes and characterises each nuclear age. If different nuclear ages are socially constructed then we need to understand how this occurs in and through places beyond the realm of 'high politics'. Subsequently, one of the core conceptual arguments of this book is that if we want to understand how the world is entering a dangerous new nuclear era we need to be attuned to how the Third Nuclear Age is constituted, made meaningful, and manifested in sites and spaces beyond the confines of much orthodox nuclear weapons scholarship. In this book, then, I hope to chronicle and investigate the causes of the Third Nuclear Age that concern the realm of 'high politics' (such as the collapse of arms control treaties) whilst also exploring the many manifestations of this dangerous new nuclear moment that exist in the realm of 'low politics' such as popular culture and everyday experiences.

Everyday life and popular culture matter in the Third Nuclear Age for several reasons. First, state policies are made intelligible and possible through broader cultural repertoires of meaning that circulate in everyday spaces such as popular culture. The actions of state leaders do not occur outside of this context; rather, these actions and policies are shaped by how those leaders apprehend the world and understand their role in it (Weldes 2014, 230). One prominent example of popular culture's influence on nuclear policy is how the 1983 television broadcast of *The Day After* depicted the effects of a nuclear war in the USA and left an impression on President Ronald Reagan. After viewing the film, Reagan wrote in his diary that the film was 'very effective and left me greatly depressed … my own reaction was one of having to do all we can to have a deterrent and to see there is never a nuclear war'. Days later, in a public speech, Reagan stated that his dream was 'to see the day when nuclear weapons will be banished from the face of the Earth' (1983), and four years after this, Reagan signed the INF Treaty and helped to abolish, for the first time, an entire class of nuclear weapons from American and Soviet arsenals.

Popular culture and the everyday matter in nuclear politics for the second reason that not only do elites make sense of the world through their lived experiences and engagement with popular culture, but so too do members of the public (Grayson, Davies and Philpott 2009; Moore and Shepherd 2010; Crilley 2021). Popular culture provides people with 'synthetic experiences' of the world that shape their identities and beliefs (Daniel and Musgrave 2017, 503). These 'synthetic experiences' are especially important with regard to issues that people have not experienced first hand – such as nuclear war. Because even though 'nobody has ever fought a nuclear war … most of us can imagine what one might be like' because millions of us have seen nuclear war and its aftermath play out on screen in films, TV shows, and videogames (Daniel and Musgrave 2017, 504). Given also that nuclear weapons are hidden away on distant military bases and nuclear policy is formulated in top secret, people's opinions and ideas about nuclear weapons and policies are shaped by how they come to know about nuclear weapons through public sites they experience in their everyday lives such as in media reports, in Hollywood films, on television, in videogames, and on social media (Gamson and Modigliani 1989; Hogg 2016; Pelopidas 2021b; Taha 2022). In short, more people have learnt about nuclear weapons by watching *Dr Strangelove* than by visiting a nuclear submarine or reading the work of Dr Henry Kissinger. Popular culture, therefore, plays a prominent role in shaping our ideas about nuclear politics.

If we are to understand the Third Nuclear Age, we consequently need to move beyond examining how it is socially constructed through elite level statements, policies, and actions. This is also a pressing issue given that there is a 'thirty-years-out-of-date archive' (Scarry 2014, 17) around our understanding of nuclear weapons policies and crises because of the classified nature of nuclear weapons even in democracies such as the USA and UK. Consequently, throughout this book I draw upon contemporary news reports and publicly available sources alongside my own personal experiences to open up broader discussions of the issues at the centre of the Third Nuclear Age. Auto-ethnographical methods of personal storytelling and self-reflection can open up 'new perspectives on political dilemmas' (Brigg and Bleiker 2010, 781) by illuminating sources of insight beyond the realm of 'high politics', disrupting what is considered as 'common sense', and incorporating those who have been excluded or silenced by traditional accounts of nuclear politics (Cohn 1987; Naumes 2015).

Whilst personal vignettes begin each chapter, the central method used to make sense of the Third Nuclear Age throughout the book is discourse analysis: a study of how language, representations, and practices give meaning to the objects, events, people, and places they represent. As the French philosopher Jacques Derrida wrote in 1984, the 'atomic age' is

> *fabulously textual*, through and through. Nuclear weaponry depends ... upon structures of information and communication, structures of language, including non-vocalizable language, structures of codes and graphic decoding ... for the moment, a nuclear war has not taken place: one can only talk and write about it. (1984, 23, emphasis in original)

Language and representations are important in constructing the Third Nuclear Age, and this book is concerned with understanding how nuclear weapons are made meaningful through how they are represented in a broad range of sources that range from official policy documents through to pop songs and social media memes. This book chronicles and critically analyses a broad range of events and issues at the outset of the Third Nuclear Age in an attempt to identify who and what is driving change, how change is occurring, how these changes manifest in society, and what can – and should – be done to avoid catastrophe. This introduction now briefly provides context for this research and expands on the conceptual contribution of the book before outlining the structure of subsequent chapters.

Everyday life and the cultural politics of nuclear exterminism

On the day the Third Nuclear Age began with the collapse of the INF Treaty, I sat down to watch the HBO drama *Chernobyl*. Like many others, I was gripped by the horror of the world's worst nuclear accident as it played out on screen. What stood out, for me, was how the danger and trauma of radiation were made so vividly visible. While the US and Russian governments were talking about the collapse of nuclear arms control by using jargon in reference to 'Mk 41 launchers' (Ministry of Foreign Affairs of the Russian Federation 2020), the 'SSC-8 or 9M729' missile and the 'noncompliant missile system' (Pompeo 2020), *Chernobyl* explicitly showed the effects of nuclear catastrophe, and demonstrated how badly governments have handled such crises.

In *Chernobyl*, terrible state policies unravelled in clearly catastrophic ways. Supposedly safe nuclear technologies were a disaster waiting to happen. Government officials were servile liars, unsuited to lead or take seriously the responsibility of great power. The lives of ordinary people and workers were torn apart by accident and incompetence. First responders confronted radioactive material without protection and paid the ultimate price. They first complained of a metallic taste in their mouths, and then appeared extremely sunburnt within minutes. Soon, their skin was cancerous, burnt black and falling from their bodies as they lay alone in hospital, their relatives prohibited from visiting them due to their enduring radioactivity. All of this, supposedly, a fiction.

Despite the creative licence taken by the producers of *Chernobyl*, the effects of radiation depicted on screen bear a striking resemblance to eyewitness accounts of the explosion and fallout from that fateful night in April 1986. Lyudmilla Ignatenko's husband Vasily was one of the first firefighters on the scene in the early hours of the morning, and he tried to fight the fire without any protective equipment. By 7 a.m. he was hospitalised, 'all swollen and puffed up. You could barely see his eyes' (Lyudmilla Ignatenko in Alexievich 2005, 6). Within a few days, 'His skin started cracking on his arms and legs. He became covered with boils. When he turned his head, there'd be a clump of hair left on the pillow' (Lyudmilla Ignatenko in Alexievich 2005. 15). When Vasily succumbed to his injuries two weeks after the accident and was laid to rest, 'they couldn't get shoes on him because his feet had swelled up … They buried him barefoot' (Lyudmilla Ignatenko in Alexievich 2005, 18–19). At the time of her hospital visits to see Vasily, Lyudmilla was seven months pregnant. When visiting Vasily's grave two months later, she went into labour and gave birth to a baby girl named Natashenka, but four hours after being born, Natashenka passed away from cirrhosis of the liver and heart malformations. These birth defects have been linked to radiation exposure – which Lyudmilla was subject to in her visits to see her dying husband. 'How could I leave him? I thought my baby was safe inside me. We didn't know anything about radiation then' Lyudmilla said in a recent interview (Lyudmilla Ignatenko in Bendix 2019).

Lyudmilla's story has stayed with me, perhaps because my fiancée Rhiannon was pregnant at the time we watched *Chernobyl*, but Lyudmilla is just one of many who have been touched by the horrors of radiation and nuclear disaster. In Japan, the term *hibakusha* (the exposed) refers to victims of the

American atomic bombing of Hiroshima and Nagasaki in August 1945. Those *hibakusha* who survived these attacks have shared stories like Lyudmilla's. They describe a 'living hell on earth' (Tsuboi in McCurry 2015) where men, women and children were burnt black, their skin swollen and peeling off, as fires as hot as 4,000 degrees Celsius raged in a 'hellscape' (Matsumoto in Rothman 2017) of rubble and destruction – a result not of accident, but of intent.

On 6 August 1945, the American B-29 bomber the *Enola Gay* (named after the pilot's mother) dropped the first nuclear weapon on the city of Hiroshima. With the destructive power of 16,000 tons of TNT, the bomb instantly killed 70,000 people and razed around 80 per cent of all the buildings in the city. When the Americans dropped a second nuclear bomb on Nagasaki three days later, 40,000 people were instantly killed, a third of the city was destroyed, and almost seven square kilometres of land were levelled flat. According to early reports from Japan, the victims 'were too numerous to count' (Braithwaite 2019, 19), and the death toll caused by the effects of radiation after the immediate bombings has never been determined with much certainty. However, by the end of 1945 it is estimated that the American nuclear weapons dropped on these cities caused a total of 210,000 deaths.

In the aftermath of the atomic bombing of Japan, the US government sought to limit and control public knowledge of their harmful and horrific radioactive consequences (Blume 2020, 2). Henry Stimson, the US Secretary of War at the time, said this censorship took place because the US government 'was anxious ... I did not want to have the United States get the reputation of outdoing Hitler in atrocities' (quoted in Bernstein 1995, 146). At the same time, Japanese research and case notes into the effects of nuclear weapons and ionising radiation were confiscated by the US military and remained classified for years. News reports were censored, and over a hundred articles published in *the New York Times* in the immediate aftermath of the bombings did not mention any information about radiation and its effects on the victims at all. The US government hoped to further develop their nuclear weapons with more destructive force, but they wanted the public to remain ignorant of their devastating radioactive effects because they did not want nuclear weapons to become 'stigmatised' (Alexis-Martin 2019a, 16). One physicist involved in the development of the American atomic bomb wrote in a government report that 'a weapon has been developed that is potentially destructive beyond the wildest nightmares of the imagination' (Smyth 1945, 223), and news of the horrors of Hiroshima and Nagasaki eventually became public knowledge through investigative journalism, activism and popular culture representations that depicted the effects of radiation

(Hershey 1946; Blume 2020; Schwab 2020). In this way, the use of nuclear weapons in Hiroshima and Nagasaki signalled the start of the First Nuclear Age, where wild nightmares of destruction, supposedly rational theories of deterrence, and optimistic dreams of disarmament became global issues that shaped the world throughout the Cold War.

The fall of the Soviet Union signalled a decline in the perceived international importance of nuclear weapons as the security concerns of the Cold War gave way to a focus on globalisation, humanitarian intervention, and the War on Terror. However, at the outset of the 2020s, nuclear weapons are once again centre stage in global politics. The collapse of the INF Treaty, emergent nuclear ambitions in Iran and North Korea, alongside heightened tensions between the USA, Russia, and China, as well as Russia's invasion of Ukraine, have all once again brought nuclear weapons to the forefront of our minds. In what many observers are referring to as 'a new nuclear age' (Legvold and Chyba 2020), this book takes its title from a telegraph written by Albert Einstein after the atomic bombing of Japan. Published in the *New York Times* in 1946, Einstein's telegraph warned that 'the unleashed power of the atom has changed everything save our modes of thinking and we thus drift towards unparalleled catastrophe' (quoted in New York Times 1946, 11). If, in 1946, the world was 'drifting' towards unparalleled catastrophe, this book documents how the world is no longer drifting but racing towards unparalleled catastrophe at breakneck speed. As political actors dismantle important arms control mechanisms, develop new nuclear weapons and means of launching them, as well as modernising and continuing to invest billions of dollars in their nuclear arsenals, the new nuclear age is wrought by uncertainty, risk, and danger. In the chapters that follow, we shall chronicle this new nuclear age, critically analyse it, and examine ideas for what may be done to avert the unparalleled catastrophe that Einstein feared.

To think through the problems and crises of the Third Nuclear Age I draw upon and develop the work of the historian and activist E. P. Thompson alongside other scholarship from the field of critical nuclear studies. As one of the earliest and most ardent supporters of the Campaign for Nuclear Disarmament during the Cold War, Thompson spent much of his life campaigning to rid the world of nuclear weapons whilst also theorising about how nuclear weapons came to be an accepted part of international politics. To do so, Thompson introduced the concept of *nuclear exterminism*, which he defined as 'those characteristics of a society – expressed, in differing degrees, within its economy, its polity, and its ideology – which thrust it in a direction whose outcome must be the extermination of multitudes' (Thompson 1982a, 20). For Thompson, the development of nuclear weapons could not sufficiently be explained by the concepts of militarism (where states build up their militaries in preparation for war) or imperialism (where states exploit other states and people) because nuclear weapons do not simply bring the world to the brink of war but take it to the brink of annihilation, and threaten to exterminate civilisation through a nuclear catastrophe from which the world as we know it is not likely to emerge. In Thompson's view, the unparalleled catastrophe of nuclear exterminism 'will not happen accidentally (even if the final trigger is "accidental") but as a direct consequence of prior acts of policy, of the accumulation and perfection of the means of extermination, and of the structuring of whole societies so that these are directed towards that end' (Thompson 1982a, 20).

Whilst the concepts of militarism and imperialism have since become key to much critical scholarship in International Relations (IR), Thompson's thinking about exterminism has not gained traction even within the field of critical security studies (cf. a brief mention in Stavrianakis and Selby 2012, 6; a short blog post by Baker 2017; and a book chapter by Pelopidas and Mian 2023). This is a shame given that Thompson's ideas have much to offer if we want to understand how and why states continue to develop and deploy weapons that have the potential to exterminate all life on earth.

I build upon Thompson's work and apply it to analysing the Third Nuclear Age. I do so by understanding nuclear exterminism as a discursive configuration of language, representations, objects, and practices found across a broad range of sites within modern societies, concerned with the build-up and preparation for nuclear war – and the inevitable extermination that would follow from those weapons being used. Exterminism is not confined to government policy, a nuclear-military-industrial complex, the military or the arms industry. Rather, it extends 'through the whole societal body' (Thompson 1982a, 21) and is a 'cumulative process' (Thompson 1982a, 24) crystallised in culture, economics, and politics. For Thompson, writing during the Cold War, exterminism was underpinned by the confrontation between the superpowers of the USA and the USSR. Nowadays, following the proliferation of potentially adversarial nuclear relationships, the development of new nuclear weapons technologies, and the resurgence of superpower confrontation between the USA and Russia, and now with China too, it seems ever more concerning that 'exterminism will reach its historical destination' (Thompson 1982a, 25) as the structuring of today's exterminism is not binary but multipolar (Baker 2017). By drawing attention to the dynamics of exterminism in the Third Nuclear Age I hope that this book follows Thompson's ethical aim of illustrating 'how to break out of this doomed logic to alternative possibilities' (Thompson 1990, 141) and helping, as John Carl Baker implores us, to highlight 'the necessity of departing from the current exterminist trajectory' (2017) in our present nuclear moment.

Conceptualising nuclear exterminism as a discourse that extends across society and politics enables us to consider our own lived experiences of nuclear politics as important sites of analysis. A key feature of Thompson's studies was an attention to 'the *lived experience* of specific historical conjunctures' (Steinberg 1996, 203–4, emphasis in original; see also Thompson 1968, 1978), and he demonstrated that the exterminism of state nuclear weapons policies are only made possible and constructed as 'common sense' and legitimate because of how they resonate with the thoughts, feelings, and experiences of members of the public (Thompson 1982b, 45). Following Thompson's thinking leads us to recognise that exterminism and the Third Nuclear Age are not only located in the realm of 'high politics', but are present in the way that we think and feel about the world around us.

The thoughts, feelings, and experiences of exterminism are not distributed evenly. Some of us will feel anxious, scared, and terrified of nuclear weapons, war, and accidents. Others will be indifferent, unaware or uncaring about nuclear weapons, perhaps due to how the world has suffered 'nuclear amnesia' (Booth 1999, 12) and seemingly forgotten about the prospect of nuclear war after the end of the Cold War (Hoskins 2018). Others will feel powerful, strong, and confident about the value nuclear weapons have either in ensuring deterrence or in being a valuable tool to defeat adversaries (Press, Sagan and Valentino 2013; Sagan and Valentino 2017; Koch and Wells 2021). Others, such as the indigenous communities affected by the mining, processing, storage, testing, use, and disposal of nuclear weapons, already live an experience of exterminism and unparalleled catastrophe (Maurer and Hogue 2020, 29–33; Choi and Eschle 2022, 1133). These different circulations of representation, interpretation, experience, and feeling that extend across society, popular culture, and public opinion – or what the feminist scholar Sara Ahmed calls 'affective economies' (Ahmed 2004, 6) – reveal the complexities of nuclear politics and make our understanding of the Third Nuclear Age messier than a simple focus on state policy and military strategy. By placing the everyday manifestations of the Third Nuclear Age at the forefront of our analysis alongside the 'high politics' of state policy, military strategy, and diplomacy, we gain a more holistic comprehension of today's nuclear issues. Understanding how the Third Nuclear Age is present and resonates across the everyday lives and lived experiences of people across the globe may also provide us with the insights needed to better address the risk of unparalleled catastrophe. To reduce nuclear risks, we of course need the likes of Joe Biden, Vladimir Putin, and Narendra Modi to take action. However, that top-down, elite action will not happen unless there is pressure from those of us below. In order to build that pressure, we therefore need to know what the Third Nuclear Age looks like to the people – all of us – who live our lives in the shadow of the bomb.

From Chernobyl to COVID-19: why we need critical nuclear studies

I began writing the notes that would become this introduction in August 2019. From then on I set out to document developments in nuclear politics over the next year and a half with the aim of keeping a 'nuclear diary' until another foundational bilateral nuclear arms control treaty between the USA and Russia, New START, was set to expire in early 2021. As I began to write this book and returned to my notes on *Chernobyl* in May 2020, amid the first lockdown of the COVID-19 pandemic, and as the UK death toll began to hit the thousands, I reread an earlier paragraph. I felt an awful sense of resonance with what was happening around me: 'Terrible state policies unravelled in clearly catastrophic ways. Government officials were servile liars, unsuited to lead or take seriously the responsibility of great power. The lives of ordinary people and workers were torn apart by accident and incompetence.' The second part of this paragraph moves on to explicitly focus on the effects of radiation, but my discussion of 'first responders' who faced a threat 'without protection and paid the ultimate price', as well as those who suffered an illness that led to them being 'laid in hospital, their relatives prohibited from visiting them', eerily described what was happening as the coronavirus tore across the planet.

Parallels between Chernobyl and the pandemic have since become prevalent in public thinking. Some commentators view China's actions in the immediate outbreak as a cover-up similar to the Soviet Union's response to Chernobyl (O'Neal 2020). Other writers draw parallels between Chernobyl and the failure of governments to prepare for a pandemic, referring to the coronavirus crisis as 'Britain's Chernobyl' (Matharu 2020) or 'Trump's Chernobyl' (Schmemann 2020). Others have pointed out that 'Today, as in 1986, people are frightened and disoriented, trying to fight something that they can't see, hear, touch or smell, even though it has already changed our lives. What was true then still seems true today: disasters know no borders' (Plokhy 2020).

I intended to start this book with the discussion of the film *Chernobyl*, as I saw it as a terrifying, effective, and convincing way of highlighting what happens in a nuclear disaster. Popular culture plays a significant role in shaping how we think about global politics (Bleiker 2001; Grayson, Davies, and Philpott 2009; Moore and Shepherd 2010; Daniel and Musgrave 2017; Crilley 2021) and the effects of radiation portrayed by the actors on screen visualise and clearly depict the all-too-real effects of radiation suffered by those who lived around the Chernobyl power plant as well as Japanese victims of nuclear weapons. The government incompetence acted out on television made clear how worrisome it is to have such people in control of nuclear technology and weapons. I did not envisage that it would foreshadow a bungled response to a global pandemic where, by the time of going to print, over 6.87 million people have lost their lives because of the negligence, incompetence, and corruption of their governments and other state leaders (Abbasi 2020; Wallace-Wells 2020; Calvert and Arbuthnott 2021; Smith *et al.* 2021).

The very same people who have built up nuclear arsenals and invested billions in the modernisation and renewal of nuclear weapons programmes in recent years have, at the same time, chronically underfunded healthcare services and ignored warnings to prepare for security threats such as pandemics. COVID-19 has caused the deaths of nearly seven million people globally since the start of the pandemic, led to record global unemployment of 6.5 per cent of the world's labour force, and caused the biggest global recession since the Second World War. Simultaneously, nine million people now die from hunger every year, and a further ten million lose their lives to air pollution. And so it seems we are already in the days of an unparalleled catastrophe. Yet, as these crises unfold, nuclear risks continue to plague the planet, and, as I write, Vladimir Putin is making nuclear threats, a new nuclear arms race is beginning, all nuclear weapons states are upgrading their arsenals, and people across the globe seem to be more supportive of nuclear weapons possession and proliferation than ever before, even if they do not support them actually being used (Clements and Thomson 2021; Egel and Hines 2021; Smetana and Onderco 2022; Sukin and Lanoszka 2022). These developments could have utterly catastrophic consequences for life on earth. The shambolic response to COVID-19 from many of the world's governments also stands as an ill omen for how many states today would handle a serious nuclear crisis, accident or confrontation.

In this book we will trace the steps that are leading us towards unparalleled catastrophe, starting from an interlinked set of puzzles such as: Why are arms control treaties collapsing? Why are states developing new nuclear weapons systems? And why do we suddenly seem so much closer to nuclear war than we have in recent history? I explore these questions by examining how the Third Nuclear Age has developed over an eighteen-month period, beginning in August 2019 with the collapse of the INF Treaty, and concluding in January 2021 when New START was extended for five years by the USA and Russia. The conclusion reflects on how events after this date, such as Russia's invasion of Ukraine, further evidence the risk of unparalleled catastrophe.

The Third Nuclear Age may have once seemed like a flash in the pan that would come and go with the reckless incompetence of the Trump administration. With the election of a new president, Joe Biden, his subsequent renewal of New START, and the commitment with Vladimir Putin that 'a nuclear war cannot be won and must never be fought' in early 2021, it may have even seemed that stability had returned to nuclear politics and international security. Vladimir Putin's 2022 invasion of Ukraine shattered this illusion. Consequently, there is a pressing imperative for critical scholarship to understand the recent events that have shaped the Third Nuclear Age, and in this book I explore how the eighteen-month period between August 2019 and January 2021 was a critical period where many of the issues that will shape the Third Nuclear Age fomented in ways that continue to be significant. Now, perhaps more than ever before, we need critical nuclear studies to challenge the existence and investment in nuclear weapons as a source of security given that they continue to pose such existential threats to all life on earth (Burke 2016, 2). Moreover, we need critical nuclear studies to explain how and why security can be otherwise, where nuclear weapons are understood as a source of insecurity, and non-proliferation and disarmament are valued as positive developments for peace (Burke 2016, 3).

This book makes the case for critical nuclear studies, and furthers and extends it, by drawing attention to the 'high politics' of the Third Nuclear Age but also the lived experiences and cultural politics of exterminism that permeate everyday spaces. Thinking about the Third Nuclear Age through the lens of critical nuclear studies, and exterminism more specifically, encourages the use of concepts and ideas from a range of diverse scholarship. The new nuclear age, I argue, is shaped by our lived experience of *nuclear culture* that consists of language, narratives, media representations, and everyday sites of analysis that give meaning to nuclear weapons, construct identities, build power relations, and grant legitimacy to certain policies and actions (Derrida 1984; Burke 2009, 2016; Fishel 2015; Mutimer 2011, 2000; Ritchie 2013; Considine 2017). As feminists have shown, nuclear politics is also underpinned by gendered ways of thinking, speaking, and acting (Cohn 1987; Eschle 2018; Acheson 2019; Alexis-Martin 2019a). Therefore, my analysis is attuned to *nuclear masculinity* and how society privileges masculine values and behaviour such as strength and aggression in the realm of nuclear politics. Recognising how the history of nuclear weapons is intertwined with the history of colonialism also leads us to recognise the importance of *nuclear imperialism* – where nuclear politics is shaped by an exploitative economic, political, social, and cultural domination of other people, states, and places by those who possess nuclear weapons (Teaiwa 1994; Gusterson 1999; Abraham 2006; Biswas 2014; Broinowski 2015).

Together, these ways of conceptualising nuclear politics draw our attention to *nuclear harms*. These harms exist in a potential, latent form since nuclear war, accident, and catastrophe could potentially kill millions of people and cause an extinction-level event for planet earth (Burke *et al.* 2016, 517). However, nuclear weapons already cause real and existing harms to indigenous communities near uranium mines and nuclear testing sites in the Global

South (Hecht 2014), as well as having ecological impacts through testing and the storage of nuclear waste, alongside harmful impacts to the functioning of democracies due to 'the authoritarian proclivities of the nuclear state' (Biswas 2014, 190; see also Scarry 2014; Pelopidas 2021a). In conceptualising nuclear exterminism as a central aspect to the Third Nuclear Age, and by drawing upon related bodies of scholarship in the field of critical nuclear studies, this book provides a theoretically innovative political intervention into contemporary global security politics.

An outline of *Unparalleled catastrophe*

I begin with a chapter that provides a brief history of nuclear weapons by documenting the key characteristics of the First and Second Nuclear Ages. It is beyond the scope of this book to provide a detailed account of the lived experience of these nuclear ages; however, the opening chapter serves to introduce readers to the broad contours and main characteristics of each nuclear age. Whilst mainly providing a brief historical overview for readers unacquainted with the history of nuclear weapons, the argument of the first chapter is that the nuclear exterminism that E. P. Thompson warned of in the early 1980s was gradually tempered by the introduction of arms control agreements and the development and consolidation of a norm around the non-use of nuclear weapons. With this history outlined, Chapter 2 then introduces recent events from the start of the Trump presidency that led to the dawn of the Third Nuclear Age, before then developing the conceptual framework that is grounded in an analysis of nuclear exterminism that informs the subsequent chapters and draws upon approaches to nuclear politics that pay attention to the role of culture, language and representation, gender, colonialism, and the planetary harms of nuclear weapons (Derrida 1984; Cohn 1987; Chaloupka 1992; Teaiwa 1994; Abraham 2006; Burke 2009, 2016; Ritchie 2013; Biswas 2014; Eschle 2018; Alexis-Martin 2019a; Pelopidas 2020).

Then, laid out in chronological order, each further chapter covers a three-month period and examines the events, issues, and developments that occurred and shaped the Third Nuclear Age. Throughout the book each chapter begins with a personal vignette that illuminates my own experience with the broader issues explored in each chapter. Whilst I attempt to explore the unfolding of the Third Nuclear Age in a global context, at times my focus is often centred on the UK and the USA. This is because, as a British citizen based in Glasgow, I have a personal interest in Britain's nuclear weapons which are based less than an hour's drive from my home. Despite

Britain's declining global significance, which began with the end of empire after the Second World War and reached a recent zenith with the Brexiteer's retreat from European Union, the United Kingdom remains enamoured of a notion that it is a significant global player, and has recently announced an increase in the cap on the number of nuclear warheads it can maintain in its operational stockpile. The intimate linkage between British nuclear weapons policy and that of the USA means that the latter is also a key focus of my analysis. This allows for a detailed exploration of the issues shaping the Third Nuclear Age in two of the countries that will determine the nuclear future of our planet given their influence in global politics, as enshrined in their permanent seats on the United Nations (UN) Security Council. Indeed, given the military supremacy of the United States, its deployment of the largest nuclear arsenal, and its ability to determine the success or failure of global arms control, it is a country worthy of study, even if the study of nuclear politics is dominated by a focus on the USA (Braut-Hegghammer 2019). My focus on the UK and USA also demonstrates that the challenges of the Third Nuclear Age do not simply begin 'over there' with the rise of China and the resurgence of Russian hostilities. Rather, I hope to map out how the problems of the Third Nuclear Age arise on our own doorstep – in the political, social, and economic structures and agents of the anglophone nuclear powers. If the UK and the USA are to have a positive impact on the world in the early twenty-first century, then we need to recognise how the Third Nuclear Age has its genesis here too. Whilst I do make reference to what happens at the dawn of this new nuclear era in other places, I hope that scholars with better local and regional expertise than I can further account for – and more authoritatively analyse – the unfolding of the Third Nuclear Age in Russia, China, and beyond.

Informed by an attention to the lived experience of nuclear exterminism, and drawing upon a diverse range of sources, the following chapters analyse the beginning of the Third Nuclear Age and make sense of it in relation to important issues in world politics such as norms and emotions, popular culture, militarisation, the development of new technologies, global health, climate change, racism, sexism, and the future of democracy. Each of the following chapters takes its title from a quote made during that three-month period, and begins with a personal vignette that highlights how the new nuclear age permeates my everyday life. Rather than being an exercise in self-indulgence, these personal insights illustrate how the Third Nuclear Age extends beyond the corridors of power and into my life on the coast of Scotland, on the streets of Glasgow, and in my own living room during months of lockdown. I hope that as well as hooking the reader into the topics of each chapter, these vignettes serve as invitations for readers to reflect on how their own experiences are imbued with political significance, and how their lives are touched by nuclear weapons in myriad ways that often go unnoticed.

Chapter 3 opens in August of 2019 with the collapse of the INF Treaty, which I argue stands as the pivotal point at which the Third Nuclear Age began. In making this case I analyse the significance of arms control and its recent unravelling, but I go beyond a narrow focus on the 'high politics' of arms control negotiations and diplomacy to demonstrate how arms control is influenced by a broader societal norm – what some experts refer to as a nuclear taboo – concerning the non-use of nuclear weapons. I then illustrate how this norm is being eroded by, for example, Donald Trump's exclamation 'I got it. I got it. Why don't we nuke them?', when hurricanes were heading to the US mainland that summer.

Chapter 4, 'This is a high time for hypersonic missiles', covers the period from November 2019 to the end of January 2020. Taking its title from a song released by Sam Fender (Newcastle's answer to a young Bruce Springsteen), this chapter explores how new nuclear weapons technologies are a dangerous portent of the Third Nuclear Age that accelerate instability and run the risk of exacerbating tensions and causing crises. I go beyond the conventional account of new technology in shaping the Third Nuclear Age and argue that popular culture is central to shaping how the world comes to know, think, and feel about technological developments and nuclear weapons.

In chronicling the events of February to April 2020, Chapter 5 engages with the coronavirus pandemic, which seemed to many as though we were living in 'The world of post-apocalypse movies'. Here, I argue that rather than being tangential to nuclear politics, global health crises – such as the COVID-19 pandemic – are exacerbated by how states prioritise nuclear weapons and military spending as solutions to security threats. This chapter therefore makes the case for conceptualising security differently, and demonstrates how this redefined understanding of security could not only better prepare the world for crises such as COVID-19 but could also help the world to recognise and address the harms that nuclear weapons cause in the Third Nuclear Age.

Chapter 6 begins with the police murder of George Floyd in May 2020. His last words – 'I can't breathe' – resonated across the world as people took to the streets to protest against police brutality and racism. Even though the police murder of a Black American man may seem a far cry from the realm of nuclear politics, I argue that the racism and white supremacy that led to George Floyd's death on the streets of Minneapolis are a structural issue that permeates and shapes state institutions as well as much thinking and policy about nuclear weapons. To illustrate this point I examine the colonial, racist history of nuclear weapons, as well as modern, orientalist fears of China in the Third Nuclear Age, as evidenced in renewed calls for the USA to test a nuclear weapon for the first time in decades on the eve of the seventy-fifth anniversary of the American atomic bombing of Japan.

Chapter 7, 'Money meant for face masks', analyses events between August and October 2020 and begins by discussing the revelation that money given to the Pentagon for face masks and medical equipment was instead funnelled to defence contractors to make jet engine parts and body armour. I argue that militarism and the entrenchment of the nuclear-military-industrial complex across economics, politics, media, and society serves to make the world less safe. In particular I focus on the absurdities of the Pentagon awarding a $13 billion contract to Northrup Grumman to build a new fleet of nuclear armed intercontinental ballistic missiles (ICBMs). Such developments reflect a staggering level of exterminism given that in a bizarre hangover from the Cold War, ICBM silos based across the American Midwest are intended to act as a 'nuclear sponge' to draw an enemy attack away from larger American cities. Also central to this chapter is the impact that militarism and nuclear weapons currently have on exacerbating climate change, and the potential climate impact of even a small nuclear war that could annihilate all life on earth.

In Chapter 8 I cover the tumultuous events of November 2020 to January 2021, and I argue that there is a democratic deficit at the heart of nuclear weapons policy. Here, the twin forces of populist authoritarianism and the backsliding of democracy create, as the poet Amanda Gorman eloquently put it in her poem written for the inauguration of President Biden, 'a force that would shatter our nation rather than share it'. The central argument of this chapter is that the authoritarian conspiracy theory influenced populist movements of the modern era pose a serious threat to states, especially when those states have leaders with the sole authority to use nuclear weapons. As the storming of the US Capitol building made clear, democratic states such as the USA are not immune to instability and violence striking at the heart of state institutions, and the recent rise of authoritarian populists presents novel challenges to security in the Third Nuclear Age.

In the concluding chapter I reflect on the dawn of the 'Third Nuclear Age' and developments since the inauguration of President Joe Biden. The central argument is that the ills of the Third Nuclear Age have not gone away with the departure of Donald Trump. Instead, as Vladimir Putin invades Ukraine and rattles his nuclear sabre, as India accidentally launches a nuclear-capable missile into Pakistan, as China builds more nuclear missile silos, and as the UK increases the cap on its nuclear warhead stockpile, many of the issues analysed throughout the book are here to stay and make the Third Nuclear Age one of potentially unparalleled catastrophe. In this final chapter, I explore what can be done to avoid such a catastrophe and draw together some of the positive developments made during the period of analysis – such as the entry into force of the Treaty on the Prohibition of Nuclear Weapons in January 2021 – to suggest where we go from here.

Current developments concerning nuclear weapons will determine the future of our planet. We cannot be complacent. This book is an attempt to trace and make sense of what's going on, by examining how the Third Nuclear Age touches our lives and gives rise to the threat of unparalleled catastrophe. In doing so I hope to provide some ideas on what we can do to avoid it. However, if we are to comprehend the dynamics of the Third Nuclear Age, we need to understand the characteristics of the nuclear ages that have come before us. To that end, the next chapter begins in 1939 with a letter written under the looming shadow of the Second World War, as two physicists urge President Roosevelt to pursue research into nuclear weapons due to fears that Nazi Germany is already doing so. This letter, and Roosevelt's response, would lead to the development and use of nuclear weapons in August 1945, and would shape global politics for decades to come.

1

'We thus drift toward unparalleled catastrophe': a brief history of nuclear weapons

> The unleashed power of the atom has changed everything save our modes of thinking and we thus drift towards unparalleled catastrophe.
>
> Albert Einstein, 25 May 1946

In 1946 Albert Einstein warned that nuclear weapons were leading the world towards 'unparalleled catastrophe'. Einstein did not always think this way. Less than a decade earlier, on 2 August 1939 (eighty years to the day before the collapse of the INF Treaty), Einstein signed and sent a very different letter to the President of the United States, Franklin D. Roosevelt. The letter was written by Einstein's friend, the Hungarian physicist Leo Szilard, who had first conceived of a nuclear chain reaction and had originally patented the idea of a nuclear reactor in 1934. The two scientists wrote to Roosevelt asking him to develop research into atomic weapons.

Szilard's eureka moment about the destructive potential of nuclear weapons came after he read *The World Set Free* by H. G. Wells – a 1914 science fiction novel. The novel predicted the development of nuclear weapons and envisioned them being used in a war so destructive it brought about a world government because the only alternative was 'the relapse of mankind to the agricultural barbarism from which it had emerged so painfully' (Wells 2009 [1914], 214). In his memoirs Szilard wrote that once he had determined the physics behind a nuclear reaction he knew that it would have world-changing impact, 'because I had read H. G. Wells' (Szilard in Weart and Weiss Szilard 1978, 18). After Berlin-based scientists Otto Hahn and Fritz Strassmann discovered the fission of uranium in December 1938, and with Europe poised for war during the summer of 1939, Szilard grew concerned that Nazi Germany would soon develop and use a nuclear weapon. Szilard reached out to Einstein, and together they wrote a letter to the President with great urgency, warning that scientists were soon likely to produce 'a nuclear chain reaction in a large mass of uranium, by which vast amounts of power and large quantities of new radium-like elements would be generated' and that this would likely 'be achieved in the immediate future' (Einstein and Szilard 1939). Szilard's letter, signed and sent by Einstein, stated that he was concerned that 'this new phenomenon would also lead to the construction of bombs, and it is conceivable – though much less certain – that extremely powerful bombs of this type may thus be constructed' (Einstein and Szilard 1939).

Einstein and Szilard made three recommendations to Roosevelt in their letter. First, they advised that the US government create a liaison with scientists working on nuclear research. Second, they suggested that the USA should secure a supply of uranium because 'the United States has only very poor ores of uranium in moderate quantities. There is some good ore in Canada and former Czechoslovakia, while the most important source of uranium is in the Belgian Congo' (Einstein and Szilard 1939). And third, they recommended that the US government fund research into nuclear science.

On 19 October – a month and a half after the outbreak of the Second World War in Europe – Roosevelt finally responded to the physicists. He addressed his letter to 'my dear professor' and told Einstein that he found his correspondence 'of such great import' that he had convened a board 'to thoroughly investigate the possibilities of your suggestion regarding the element of uranium' (Roosevelt 1939). These actions, brought about by scientific developments inspired by science fiction stories, set the First Nuclear Age in motion. As Einstein and Szilard would both later come to regret, it was their letter that eventually led to the development of nuclear weapons through the Manhattan Project, and their subsequent use on the cities of Hiroshima and Nagasaki in August of 1945. It was Einstein and Szilard's letter that began the chain reaction of scientific breakthroughs and technological achievements that ultimately resulted in the deaths of over 200,000 people.

The first scientific proof that confirmed Einstein and Szilard's fears that a nuclear weapon could be created came in March 1940, when two refugee physicists – Rudolf Peierls and Otto Frisch – who had fled Nazi Germany and now worked at the University of Birmingham in England, determined that uranium could indeed be used to create a 'super-bomb' whereby 'Effective protection is hardly possible' (Frisch and Peierls 1940a).

In a detailed memorandum on their research, Peierls and Frisch stated that, 'as a weapon, the super-bomb would be practically irresistible' but that 'owing to the spread of radioactive substances with the wind, the bomb could probably not be used without killing large numbers of civilians, and this may make it unsuitable as a weapon for use by this country' (Frisch and Peierls 1940b). Despite this, under the assumption that Nazi Germany had or would be seeking such a weapon, they suggested that 'The most effective reply would be a counter-threat with a similar bomb. Therefore it seems to us important to start production as soon and as rapidly as possible, even if it is not intended to use the bomb as a means of attack' (Frisch and

Peierls 1940b). With these few sentences, the idea of nuclear deterrence was born. By the end of the year, as the war raged on, a group of British scientists reported to the British and American governments that a uranium bomb would be 'likely to lead to decisive results in the war' and that work on it should be of 'the highest priority and on the increasing scale necessary to obtain the weapon in the shortest possible time' (MAUD Committee 1941).

In response, Roosevelt approved a secret programme to develop a nuclear weapon in October 1941. The programme became known as the Manhattan Project, and on 16 July 1945 they detonated the first nuclear bomb in the desert of New Mexico with the explosive force of 22 kilotons of TNT. Those present referred to the Trinity test explosion as 'a vision from the Book of Revelation' (Chadwick in Braithwaite 2019, 63), and an 'awesome roar [that] warned of doomsday' (Farrell in Braithwaite 2019, 63). Less than a month later, the crew of the *Enola Gay* dropped the 'Little Boy' bomb on Hiroshima, and the crew of *Bockscar* dropped 'Fat Man' on Nagasaki – 130,000 people were killed instantly. By the end of 1945, another 84,000 would die from the effects of radiation.

The American atomic bombing of Hiroshima and Nagasaki had a profound impact on Einstein. Having played a fundamental role in the dawn of the atomic age, he soon expressed remorse for his contribution to the creation of nuclear weapons. In May 1946 the *New York Times* published a plea for support Einstein had telegrammed to fellow scientists and other prominent American citizens. In this telegram Einstein wrote: 'Our world faces a crisis as yet unperceived by those possessing power to make great decisions for good or evil. The unleashed power of the atom has changed everything save our modes of thinking and we thus drift towards unparalleled catastrophe' (quoted in New York Times 1946, 11). Despite these concerns, the 'immense crisis' (Einstein in New York Times 1946, 11) of nuclear weapons never went away. By 1949 the Soviet Union had developed and tested nuclear weapons. By 1953 both the Americans and the Soviets had tested more powerful thermonuclear weapons, the destructive power of which was measured in millions of tonnes of TNT rather than thousands. Nuclear weapons soon proliferated to other states such as the UK, France, and China, who developed their own bombs, and today there are now nine states armed with nuclear weapons: the USA, Russia, UK, France, China, India, Pakistan, Israel, and North Korea.

During the course of the Cold War, in the face of nuclear proliferation, crises, and close calls of nuclear confrontation, states negotiated various bilateral and multilateral arms control treaties in order to limit the proliferation of nuclear weapons to others, and to limit the number of nuclear weapons that they could possess. Until recently, these treaties have been developed, renewed, and adhered to in various ways. However, the global arms control regime is now unravelling. As the world faces unprecedented challenges from the COVID-19 pandemic, climate change, and rising authoritarian populist movements, alongside renewed tensions between global superpowers, the threat of nuclear weapons looms larger than it has for decades. While Einstein warned in 1946 that the world was 'drifting' towards unparalleled catastrophe, we are now no longer drifting, but are being actively driven towards unparalleled catastrophe by political actors who should know better, and by political, economic, and social systems that perpetuate a world where nuclear weapons are deemed to be an acceptable, if not necessary, risk to all of life on planet earth. In later chapters I explore how this is so. However, before examining the events that demarcate the dawn of the Third Nuclear Age, this chapter provides further historical context, and explores the central characteristics of the First and Second Nuclear Ages. This chapter illuminates the broad contours of earlier nuclear ages and argues that arms control agreements, steps towards nuclear disarmament, popular movements against nuclear weapons, and the consolidation of a norm around the non-use of nuclear weapons at the end of the First Nuclear Age and throughout the Second served to assuage the nuclear exterminism that E. P. Thompson warned of in the early 1980s.

The First Nuclear Age

To understand the Third Nuclear Age, we need to understand the nuclear ages that have come before. This is because even if these ages are social constructs, the agents, ideas, and policies that characterised them had real-world effects (Futter and Zala 2021). The First Nuclear Age has its genesis in the pioneering radioactivity research of the early twentieth century. It was started in earnest by Einstein and Szilard's letter to Roosevelt that prompted the development of nuclear weapons and their use by the USA during the Second World War. As the Second World War ended and the Cold War began, nuclear weapons became central to the security strategies of the USA and the Soviet Union. During the First Nuclear Age, which ended with the fall of the Soviet Union in 1991, the UK, France, and China also developed, tested, and declared their nuclear capabilities. At the same time, South Africa, Israel, and India developed and tested nuclear weapons but did not declare their nuclear status. Even with six other nuclear-armed states, the First Nuclear Age is marked by superpower competition between the USA and the Soviet Union, mainly because their nuclear arsenals dwarfed those of other states.

The First Nuclear Age also gave rise to the theory of deterrence. In one of the first examinations of the impact of nuclear weapons on global politics, Bernard Brodie noted that 'thus far the chief purpose of our military establishment has been to win wars. From now on its chief purpose must be to avert them. It can have almost no other useful purpose' (Brodie 1946, 62). Subsequently, the basic logic of deterrence – the idea that nuclear weapons are necessary in order to prevent other states from attacking and using them – has become a foundation of much thinking about nuclear weapons and international security in both theory and practice. Prominent International Relations scholars have even argued that more nuclear-armed states may make the world safer (Waltz 2003), and during the Cold War nuclear weapons were seen to be essential in preventing the Soviet Union from invading Europe.

Just a few months before the Soviet Union tested its first nuclear weapon in 1949, Western European states came together with the USA and Canada to sign the North Atlantic Treaty, thereby creating a security umbrella where 'an armed attack against one or more of them ... shall be considered an attack against them all' (NATO 1949). As the Soviet Union went on to detonate its first nuclear weapon, the North Atlantic Treaty Organization was set up to implement the treaty and to act as an organised military alliance to deter Soviet expansionism, curtail nationalist militarism in Europe, and promote European integration. Even if NATO did not declare itself a nuclear alliance until 2010 (Egeland 2020a), nuclear deterrence came to play a key role in its strategy, where NATO relied on the maintenance of nuclear weapons and the threat of retaliating with them in response to potential Soviet aggression (Heuser 1995).

Deterrence was given further credence during the 1960s when the development of intercontinental ballistic missiles gave rise to the idea of mutually assured destruction (MAD) within academic thinking and policy-making circles. According to the theory of MAD, the large-scale use of nuclear weapons by either the USA or the Soviet Union would result in massive retaliation in kind from the other, and would therefore result in the destruction of both. The logic of MAD therefore supported the idea that deterrence would prevail in ensuring an uneasy peace where nuclear weapons would never be used since it would be irrational for any leader to use them and risk the destruction of their own state. In 1953 the recently re-elected British prime minister Winston Churchill evoked a vision of MAD by looking towards a day 'when the advance of destructive weapons enables everyone to kill everybody else [as] nobody will want to kill anyone at all'. For Churchill, it was a 'comforting idea' that 'a war which begins by both sides suffering what they dread most ... is less likely to occur than one which dangles the lurid prizes of former ages before ambitious eyes'. He closed his speech that day by stating that 'we, and all nations, stand, at this hour in human history, before the portals of supreme catastrophe and of measureless reward. My faith is that in God's mercy we shall choose aright' (Churchill 1953), placing the fate of the earth in God's hands.

Several years later, in his farewell speech to Parliament, Churchill foreshadowed the significance that deterrence and MAD would play throughout the entirety of the First Nuclear Age. He said that 'we see the value of deterrents' because through 'a process of sublime irony' the world has 'reached a stage in this story where safety will be the sturdy child of terror, and survival the twin brother of annihilation' (Churchill 1955). This balance of safety and terror, and the thin line between survival and annihilation produced by deterrence and MAD, would continue to characterise the First Nuclear Age until its end in 1991.

Alongside the concepts of deterrence and MAD, the First Nuclear Age was also characterised by the development of tactical nuclear weapons alongside strategic nuclear weapons. Unlike strategic nuclear weapons which are designed to be delivered by large missiles and long-distance bomber aircraft (therefore playing a strategic role in threatening the interior land mass of adversaries and deterring them from committing undesirable acts), tactical nuclear weapons are designed to be used on the battlefield by artillery units or short-range means of deployment. One of the smallest nuclear weapons ever deployed was called the 'Davy Crockett': a warhead that could fit inside a backpack and was also known as the 'atomic bazooka'. Given that the range of the Davy Crockett was only 1.25–2 miles, the crew who launched it risked being killed by the fallout from their very own weapon. Despite this, in 1956, the US Army requested an incredible total of 151,000 nuclear weapons – 106,000 of which were for tactical battlefield use (Assistant Secretary of Defense 1978, 50). Although this request for so many nuclear weapons was never met, the US nuclear arsenal peaked at just over 31,000 nuclear warheads in 1967. The total number of nuclear weapons in the world reached a total peak in 1986, with 64,449 nuclear weapons in existence: of which the USA had 23,317 and the USSR had 40,159. The fluctuating volume of nuclear weapons during this period was caused by two other features characteristic of the First Nuclear Age: nuclear arms races and attempts to avoid these crises through the development of arms control mechanisms.

During the First Nuclear Age, the number of nuclear weapons reached dizzy heights due to how the prevailing logic of deterrence in the USA and the Soviet Union led both states to seek a military advantage by gaining more nuclear weapons than the other. In the absence of international control of nuclear weapons, the military director of the Manhattan Project, General Leslie Groves, said in 1946 that 'if there are to be atomic bombs in the world, we must have the best, the biggest, and the most' (quoted in Schlosser 2013, 75). This thinking shaped the First Nuclear Age as arms races became a common feature of the Cold War. These were often driven by the development of new technologies. In the 1950s the development of long-range bomber aircraft led to US concerns of a 'bomber gap' with the Soviet Union due to fears that they had more of these aircraft and a better capability of attacking the United States with nuclear weapons. The US government raised similar concerns later in the Cold War as the development of ICBMs led to fears of a 'missile gap'. In 1961 the CIA estimated that the Soviet Union had approximately 500 long-range missiles, whilst Air Force Intelligence warned that the Soviets might potentially have over 1,000. Soon though, satellite and aerial photography revealed that the Soviet Union only had four missiles that could actually reach the US mainland (Schlosser 2013, 269). Soviet disinformation designed to deter the USA – such as Khrushchev's claims that the Soviet Union was producing over 250 long-range missiles a year – was not critically analysed by US officials and thus contributed to the build-up of an arms race.

In realising that there was no such missile gap, and viewing the nuclear arms race as a source of insecurity that threatened the future of Earth, President John F. Kennedy advocated global nuclear disarmament in a speech to the UN in September of 1961. Kennedy pointed out that 'in a spiralling arms race, a nation's security may well be shrinking even as its arms increase', and he claimed that 'the risks inherent in disarmament pale in comparison to the risks inherent in an unlimited arms race' (Kennedy 1961). The young president warned his fellow world leaders that

> every inhabitant of this planet must contemplate the day when this planet may no longer be habitable. Every man, woman and child lives under a nuclear sword of Damocles, hanging by the slenderest of threads, capable of being cut at any moment by accident or miscalculation or by madness. The weapons of war must be abolished before they abolish us. (Kennedy 1961)

For these reasons Kennedy announced his intention to 'challenge the Soviet Union, not to an arms race, but to a peace race – to advance together step by step, stage by stage, until general and complete disarmament has been achieved'. As he closed his speech, Kennedy had his eyes set on the future. He claimed that those present in the room would be remembered

> either as part of the generation that turned this planet into a flaming funeral pyre or the generation that met its vow 'to save succeeding generations from the scourge of war'... Never have the nations of the world had so much to lose, or so much to gain. Together we shall save our planet, or together we shall perish in its flames. (Kennedy 1961)

Despite the Cuban missile crisis taking place the year after this speech, followed by Kennedy's assassination a year later – his dream of international cooperation to move towards global disarmament would soon begin to take form through various arms control mechanisms.

In 1963, the Soviet Union, the USA, and Great Britain signed the Partial Test Ban Treaty and agreed to stop testing nuclear weapons in the atmosphere, in outer space, and under water. This was a stepping stone to one of the most important nuclear arms control agreements of the twentieth century – the Treaty on the Non-Proliferation of Nuclear Weapons (Non-Proliferation Treaty/NPT). After four years of negotiations, the NPT was signed in 1968 and entered into force in 1970. It begins by stating that the signatories are 'considering the devastation that would be visited upon all mankind by a nuclear war and the consequent need to make every effort to avert the danger of such a war and to take measures to safeguard the security of peoples'. The NPT then goes on to note that its adherents are

> Desiring to further the easing of international tension and the strengthening of trust between States in order to facilitate the cessation of the manufacture of nuclear weapons, the liquidation of all their existing stockpiles, and the elimination from national arsenals of nuclear weapons and the means of their delivery pursuant to a Treaty on general and complete disarmament under strict and effective international control. (United Nations 1968)

Subsequently, the NPT sets out several key responsibilities for signatories. Nuclear-armed states are prohibited from transferring nuclear weapons technologies to non-nuclear states, and these states are in turn prohibited from receiving or manufacturing such weapons. At the same time, the NPT outlines that states can pursue 'peaceful nuclear activities' such as nuclear energy, and it created the International Atomic Energy Agency to act as a central organisation to oversee and verify the peaceful use of nuclear technology. The NPT also recognises that signatories will pursue 'effective measures relating to cessation of the nuclear arms race at an early date and to nuclear disarmament' whilst also seeking 'a treaty on general and complete disarmament under strict and effective international control' (United Nations 1968).

Originally agreed for twenty-five years, the NPT was signed by the Soviet Union, the USA, Great Britain, and forty other countries. China and France – the two other nuclear powers at the time – refused to sign until 1992. Over time, the NPT became one of the most widely supported international treaties, and now 191 countries have signed it. As such, the NPT is the only binding commitment from nuclear weapons states to the goal of global disarmament – even if, as critics rightly argue, nuclear weapons states have not taken this commitment seriously (Biswas 2014). In the First Nuclear Age, alongside signing the NPT, several states created nuclear-weapon-free zones (NWFZ). The 1968 Treaty of Tlatelolco banned the possession, testing, use, or deployment of nuclear weapons in Latin America and the Caribbean. The 1986 Treaty of Rarotonga did the same in the South Pacific.

The efforts of states to disarm were driven by the growth of a popular, global anti-nuclear protest movement. In the UK, the Campaign for Nuclear Disarmament (CND) was formed in 1958 in response to a government report that outlined British support for the bomb and admitted that 'some unforeseen circumstances might spark off a world-wide catastrophe' (Minnion and Bolsover 1983, 1). CND campaigned for unilateral British nuclear disarmament, and it would go on to become one of the most prominent protest movements in the world. Their logo, designed by the artist Gerald Holtom, and based on the flag semaphore characters for N and D (standing for nuclear disarmament) would become a 'universally recognised peace symbol', once described as 'probably the most powerful, memorable and adaptable image ever devised for a secular cause' (Driver 1964, 58). In 1982, a group of women set up a protest camp outside the US Air Force base at RAF Greenham Common, and in December of that year 30,000 women joined hands around the perimeter to 'embrace the base' (Laware 2004), becoming another global symbol of the nuclear disarmament movement. That same year, in New York on 12 June, the largest anti-nuclear protest the world has ever seen took place as one million people protested against the bomb. Throughout the First Nuclear Age, African American activists also played a pivotal role in the US anti-nuclear movement (Intondi 2015) and research suggests that the activities of anti-nuclear activists in the 1980s mobilised anti-nuclear sentiment in the public sphere and had an impact on policy makers moving towards nuclear arms control agreements and gradual disarmament at this time (Meyer 1995; Santese 2017).

Anti-nuclear movements were influenced by popular culture that made the horror of nuclear destruction loom large in the public imagination. The early days of the First Nuclear Age saw the publication of several popular novels such as *On the Beach* (1957) and *A Canticle For Leibowitz* (1959) set in a world after a nuclear war. Around the same time, Stanley Kubrick's *Dr Strangelove* (1964) satirised the 'rational' world of nuclear strategists with cutting insights like 'Gentlemen you can't fight in here! This is the war room!' exposing the ludicrous paradoxes of nuclear policy. Other films such as *Planet of the Apes* (1968) provided a fantastical vision of a world turned upside down in a post-apocalyptic nuclear landscape. On finding out that the planet of the apes is in fact Earth after a nuclear war, Charlton Heston's lead character exclaims, 'We finally really did it. You maniacs! You blew it up! Ah, damn you! God damn you all to hell!'

Throughout the First Nuclear Age the genre of post-apocalyptic fiction set after a nuclear catastrophe grew exponentially, and in the later stage of the Cold War blockbusters such as *Mad Max* (1979) and *The Terminator*

(1984), television shows and movies like *The Day After* (1983), *Threads* (1984), and *When the Wind Blows* (1986), as well as a diverse range of popular musical hits, from Kate Bush's *Breathing* (1980), Nena's *99 Luftballoons* (1983), and Iron Maiden's *2 Minutes to Midnight* (1984), reflected and shaped widespread concerns about the potential large-scale destruction of nuclear exterminism (Brians 1987; Lipschutz 2001; Williams 2009; Cordle 2017).

Popular anti-nuclear culture and protest movements were also influenced by the experience of nuclear testing, crises, accidents, and close calls. Concerns about fallout and the harmful ecological impact of nuclear weapons were popularised through films such as *Godzilla* (1954) where an ancient dinosaur is awakened by nuclear testing. *Godzilla* was made in response to the deaths of the Japanese crew on the fishing vessel *Lucky Dragon No. 5* who were poisoned by radioactive ash carried to their vessel – outside of the official danger zone – by the Bravo test of the first American hydrogen bomb in the Marshall Islands (Pearce 2018, 30).

Other events throughout the First Nuclear Age also led to a growing sense that nuclear weapons would exterminate life on planet earth either by deliberately, inadvertently, or accidentally instigating a nuclear war. In 1961, a bomber carrying nuclear weapons broke up over Goldsboro, North Carolina and two nuclear weapons fell to earth. One bomb broke up on impact, and on the other, five of the six safety devices failed when it hit the ground. As Robert McNamara, the US Defense Secretary, said at the time: 'by the slightest margin of chance, literally the failure of two wires to cross, a nuclear explosion was averted' (Center for Defense Information 1981). In the 1960s nuclear forces were put on high alert after a series of false alarms, including a US radar detecting incoming Soviet missiles which turned out to be a moon rise over Norway. US nuclear armed planes were also scrambled during the Cuban missile crisis after an intruder alarm was set off by a bear climbing a fence at an Air Force base.

The Cuban missile crisis of October 1962 is widely considered as 'the moment when humankind came closest to Armageddon' (Scott and Hughes 2015, 234) after the USA detected Soviet missiles on the island of Cuba capable of striking the American mainland. President Kennedy was advised to strike or even invade Cuba, yet catastrophe was averted when Khrushchev agreed to remove the Soviet missiles on Cuba if Kennedy removed US missiles based in Turkey. In the 1960s, nuclear weapons were accidentally dropped over Palomares, Spain, were lost at sea in the Pacific, and were destroyed in fires on planes at the Air Force base in Thule, Greenland. Then, as the decades went by, an explosion at an ICBM missile silo in Arkansas in 1980, and at the nuclear power plant in Chernobyl in 1986, led to widespread realisation about the dangers of nuclear technologies. Although it remained secret until 1998, in 1983 the world narrowly avoided nuclear war because a Soviet soldier named Stanislav Petrov ignored a message on the early warning system he was monitoring which said, with 'maximum certainty', that the USA had launched nuclear missiles at the Soviet Union. Petrov thought that the United States would launch an all-out attack with more than five missiles, so he ignored protocol and didn't report the incident to his superiors who would likely have retaliated by launching nuclear weapons at the USA. Petrov's actions gained him the moniker of 'the man who saved the world' for his role in averting nuclear catastrophe. At the end of the First Nuclear Age, even the head of Strategic Air Command, General George Lee Butler, stated that 'we escaped the Cold War without a nuclear holocaust by some combination of skill, luck, and divine intervention, and I suspect the latter in greatest proportion' (quoted in Schlosser 2013, 457). Research also suggests that luck played a far more prominent role in avoiding nuclear exterminism than effective control or risk management did throughout and beyond the First Nuclear Age (Pelopidas 2017, 2020).

As policy makers were brought to act in response to the dangers of nuclear crises and accidents, and as people protested in support of banning the bomb, some states came together to ban nuclear weapons from their territory, and the Soviet Union and the USA worked to develop bilateral agreements that would slow down the nuclear arms race and place limits and controls on, as well as reducing, their nuclear arsenals. The Strategic Arms Limitation Talks (SALT I) took place between the two superpowers from 1969 to 1972 and limited the number of ballistic missiles both sides could have. This led to the signing of the Anti-Ballistic Missile Treaty which limited the use of technologies that could be used to defend against long-range missiles. From 1972 to 1979, the second round of Strategic Arms Limitation Talks (SALT II) between the Soviets and the Americans aimed to add further limits to strategic nuclear weapons and launchers. President Jimmy Carter and his Soviet counterpart Leonid Brezhnev signed the SALT II treaty in Vienna on 18 June 1979. However, due to the Soviet invasion of Afghanistan, the US Senate refused to ratify it. Nevertheless, the USA and the Soviet Union voluntarily followed the arms limits in the years that followed.

In 1982 the superpowers began the Strategic Arms Reduction Talks (START) when President Reagan announced his intentions to build upon SALT I and II by not only limiting nuclear arsenals but reducing them. Reagan's 1983 announcement of a space-based missile defence system in the Strategic Defense Initiative (better known as 'Star Wars') caused the Soviets to withdraw from START, but talks eventually resumed in 1985. They eventually resulted in Reagan and Gorbachev ratifying the Intermediate-Range Nuclear Forces (INF) Treaty in June 1988. This treaty banned both countries from having short-, medium-, and intermediate-range ground-based missiles (both nuclear armed and non-nuclear ones) which could be used at distances between 500 and 5,500 km. The INF Treaty was in place until the USA and Russia formally withdrew from it in August 2019, and now there is no limit on these weapons.

The START talks would eventually culminate in the summer of 1991 when George H. W. Bush and Mikhail Gorbachev signed the START I Treaty. This barred the United States and Soviet Union from deploying more than 1,600 strategic nuclear delivery vehicles (such as missiles and bombers) and limited them both to 6,000 nuclear warheads. Given that only five years earlier the USA and Soviet Union had more than 63,000 nuclear weapons between them, these reductions and limits were an extraordinary achievement. Moreover, in September of 1991, Bush senior announced on national television that 'America must lead again ... we can now take steps to make the world a less dangerous place than ever before in the nuclear age' and declared that he was eliminating 'all of our nuclear artillery shells and short-range ballistic missile warheads' (Bush in Koch 2012, 24--5). This unilateral decision was reciprocated by Gorbachev, who agreed to eliminate tactical 'battlefield' nuclear weapons. These presidential nuclear initiatives complemented the START I Treaty, and have been referred to as 'the most spontaneous and dramatic reversal of the Cold War arms race' (Hoffman 2009, 383). Even with these progressive steps to reduce the risk of nuclear catastrophe in place, the START I Treaty was delayed from entering into force until 1994. The cause of this delay came in the winter of 1991 as the Soviet Union collapsed and the Second Nuclear Age began.

The Second Nuclear Age

On Christmas Day in 1991, Mikhail Gorbachev announced his resignation as leader of the Soviet Union. In a televised address he said, 'We live in a new world. The Cold War has ended, the arms race has stopped, as has the insane militarization which mutilated our economy, public psyche and morals. The threat of a world war has been removed' (Gorbachev 1991). The Berlin Wall had fallen two years earlier, and peaceful revolts and declarations of national independence had swept across the Eastern bloc. On the day after Gorbachev's speech, the USSR officially dissolved, thereby heralding the dawn of the Second Nuclear Age where many policy makers and experts, such as Gorbachev himself, felt that the world was moving away from the nuclear exterminism that had characterised the Cold War. The First Nuclear Age had been characterised by the proliferation of nuclear weapons, theories of deterrence, arms races, and measures to counter them through nuclear arms control. The Second Nuclear Age would share similar features, though new challenges and opportunities for disarmament would arise as the geopolitical landscape shifted with the end of the Cold War.

As the Soviet Union collapsed, the newly independent states of Ukraine, Belarus, and Kazakhstan found themselves in charge of vast amounts of nuclear weapons. In 1991, Ukraine came into possession of the third largest nuclear arsenal in the world. Approximately 1,900 strategic and 2,000 tactical nuclear weapons that had formerly belonged to the USSR were based on Ukrainian soil, though the country did not have the ability to use or launch them. With the political, social, and economic upheaval of the time, concerns abounded about the risks of there suddenly being four nuclear-armed states in a region where there had previously been only one, especially given that these new states lacked the resources to safely and securely store their nuclear weapons, let alone maintain them. Subsequently, at the end of 1991, Ukraine, Belarus, and Kazakhstan agreed to return their inherited stock of tactical nuclear weapons to Russia, and by 1 July 1992 they had all done so. The issue of strategic nuclear weapons proved somewhat trickier to resolve. The USA and Russia engaged the three newly founded states in a dialogue which culminated in the 1992 Lisbon Protocol. This agreement made Ukraine, Belarus, and Kazakhstan party to START I, and signalled that they would join the NPT as non-nuclear states and forswear their nuclear weapons. By the end of 1996, all three had transferred the last of their nuclear weapons to Russia.

In 1995 the NPT was indefinitely extended, and in 1996, other arms control mechanisms met important milestones. In January, the US Senate ratified START II. This agreement had originally been signed by George H. W. Bush and Boris Yeltsin in 1993, and it banned the use of multiple independent targetable re-entry vehicles (MIRVs) – a missile payload containing several nuclear warheads capable of hitting different targets – on intercontinental ballistic missiles (ICBMs). The Russian Duma, however, refused to ratify START II and it never entered into force, though it would come to be bypassed by the Strategic Offensive Reductions Treaty (SORT) signed by George W. Bush and Vladimir Putin in 2002. Returning to 1996, in September, the UN adopted the Comprehensive Nuclear Test Ban Treaty (CTBT) which aimed to ban all nuclear explosions in all environments. Yet, India, Pakistan, and North Korea have not signed the treaty, and, despite signing it, the USA, China, Iran, Israel, and Egypt have not ratified it. Due to this, the CTBT is still to enter into force as international law, even if most states have abided by it informally. Despite these limitations, both START II and the CTBT signal moves towards international agreements on arms control and represent serious attempts to limit the harms, risks, and potential for exterminism caused by nuclear weapons during the Second

Nuclear Age. When President Bill Clinton spoke to the UN General Assembly at the signing of the CTBT, he claimed that it would

> help to prevent the nuclear powers from developing more advanced and more dangerous weapons. It will limit the ability of other states to acquire such devices themselves. It points us toward a century in which the roles and risks of nuclear weapons can be further reduced and ultimately eliminated. (Clinton 1996)

For Clinton, one of the strengths of the CTBT was that it would 'create an international norm against nuclear testing' and his priority goals for the future included reducing the American and Russian nuclear arsenals and making 'deep reductions irreversible', whilst also aiming to prevent the spread of nuclear weapons 'by strengthening the Nuclear Non-Proliferation Treaty' (Clinton 1996). Boris Yeltsin, Clinton's Russian counterpart, shared similar views, later describing the CTBT as the 'most important instrument for strengthening the nuclear proliferation system' (Yeltsin in Jamestown Foundation 1999).

Alongside these commitments, bilateral arms control agreements would continue between the USA and Russia through SORT in 2002, and they would culminate in the signing of New START by President Barack Obama and the Russian president Dmitry Medvedev in April 2010. At the beginning of his presidency, Obama spoke of his desire for nuclear disarmament, announcing 'America's commitment to seek the peace and security of a world without nuclear weapons' (Obama 2009). New START was one of several 'concrete steps towards a world without nuclear weapons' that Obama oversaw which included reducing the role of nuclear weapons in American national security strategy, and negotiating the 2015 Joint Comprehensive Plan of Action (JCPOA/Iran Deal) to prevent Iran from developing nuclear weapons.

Even if the actions of the Obama administration never quite lived up to their lofty ambitions and the promise of a nuclear-weapon-free world, when ratified in February 2011 New START did help to reduce the number of nuclear weapons America and Russia possessed. Under the limits of New START, both countries could only deploy 700 missiles and bombers to launch their nuclear weapons, with a total limit of 1,550 nuclear warheads each. At the time of writing, New START has led to both states approximately halving their deployed arsenals of missiles and bombers, whilst also reducing their number of warheads by roughly two thirds. Even though New START doesn't include tactical nuclear weapons, and doesn't limit the stockpiled and retired nuclear weapons yet to be dismantled by both states, it has succeeded in reducing the number of deployed nuclear weapons and launchers whilst also building trust between the two nations through inspection, tracking, and verification measures that increase transparency and predictability (Gottemoeller 2011).

As the nuclear arms control expert Joe Cirincione suggests, 'New START implementation has been an unequivocal success story' (Cirincione 2018). Evidence for this claim is demonstrated by the fact that even as relations between the USA and Russia deteriorated after Russia's invasion of Crimea, intervention in Syria, and meddling in the 2016 US presidential election, both the United States and Russia continually met the treaty limits of New START and implemented the treaty including its verification measures (Williams 2018). New START was therefore a foundation of bilateral nuclear arms control in the Second Nuclear Age and it entered into force for ten years. Despite being threatened with collapse under the Trump administration, President Biden and President Putin extended the treaty for another five years in January 2021. However, in February 2023 Putin announced that Russia was suspending its participation in New START. In a lengthy speech, Putin stated that Russia would no longer allow US inspectors into Russia to conduct inspection activities, whilst also threatening to resume nuclear weapons tests. As it stands, the future of the last major nuclear arms control treaty between the two largest nuclear powers hangs in the balance as we enter the Third Nuclear Age.

During the Second Nuclear Age the development of more nuclear-weapon-free zones also signalled the salience of cooperative attempts to limit nuclear harms and temper nuclear exterminism. The 1997 Treaty of Bangkok, and the 2009 Treaties of Pelindaba and Semipalatinsk made the respective areas of South East Asia, Africa, and Central Asia NWFZs. In 2000, Mongolia also became a nuclear-weapon-free zone after declaring that the possession, transport, stationing, or testing of nuclear weapons were prohibited there.

Even with the success of nuclear arms control, the Second Nuclear Age was wrought by two major challenges: horizontal nuclear proliferation and the joint spectres of nuclear terrorism and rogue states. Whereas attempts to limit the proliferation of nuclear weapons to the former states of the Soviet Union were successful, several other states developed nuclear weapons only after the Cold War had ended. After India tested thermonuclear weapons on 11 May 1998, Pakistan surprised the world fifteen days later by exploding its own nuclear weapons underground in the mountainous Ras Koh Hills area of Balochistan – near the borders of Iran and Afghanistan. Pakistan gained nuclear weapons technology through the work of scientists such as Abdul Qadeer Khan who is known as 'the father of the bomb' in his home country. However, not only did Khan develop nuclear weapons for his homeland, he also sold technology that could be used to make nuclear weapons to numerous international customers including Iran, North Korea, and Libya.

Fears of these states obtaining nuclear weapons characterised the Second Nuclear Age. Due to their departure from international norms, their authoritarian leadership, and history of hostility towards nuclear powers such as the USA, these states were seen as unstable regimes which would threaten international security if they were to obtain nuclear weapons. After 9/11 and the declaration of a Global War on Terror against an 'axis of evil' (composed of Iraq, Iran, and North Korea), the Bush administration used the prospect of Saddam Hussein's Iraq having nuclear weapons as a pretext for intervention. In late 2002, Condoleezza Rice said in an interview with CNN that 'We know that he [Saddam] has the infrastructure, nuclear scientists to make a nuclear weapon' and that the USA was reluctant to wait for UN inspectors to search Iraq for evidence of weapons of mass destruction (WMDs) because 'we don't want the smoking gun to be a mushroom cloud' (quoted in Blitzer 2003). As the nuclear politics expert Gabrielle Hecht puts it, at the time 'war plans were in motion' (Hecht 2014, 2), and on 19 March 2003 the USA, alongside a 'coalition of the willing', invaded Iraq. Three days before this, Libyan leader Muammar Gaddafi saw the writing on the wall and sent an envoy to President Bush to say he was willing to dismantle his country's nascent nuclear weapons programme. In December of that year, Gaddafi made that announcement to the world. By then it was also clear that Iraq, its infrastructure destroyed and its people suffering under a post-invasion occupation, had had no nuclear weapons or weapons of mass destruction in the first place.

Three years after the Bush administration's invasion of Iraq, and after Libya's commencement of nuclear disarmament, global fears of a nuclear-armed 'rogue state' became a reality as North Korea tested its first nuclear weapon. North Korea had ratified the NPT in 1985, but withdrew in 2003, and in October 2006 it exploded a 1 kiloton nuclear bomb underground. Over the course of a tumultuous few years, the International Atomic Energy Agency sought to engage North Korea in talks, though these failed, and in May 2009 North Korea conducted its second nuclear test. This 2.7 kiloton explosion was detected by the international community because it caused an earthquake at the test site. Further nuclear tests took place in 2013, 2016, and 2017, alongside the testing of long-range missiles capable of reaching the US mainland. In condemning the 2016 North Korean nuclear tests, President Obama noted that 'North Korea stands out as the only country to have tested nuclear weapons this century' and that the US was committed 'to take necessary steps to defend our allies in the region, including through … the commitment to provide extended deterrence, guaranteed by the full spectrum of U.S. defense capabilities' (Obama 2016).

Throughout the Second Nuclear Age, due to the break-up of the Soviet Union and the proliferation of nuclear-armed states, many policy makers and academic analysts were concerned that theories of deterrence were no longer relevant. Grounded in oriental, colonial understandings of order, 'Western' states viewed these 'rogue states' – and others such as Pakistan – as being beyond the confines of rationality due to the political extremism of their governing regimes (Hecht 2014). Alongside these concerns, many 'Western' states were worried about the threat of nuclear terrorism, especially after the events of 9/11 made the dangers of mass casualty acts of suicidal violence conducted by non-state actors all too apparent. As terrorists were now willing to kill thousands of people by sacrificing themselves without providing any warning or making political demands, states were concerned that nuclear deterrence was no longer relevant as non-state terrorist actors could not be deterred from attempting to obtain and use a nuclear device to inflict untold damage.

In October 2002, in the build-up to the invasion of Iraq, George W. Bush warned that Saddam Hussein was 'on a drive toward an arsenal of terror' and 'seeking nuclear weapons' (Bush 2002). That same month, the second season of the popular American TV drama *24* saw its special agent protagonist Jack Bauer attempt to find and dispose of a nuclear bomb planted by terrorists in Los Angeles. Whilst he was successful in this season, several years later, in the sixth season of *24*, Bauer watched in horror as terrorists detonated a nuclear bomb and destroyed the LA neighbourhood of Valencia. These acts of nuclear terrorism, though fictional, highlight how fears of nuclear armed terrorists were prominent in the popular imagination throughout the Second Nuclear Age, especially during the War on Terror, where alongside intervening in states that were allegedly linked with terrorists, the international community made securing fissile material such as uranium and plutonium a top priority. Anxieties around nuclear exterminism remained apparent in other popular cultural artefacts throughout the Second Nuclear Age (Taylor 1998; Jacobs 2010; Fey, Poppe, and Rauch 2016) such as military first-person shooter videogames *Call of Duty* and *Battlefield* and the post-apocalyptic nuclear wastelands of the *Fallout* and *Metro 2033* games. Around this time, a small but committed 'prepper' movement began to grow across the USA, where preppers prepare for doomsday by building bunkers, learning survival skills, and stockpiling resources in case of nuclear war (Garrett 2020). Despite these examples, throughout the Second Nuclear Age fears of nuclear extremism 'receded with the Cold War' (Latham 2016, 365) and played a less prominent role in popular culture and the public imagination than they did throughout the First Nuclear Age.

Alongside the waning of nuclear weapons as a source of anxiety in popular culture, the accidents and close calls of the Second Nuclear Age also failed to capture the public imagination in ways that the likes of the Cuban missile crisis and Chernobyl did. This is not to say that there were no nuclear crises during this time. In 1995 a Russian early warning system detected a missile launch from Norway, and in response Russia put its nuclear forces on full alert as Boris Yeltsin prepared for a retaliatory launch and became the first world leader in history to activate his nuclear briefcase and retrieve nuclear launch codes. Thankfully, Russian leaders realised that there were no other missiles being launched, and it turned out that the early warning system had detected a Norwegian rocket launched for scientific purposes. The Norwegians had told the Russians about the scheduled launch but the information failed to reach the appropriate personnel (Schlosser 2013, 478).

More recently, in 2003, half of all US Air Force units in charge of nuclear weapons failed safety and security checks even though they had advance warning of the inspections, and in 2007 a US B-52 bomber was erroneously loaded with live nuclear-armed missiles, then left without special guard overnight before being flown over 1,500 miles from North Dakota to Louisiana where it sat for another eight hours without guards before anyone realised the plane had nuclear weapons strapped to its wing. Commenting on the incident, a retired Air Force General who was commander of US Strategic Command between 1996 and 1998 said: 'I have been in the nuclear business since 1966 and am not aware of any incident more disturbing' (Habiger in Warrick and Pincus 2007). In October 2010, an American ICBM launch control centre lost communication with fifty missile silos carrying nuclear warheads. Due to a malfunctioning computer chip, American safeguards to prevent the unauthorised launch of nuclear weapons were compromised. Since then, US nuclear weapons have been found to be vulnerable to hacking (Futter 2018), US personnel responsible for overseeing nuclear weapons have been found asleep in charge of ICBMs, been sacked for using drugs and heavy drinking (McCarthy 2014), and one in five of the Air Force's nuclear missile officers were found to have cheated in proficiency tests (BBC News 2014). At the time of these revelations the commander in charge of the Air Force's nuclear weapons stated that the biggest threat to America 'is an accident. The greatest risk to my force is doing something stupid' (Kowalski quoted in Harkinson 2014). Yet, despite the prospect of inadvertent nuclear exterminism through accident or incompetence, these issues failed to capture our imaginations, mainly because of an illusion of competent command and control over nuclear weapons coupled with a growing sense that there was a strong norm around the non-use of nuclear weapons that would keep us safe from exterminism.

Even with concerns about the efficacy of deterrence in the Second Nuclear Age – due to the proliferation of nuclear powers and terrorist actors who would not be susceptible to deterrence – ideas about a 'nuclear taboo' (Tannenwald 2007) became prominent in academic and policy circles. According to the IR expert Nina Tannenwald, deterrence is not sufficient to explain the non-use of nuclear weapons after 1945, and for her, the reason that nuclear weapons have not been used since the US bombing of Nagasaki is because 'a powerful taboo against the use of nuclear weapons has developed in the global system … [and] has stigmatised nuclear weapons as unacceptable weapons' (Tannenwald 2007, 2). Through the development of what some view as a strong global norm, states such as the USA have not used nuclear weapons (even when they potentially could have used them against, for example, non-nuclear-armed enemies) as 'states are not free to resort to nuclear weapons without incurring moral opprobrium or political costs' (Tannenwald 2007, 362). Critics of this position have argued that instead of a taboo, there is only a much weaker tradition of non-use because states are actually prepared to use nuclear weapons and often outline how and why they would do so in their nuclear strategies and military doctrine (Paul 2009, 2010). Either way, the decades-long history of nuclear weapon non-use as well as the strengthening of nuclear arms control and tangible steps towards nuclear disarmament throughout the Second Nuclear Age had 'brought about important benefits' (Freedman 2013, 105), even if they did not constitute a 'golden age' of disarmament (Egeland 2020b, 1387), and instead led to a sense that the threat of planetary nuclear catastrophe was largely one of the past. Indeed, nuclear arms control and the nuclear taboo have recently been criticised for sustaining the existence of nuclear weapons and allowing states to continue to possess nuclear weapons rather than abolishing them for good (Acheson 2022; Pelopidas and Mian 2023). Therefore, whilst arms control and the nuclear taboo are perhaps necessary to reduce the risk of nuclear catastrophe, they are not sufficient to remove that risk altogether – a fact that has become all too apparent at the dawn of the Third Nuclear Age.

Conclusion

The First Nuclear Age was set in motion by Einstein and Szilard's letter to President Roosevelt encouraging him to develop nuclear weapons. Those weapons were eventually used by the Americans when they dropped them on the Japanese cities of Hiroshima and Nagasaki in August 1945. Although this led to Einstein warning of a world drifting towards unparalleled catastrophe and regretting his role in developing nuclear weapons, it was not until much later that states began to implement nuclear arms control and disarmament measures to avoid disaster. After a Cold War characterised by nuclear proliferation, bilateral superpower competition, arms races, popular culture concerned with nuclear apocalypse, and a series of nuclear crises and accidents that captured the public's attention and led to mass protests against nuclear weapons, the treaties and agreements of the late 1980s worked to relieve concerns of nuclear exterminism that E. P. Thompson had written of earlier that decade.

The Second Nuclear Age was brought about by the end of the Soviet Union. It was defined by concerns about nuclear proliferation, successful attempts to prevent that in the former Eastern bloc, as well as continued bilateral and multilateral commitments to nuclear arms control and the reduction of nuclear arsenals in the USA and Russia. It was also defined by the breakout of a nuclear-armed Pakistan and North Korea, alongside concerns about Iran developing the bomb, and fears of rogue states and nuclear terrorism. With more nuclear-armed states, the Second Nuclear Age saw a shift of attention from the threat posed by superpower conflict towards a new focus on the possibility of regional powers – with weak institutions, and often engaged in active, protracted conflicts – waging nuclear war (Narang 2014). In the context of a Global War on Terror, fears of nuclear exterminism gave way in the Second Nuclear Age to worries about localised terrorist attacks using dirty bombs or crude nuclear devices, as scholars debated the strength of a norm or a tradition around the non-use of nuclear weapons that had persisted since 1945. Even so, the challenges and concerns of these earlier nuclear ages are still with us, and while the First Nuclear Age ended with the world-changing collapse of the Soviet Union, the Second Nuclear Age gave way to the Third through a series of events beginning with the election of Donald Trump as US President in 2016. The next chapter outlines current insights into the dawn of the Third Nuclear Age and builds upon them by making a detailed case for how and why critical nuclear studies can help in understanding recent events through a renewed conceptualisation and attention to E. P. Thompson's idea of nuclear exterminism.

2

'Fire and fury like the world has never seen': understanding the Third Nuclear Age

> North Korea best not make any threats to the United States. They will be met with fire and fury like the world has never seen.
>
> Donald Trump, 8 August 2017

In March 2016, Donald Trump was on the campaign trail in Milwaukee, Wisconsin. In a town hall event broadcast on CNN, Trump was asked about the topic of nuclear weapons and what he thought about them. In response he went off on a tangent, taking umbrage at the notion of extended deterrence for US allies near North Korea such as Japan and South Korea. Trump claimed that 'We are supporting them, militarily, and they pay us a fraction, a fraction of what they should be paying us.' He went on to say that 'at some point we have to say, you know what, we're better off if Japan protects itself against this maniac in North Korea, we're better off, frankly, if South Korea is going to start to protect itself' (Trump in CNN 2016). Trump appeared to be suggesting that nuclear proliferation may be the best solution to reducing the American deficit whilst simultaneously ensuring the security of American allies neighbouring North Korea. However, moments later, Trump contradicted himself when he was asked if it was okay for Japan and South Korea to have nuclear weapons:

> I don't want more nuclear weapons. I think that – you know, when I hear Obama get up and say the biggest threat to the world today is global warming, I say, is this guy kidding? The only global warming – the only global warming I'm worried about is nuclear global warming because that's the single biggest threat. So it's not that I'm a fan – we can't afford it anymore. (Trump in CNN 2016)

In response, and probably bewildered by the idea of 'nuclear global warming', Hillary Clinton pointed out how Trump's ideas were 'dangerously incoherent'. She highlighted that 'They're not even really ideas – just a series of bizarre rants', saying, 'This is not someone who should ever have the nuclear codes – because it's not hard to imagine Donald Trump leading us into a war just because somebody got under his very thin skin.' Clinton closed her speech by saying that 'making Donald Trump our commander-in-chief would be a historic mistake' (Clinton in Reilly 2016).

At 2.30 a.m. on Wednesday 9 November 2016, after a night of unforeseen election results, the state of Wisconsin declared for Donald Trump. Now that he was over the threshold of 270 electoral college votes, Clinton's concerns of a historic mistake became a reality: Trump was now the President Elect. By 2.35 a.m. Clinton had called Trump to concede defeat, and fifteen minutes later he took to the stage to make his victory speech. The world watched on. Few had seen this coming.

In the wake of Donald Trump's 2016 election victory, this chapter introduces the central features of the Third Nuclear Age as others have so far articulated them. Given that, in this new era, 'much of what we know about nuclear weapons and deterrence is up for reassessment'(Wirtz 2018, 335), I highlight the need for novel approaches to the analysis of nuclear weapons grounded in critical approaches to global politics such as those that focus on the importance and intersections of identity, representation, emotions, culture, race, gender, political economy, and the environment. I outline how the concept of nuclear exterminism can help us think through and make sense of the Third Nuclear Age beyond the realm of 'high politics'. I develop and build upon critical nuclear studies to inform the subsequent analysis, and make clear how this approach can help to understand, analyse, challenge, and overcome the limitations of traditional thinking that has dominated the domains of theory and practice in the realm of nuclear weapons since their inception.

The dawn of the Third Nuclear Age

The election of Donald Trump is a watershed moment that signals the beginning of the end of the Second Nuclear Age. Soon after his election victory, on 22 December Trump tweeted that 'The United States must greatly strengthen and expand its nuclear capability until such time as the world comes to its senses regarding nukes.' Several days later, Trump told a reporter 'Let it be an arms race … We will outmatch them at every pass and outlast them all' (Trump quoted in Pilkington 2016). All of a sudden, decades of commitment to nuclear arms control and the slow but steady reduction of global nuclear arsenals began to unravel.

Trump's commitment to increasing the US nuclear arsenal was made evident in July 2017 when he asked military leaders at the Pentagon for a tenfold increase in the number of nuclear weapons in his country's possession. After being shown a chart of America's nuclear stockpile at its height during the Cold War, Trump told his team he wanted 32,000 nuclear weapons – the same number shown on the chart (Kube *et al.* 2017). After Trump left this meeting, Rex Tillerson, the then Secretary of State, referred to him as a 'fucking moron'. Within a few months, Trump had fired Tillerson and the US Department of Defense had released the Trump administration's Nuclear Posture Review.

The 2018 Nuclear Posture Review (NPR) set out the role that nuclear weapons play in US security strategy and signalled a stark contrast with the Obama administration's approach to nuclear weapons. Whereas the 2010 NPR overseen by Obama opened by outlining a road map 'for reducing nuclear risks to the United States, our allies and partners, and the international community' and claimed that 'a world without nuclear weapons will not be achieved quickly, but we must begin to take concrete steps today' (Department of Defense 2010, i), the 2018 NPR had a rather different tone. It began by warning of 'Moscow's decided return to Great Power competition', China's pursuit of 'new nuclear capabilities', as well as the threats posed by North Korea, Iran, and nuclear terrorism (Department of Defense 2018, 1). The 2018 NPR even articulated policies such as the development of 'low yield' nuclear weapons and dual-use technologies for nuclear and non-nuclear warheads. The 2018 NPR legitimises these steps by claiming that global threats have increased in recent years, arguing that Obama's strategy of leadership by example has failed, and noting that great power rivalry is once again the defining characteristic of global politics with a resurgent Russia and a China on the rise (Smetana 2018, 139). As Obama advocated for nuclear disarmament, he sought to make American security strategy less reliant on nuclear weapons. Within two years of taking office, Trump reversed those steps (Brown 2018).

Prior to 2019, commentators noted that Trump's views, rhetoric, and policies on nuclear weapons 'are largely consistent with past Republican administrations, especially those of Ronald Reagan and George W. Bush' (Michaels and Williams 2017, 56), suggesting that Trump represented more continuity than change when it came to nuclear weapons policy. Similarly, in their 2019 book *The Ordinary Presidency of Donald J. Trump*, Herbert, McCrisken, and Wroe claim that 'In style, process, words, rhetoric and promises made, Trump is a most extraordinary president. But in substance, policy, deeds, action and promises kept, Trump's presidency is not extraordinary. Indeed, it is ordinary – largely conventional, orthodox and conservative, rather than revolutionary or radical' (Herbert, McCrisken, and Wroe 2019, 4). According to this view, like those other Republican leaders before him Trump may talk the hawkish talk, but he is constrained, when it comes to walking the nuclear walk, by other institutions and norms. While, at the time of their writing, such arguments could be valid, events that occurred after these claims present a grimmer picture and suggest that Trump marks a point of departure that brought about the Third Nuclear Age.

Take, for example, the 2017 confrontation between President Trump and North Korea. At the time, the playground insults of Trump calling Kim Jong-un 'little rocket man' and threatening that North Korea 'will be met with fire and fury like the world has never seen' made headlines across the world (Zeleney, Merica, and Liptak 2017). What was less well known was that Trump administration officials were so concerned about the prospect of nuclear war that the then Defense Secretary James Mattis had a flashing light installed in his bathroom in case 'an alert came while he was showering' (Hohmann and Alfaro 2020). According to Trump himself, war with North Korea was 'much closer than anyone would know' (Trump in Woodward 2020, 205), and US Strategic Command had reviewed and updated operational plans for regime change in North Korea that included the use of up to eighty nuclear weapons.

As North Korea launched a missile over Japan on 29 August 2017, the US military was 'ready to fire' (Woodward 2020, 96), yet even though government officials wondered if they were on 'the edge of Armageddon' (Woodward 2020, 97) the crisis didn't escalate. However, the very real possibility of recommending a nuclear strike against North Korea weighed heavily on the mind of Mattis. After an argument with Trump where Mattis defended US support of South Korea, the President turned to one of Mattis's aides and said, 'My fucking generals are a bunch of pussies' (Trump in Woodward 2020, 56). These playground insults belie the fact that 'the world was perilously close to nuclear conflict in 2017' (Jackson 2018, 193), and, by the end of 2018, prompted by Trump's decision to withdraw US troops from Syria, Mattis had quit as Secretary of Defense. He later explained his decision, pointing out that 'I was basically directed to do something that I thought went beyond stupid to felony stupid, strategically jeopardizing our place in the world and everything else, that's when I quit' (Mattis in Woodward 2020, 162).

In the face of such revelations, not to mention the abject failure of the Trump administration to de-escalate tensions on the Korean peninsula despite face-to-face meetings between Trump and Kim Jong-un in 2018 and 2019 (Stein 2019), the view of Trump as an 'ordinary' president seems misplaced. The subsequent withdrawal from the INF Treaty in August 2019, serious efforts to test American nuclear weapons in the summer of 2020, and the failure to renew New START during his time in office all indicate that the view of Trump as a bellowing but benign President is perhaps rather naive. Even though Trump's Republican predecessors were bellicose and engaged in military intervention and a Global War on Terror, at least in the realm of nuclear weapons they made several efforts to reduce America's nuclear arsenal and to promote international arms control. Trump, in contrast, sought to do the opposite. He actively wanted to increase America's nuclear arsenal while also undermining arms control, and he even came close to nuclear confrontation during his presidency.

Writing in March 2019, political experts Trevor McCrisken and Maxwell Downman pointed out that even if Trump's 'peace through strength' approach to nuclear weapons policy did reflect a certain level of continuity with previous administrations, it still creates 'risks for arms-control and non-proliferation' (McCrisken and Downman 2019, 294), and that if US allies 'hope to forestall a renewed arms race and aspire to a world free from the threat of nuclear annihilation' (McCrisken and Downman 2019, 279) they need to assert a different vision of global security given concerning developments that have taken place under Trump. Even though Trump did not use or test a nuclear weapon, allies, institutions, and norms failed to prevent him from playing a pivotal role in heralding the dawn of a Third Nuclear Age – one where unparalleled catastrophe is closer than ever before.

As decades of critical scholarship has demonstrated, the rhetoric, language, discourse and style of political leaders, government officials, media institutions, and others, are not tangential to 'action', 'policy', and 'deeds.' Instead, they are constitutive of them (Cohn 1987; Campbell 1992; Chaloupka 1992; Bleiker 2001; Biswas 2014). Trump's exceptional 'style, process, words, rhetoric and promises' are not beside the point as some would claim (Herbert, McCrisken, and Wroe 2019, 4). Rather, they are the point itself. Language, rhetoric, media, and performative practices such as Trump's aggressive expressions of anger – or what critical theorists call discourse – matter because they give meaning to the world, create identities, position subjects in relation to one another, and create the conditions of possibility for what can and does happen in the world.

Discourse and language matters when it comes to nuclear weapons. In 1984, the French poststructural theorist Jacques Derrida proclaimed that the atomic age is '*fabulously textual*, through and through. Nuclear weaponry depends … upon structures of information and communication, structures of language, including non-vocalizable language, structures of codes and graphic decoding … for the moment, a nuclear war has not taken place: one can only talk and write about it' (1984, 23, emphasis in original). Given that we can still only imagine, talk, and write about a nuclear war, when we come to assess the Third Nuclear Age we should not reject language and representation as unimportant; we should place them at the forefront of our analysis.

Unfortunately, as we shall see later in this book, the risks and dangers of the Third Nuclear Age did not end with Trump's departure from office.

If the Third Nuclear Age was foreshadowed by the election of Trump, his threats of 'fire and fury', and his Nuclear Posture Review in 2018, it was in 2019 that it began in earnest. According to nuclear weapons experts, 2019 was 'the point of no return' (Miller and Narang 2019) and 2020 subsequently began as 'the year to worry about nuclear weapons' (Braut-Hegghammer 2020). The following chapters of this book trace the development of the Third Nuclear Age in detail, beginning from 2 August 2019 – the date the United States formally withdrew from the INF Treaty. Before we turn to the events that define this new nuclear age in detail, it's worth briefly exploring the broad contours of the Third Nuclear Age as others have so far observed it.

According to political scientists Robert Legvold and Christopher Chyba, the new nuclear age presents dangers 'at least as great as those during the Cold War' (2020, 6). These dangers arise for several reasons. First, with the proliferation of nuclear weapons to more and more states, we have entered an era marked not by bilateral superpower competition and confrontation, but by a multipolar world where 'competitive and potentially adversarial nuclear relationships have expanded' (Legvold and Chyba 2020, 7). Now, disagreements between India and Pakistan, India and China, China and the USA, the USA and North Korea, and so on all run the risk of escalating towards nuclear confrontation. Whereas in the past, nuclear confrontation was generally centred on one relationship (between the USA and Russia), we now face multiple relationships deteriorating and sparking crisis and catastrophe. With the 'rise of China', we see three superpowers entering an arms race 'the likes of which the world has never seen' (Miller and Narang 2019). Furthermore, the world's attempts to halt the development of North Korea's nuclear weapons programme have themselves stalled, and efforts to prevent Iran from developing nuclear weapons have entered reverse rather than moving forward. Iran is now estimated to be only six to ten months away from producing enough enriched uranium for a nuclear warhead, and this is closer than ever before. The Trump administration's decision to tear up the Iran deal is the reason for this worrying development.

The proliferation of nuclear weapons to other states also looks set to increase, as states such as Saudi Arabia, South Korea, and Turkey have all expressed an interest in enriching uranium and developing nuclear capabilities. The cause of this once again lies with the Trump administration, which called into question security commitments to US allies (Miller and Narang 2019). Even US allies in Europe expressed concern about practices of extended deterrence under the Trump administration, leading the French president Emmanuel Macron to float the idea that French nuclear weapons could replace US ones as a supposed guarantor of security in Europe (Macron 2020).

Second, the development of new technologies that are intended to enhance nuclear deterrence by making nuclear weapons more usable (and the threat of nuclear retaliation more credible), alongside technologies that blur the distinction between nuclear and conventional weapons, present novel challenges (Futter and Zala 2021). Low-yield nuclear weapons notably lower the threshold for nuclear war as they are designed to be used on the battlefield, and dual-use technologies (that can be used for nuclear and conventional warheads) such as hypersonic missiles increase uncertainty and make decision making more difficult in times of crisis.

It is also increasingly apparent that the concepts used to understand and strategise nuclear weapons are 'undergoing unpredictable change' (Legvold and Chyba 2020, 8). Given that nuclear deterrence and MAD provided the cornerstones of strategic and political thinking during the Cold War, their current erosion due to the development of 'limited nuclear options' in both the US and Russian arsenals suggests that much of what we know, or presume to know, about the risks of nuclear war needs to be rethought.

In addition, international norms such as the nuclear taboo are blatantly undermined and eroded by 'the development of weapons for limited, and therefore more plausible, nuclear use' (Legvold and Chyba 2020, 8). Here, the 'no-first-use' nuclear weapons policies of China and India are under threat, as China perceives itself to be threatened by the USA, and India seeks exceptions to its own doctrine. Other nuclear weapons states, including both the United States and Russia, reject the idea of 'no-first-use' and still threaten to be the first to use nuclear weapons in a conflict if they deem it necessary. Russia's invasion of Ukraine has been accompanied by blatant threats of nuclear use, where Putin himself has stated that he will cause 'consequences you have never seen' against anyone who opposes his invasion of Ukraine.

Finally, while these changes and developments continue to have unforeseen impacts, we are still faced with the dangers of earlier nuclear ages. Frosty relations between the USA and Russia have led some observers to suggest that we are in an era of a 'new Cold War' (Lucas 2014), where dialogue, constructive bilateral nuclear negotiations, and effective arms control agreements seem a distant memory as key treaties have collapsed and neither the USA nor Russia seems truly committed to their revival or the development of new treaties. Even by renewing New START for five years, as Russia and the USA did in early 2021, without further commitments to increasing arms control we run the risk that the nuclear football has simply been kicked into the long grass when New START expires in 2026. The situation is compounded by Putin's invasion of Ukraine, the cessation of strategic dialogue between Russia and the USA, and Russia's 2023 suspension of its participation in New START.

Further measures to reduce nuclear arsenals or move the world towards nuclear disarmament also seem distant, especially when China is building more silos for its nuclear weapons, India and Pakistan are modernising their arsenals, and the United Kingdom is increasing the number of nuclear warheads it can possess in its operational stockpile. Yet the January 2021 passing into force of the Treaty on the Prohibition of Nuclear Weapons as the first legally binding comprehensive ban on nuclear weapons signals a glimmer of hope. These issues, and more, will be discussed in detail in subsequent chapters. In the next chapter I argue that just as the detonation of the atomic bomb over Hiroshima in August 1945 marked the beginning of the First Nuclear Age, the official withdrawal of the USA and Russia from the INF Treaty in August 2019 stands as a clear starting point for when the world entered the Third Nuclear Age (Miller and Narang 2019). Before we examine the dawn of this new nuclear age, I now demonstrate the utility of conceptualising and studying the concept of nuclear exterminism to enhance the project of critical nuclear studies – grounded in feminist, post-/decolonial, poststructural, and ecological thinking – and to understand how we are heading towards unparalleled catastrophe and what we can do about it in the Third Nuclear Age.

Analysing the Third Nuclear Age: towards a critical nuclear studies

Since the development, testing, and use of nuclear weapons in 1945, International Relations scholarship has been concerned with studying nuclear weapons and their effects on global politics. For much of this history, the majority of scholarship has been conducted by mainstream theories that adopt a perspective of problem solving, where research 'takes the world as it finds it, with the prevailing social and power relationships and the institutions into which they are organised, as the given framework for action' (Cox 1981, 128). In this vein, many of the oft-cited experts on nuclear weapons – from Bernard Brodie to Herman Kahn, via Henry Kissinger and Kenneth Waltz – have adopted a problem-solving perspective where they aim to understand nuclear weapons so as to make states and international institutions 'work smoothly by dealing effectively with particular sources of trouble' (Cox 1981, 128–9). Within the confines of traditional, problem-solving, and 'realist' scholarship, the study of nuclear weapons has been underpinned by a focus on states as sovereign, self-interested rational actors, who operate in an anarchical international system and attempt to wield power by coercing others into doing what they want them to do. In this line of thinking, the aim of research on nuclear weapons comes to be about strategising on how best to deter and defeat other nuclear states, how to balance power between competing superpowers, and how to legitimise and maintain large arsenals of nuclear weapons (see for example Sagan 1996; Debs and Monteiro 2017; Kahn 2017; Freedman and Michaels 2019; Kissinger 2019; Green 2020; Schelling 2020).

Since the 1980s, this approach to International Relations in general, and nuclear weapons in particular, has been challenged by critical perspectives (Derrida 1984; Cohn 1987; Chaloupka 1992; Abraham 2006; Burke 2009; Egeland 2021). In contrast to problem-solving theory, a critical approach 'does not take institutions and social and power relations for granted but calls them into question by concerning itself with their origins and how and whether they might be in the process of changing' (Cox 1981, 129). In questioning the underpinning assumptions of common sense and what is often taken for granted in global politics, 'Critical theory allows for a normative choice in favour of a social and political order different from the prevailing order' (Cox 1981, 130). By this logic, that which is taken to be natural and unchanging in global politics – such as states as the primary form of human political organisation operating in an anarchical international system – are in fact historically contingent and socially constructed. As Alexander Wendt has noted, 'anarchy is what states make of it' (Wendt 1992, 395), therefore understanding how states come to develop, articulate, and represent their identities and interests is of paramount concern in global politics (Campbell 1992; Doty 1996; Hansen 2013).

Alongside this attention to the social construction of identities and interests, critical approaches to global politics recognise that 'theory is always for someone and for some purpose' (Cox 1981, 129) and note that the majority of problem-solving theory – especially that on the topic of nuclear weapons – has been conducted in service of states in order to legitimise and justify their actions or to pursue their own interests and power. Such traditional approaches have led to the development of an academic discipline that serves the interest of powerful states by legitimising nuclear weapons as necessary tools of survival in a world of self-interested, hostile 'others' who need to be deterred. Throughout the Cold War, these traditional theories enabled 'the crudest fanaticism … to masquerade as realistic and responsible policy' (Walker 1990, 21) and have led to 'the most powerful structures of violence the world has ever known' (Walker 1990, 20). Given this, and in recognition of the fact that traditional approaches to global politics have done little to prevent the world from heading towards unparalleled catastrophe, I adopt a critical approach to analyse and make sense of the Third Nuclear Age.

The analysis herein is underpinned by, and aims to build upon and develop, scholarship in the area of critical nuclear studies that draws upon feminist, post-/decolonial, poststructural, and ecological thought. These strands of thinking contributed to the deepening and broadening of IR and security scholarship in the late 1980s and early 1990s, and have contributed to a burgeoning field of 'critical nuclear studies' (Burke 2016, 4). These critical bodies of scholarship have contributed to the development of security studies and IR by opening up the referent object of security from the previous focus on militaries and sovereign states to accounts of human, economic, and social security where the object to be secured includes 'individuals and the whole of humanity' (Booth 2005, 14). This move has enabled an expanded agenda that aims not to serve the interest of powerful states but to develop 'more promising ideas by which to overcome structural and contingent human wrongs' (Booth 2005, 16). The mainstream of thought, study, and action in nuclear weapons scholarship serves to marginalise 'critical perspectives and voices' (Burke 2016, 2), and the nascent body of critical scholarship on nuclear weapons has two central features: first, 'a political and normative challenge to the existence of nuclear weapons and the acceptability of deterrence', and second, a desire to explain how and why non-proliferation and disarmament would be beneficial to the world (Burke 2016, 3). The following chapters therefore seek to illuminate and interrogate the recent developments of the Third Nuclear Age from a critical perspective whilst also serving as a warning of how we are racing towards unparalleled catastrophe.

Beyond these two broad features, the thinking that underpins the subsequent analysis builds upon decades of critical scholarship on nuclear weapons, and is indebted to a broad range of research. Rather than being based in the silo of one critical perspective, I draw upon multiple theories and viewpoints to understand the imminent catastrophes facing the planet. As the critical theorist Jairus Grove has noted, if we want to address the myriad ills of the modern moment's interlinked crises of potential nuclear annihilation, war, climate change, rising authoritarianism, and other planetary crises – what he refers to as the 'fathoms of shit we are in as a community of species' or the 'savage ecology' (Grove 2019, 11) of contemporary global politics – then we need to draw upon different perspectives and examine the collective impact of multiple issues on the world today.

In recent years we have seen the fragile masculinity of state leaders bring us close to nuclear war, as when Donald Trump and Kim Jong-un compared the size of their nuclear buttons and Donald Trump tweeted, 'I too have a Nuclear Button, but it is a much bigger & more powerful one than his, and my Button works!' (quoted in Cohn 2018). We have seen a global coronavirus pandemic highlight the vulnerability of human life whilst also demonstrating the inefficacy of traditional military security measures in keeping us safe and making it clear just how ill prepared the world is for cataclysmic events

(Fihn and Sanders-Zakre 2020; Futter *et al.* 2020). We have seen the police murder of Black people draw attention to how the state, and institutions involved in nuclear politics, produce and sustain racial hierarchies through their histories, logics, and cultures (Zvobgo and Loken 2020; Turner *et al.* 2020). We have seen states commit billions of dollars to increasing their nuclear arsenals and modernising obsolete nuclear weapons largely due to the lobbying activities of defence contractors and a nuclear-military-industrial complex (Belcher 2020). We have seen a riot of far-right conspiracy theorists storm the US Capitol and get within metres of Vice President Mike Pence and the 'nuclear football' he would use to launch nuclear weapons if the President was incapacitated (Borger 2021).

The Third Nuclear Age is marked by an intersection of issues and crises. It is not that sexism, or militarism, or racism, or imperialism, or neoliberal market forces, or populism, etc. are *the* most singularly important issues shaping the current crises we face. Rather, these issues and factors are not 'mutually exclusive categories of experience and analysis' (Crenshaw 1989, 139), and as Black feminists have argued for decades, it is the intersectionality of how these issues come together, collide, and even at times contradict and contrast that shapes the construction of the social world (Crenshaw 1990, 1245). What we need, therefore, to understand the Third Nuclear Age is a critical approach to nuclear weapons that recognises the significance of intersectionality, and casts a broad net to theorise, analyse, and hopefully overcome the challenges of today (Acheson 2021; Choi and Eschle 2022). By drawing together various strands of critical thinking about nuclear weapons, the rest of this chapter outlines a critical nuclear studies that conceptualises the role of nuclear exterminism in shaping the Third Nuclear Age.

Some of the earliest and most influential critical work on nuclear weapons came from feminist perspectives, and my approach to the study of nuclear weapons is feminist. It recognises that the existence and maintenance of nuclear weapons is made possible by gendered ways of thinking, speaking, and acting (Cohn 1987; Teaiwa 1994; Eschle 2018; Acheson 2019; Alexis-Martin 2019a; Choi and Eschle 2022). Following feminist scholarship and activism, I recognise the importance of patriarchal social structures – that privilege masculinity and men over femininity and women – as having an impact on how nuclear weapons are legitimised and strategised. As Carol Cohn wrote in the late 1980s, the gendered language used to talk about nuclear weapons – where state leaders compare missile size, payloads, and talk of warheads having a 'soft lay down' and 'penetrating' enemy targets – fetishises nuclear weapons and also serves to domesticate, sanitise, and 'tame the wild and uncontrollable forces of nuclear destruction' (Cohn 1987, 698). Such ways of speaking and thinking about nuclear weapons in abstract euphemisms, and 'friendly, sexy acronyms' – ICBMs, MIRVs, SLBMs (submarine-launched ballistic missiles)! – functions to obscure and silence the fact that these weapons can cause untold violence and horror (Cohn 1987, 709).

To this end, my critical approach to nuclear weapons develops and is attuned to a concept of *nuclear masculinity*. Feminists have long drawn attention to military masculinity – the notion that society privileges and glorifies masculine participation in violence and war and the associated values of heterosexuality, aggression, strength, and toughness (Henry 2017, 16–17; see also Enloe 2014). Building upon this research, in the realm of nuclear weapons policy and strategy, we are confronted with nuclear masculinity, where ideas, language, and practices regarding the ultimate weapon of destruction are shaped by gender and the privileging of masculinity. As Carol Cohn noted after the 2017 spat between Donald Trump and Kim Jong-un about the size of their nuclear buttons, 'the literal button or penis size of Mr. Trump or Mr. Kim matters not at all, their need for the world to believe that they are manly men does' (Cohn 2018). Conceptions of gender – of what it means to be a man – shape nuclear policy, and a critical approach to nuclear weapons is feminist and works to draw attention to how gender and masculinity function in the Third Nuclear Age.

A critical approach to nuclear weapons is also decolonial. It is committed to opposing the imperialism of nuclear weapons and drawing attention to how empire, race, colonialism, and white supremacy have shaped the historical development and modern existence of nuclear weapons (Teaiwa 1994; Gusterson 1999; Abraham 2006; Biswas 2014; Alexis-Martin 2019a). Following postcolonial and decolonial scholarship that draws attention to 'the global unequal order that sustains the desire for and production of nuclear weapons' (Biswas 2014, 74), a critical approach to nuclear weapons recognises how nuclear weapons are 'always already harmful' (Biswas 2014, 197) to many people across the planet. Whilst the unparalleled catastrophe of nuclear war has not yet happened, for many, the existence of nuclear weapons has already had catastrophic effects (Maurer and Hogue 2020, 29–33; Choi and Eschle 2022, 1133). Indigenous communities on Pacific islands (Teaiwa 1994), as well as Native Americans on the US mainland (Voyles 2015), have been massively affected by nuclear testing – displaced from their homes and subject to the adverse health effects of nuclear fallout. Furthermore, during the Cold War, vast amounts of the 'Western' world's uranium – the fissile material used in nuclear weapons – came from across Africa, and miners of uranium in Niger, South Africa, Congo, and elsewhere across the African continent have been subject to severe radioactive health risks. The reliance of the 'West' on African uranium miners is but one example of people in the Global South being exploited in order to sustain the nuclear capabilities of other states (Hecht 2014). Today, a 'nuclear apartheid' (Maddock 2010; Biswas 2014) persists in global politics where there are stark 'material inequities in the distribution of global nuclear resources – inequities that are written into, institutionalized, and legitimized through some of the major arms-control treaties, creating an elite club of nuclear "haves" with exclusive rights to maintain nuclear arsenals that are to be denied to the vast majority of nuclear "have-nots"' (Biswas 2001, 486).

This exclusionary global nuclear order is underpinned by inequalities, racism, white supremacy, and colonialism. Mainstream approaches to global politics are also built upon these very ideas and are often blind to their impact in international affairs (Doty 1996; Henderson 2013; Vitalis 2015; Zvobgo and Loken 2020); however, a critical approach to nuclear weapons recognises their importance. In adopting a post-/decolonial perspective, we are attuned to 'nuclear orientalism' (Gusterson 1999, 113). This means that we recognise that in 'Western' public discourse, 'our' nuclear weapons are deemed to be safe, guarantors of security, whereas those of 'others' are perceived to be dangerous problems, and objects of insecurity. Following Edward Said's work on orientalism – where the 'West' is deemed to be rational, modern, enlightened, and civilised, and the rest of the world is depicted as being emotional, backwards, unenlightened, and barbaric (Said 1978) – a critical approach to nuclear weapons aims to understand how orientalist, racist, and white supremacist ideas shape nuclear weapons policies, strategies, and culture (Teaiwa 1994).

Subsequently, a post-/decolonial approach to nuclear weapons explores nuclear apartheid (how the global nuclear order is divided between nuclear weapons states and those who are unable to have them) alongside nuclear orientalism (how the global nuclear order is underpinned by ideas and discourses of otherness) and *nuclear imperialism*. Nuclear imperialism is characterised by an exploitative economic, political, social, and cultural domination of other people, states, and places by others with possession of nuclear technologies (Broinowski 2015). We see nuclear imperialism occurring in the mining of uranium in Africa, the testing of nuclear weapons by 'Western' countries in the Pacific, Soviet testing of nuclear weapons in Kazakhstan, and in the persecution of communities such as Uyghur Muslims who live in areas where China bases some of its nuclear weapons (Alexis-Martin 2019b). Throughout what follows, I draw upon the concept of nuclear imperialism and the associated concepts of nuclear apartheid and nuclear orientalism to help make sense of developments in the Third Nuclear Age.

The critical approach to nuclear weapons adopted herein is also influenced by poststructural and interpretive scholarship that recognises the importance of discourse, representation, and identity in shaping today's nuclear politics (Derrida 1984; Burke 2009, 2016; Mutimer 2011, 2000; Ritchie 2013;

Fishel 2015; Considine 2017). Here, discourse – understood as systems of signification that give meaning to what happens and exists in the world, such as language, visual media, music, and other meaning-making practices – plays a central role in shaping identities, interests, emotions, and what is thought, said, and done in global politics (Campbell 1992; Milliken 1999; Bleiker 2001; Hansen 2013). A critical approach to nuclear weapons therefore pays attention to representation, and how language, media, and practices function to represent nuclear weapons in ways that serve to legitimise their existence and grant authority and power to those who possess them. A rich body of work has developed in this area, and has so far problematised the role that reason plays in nuclear strategising (Burke 2009), drawn attention to the importance of narrative in shaping constructions of memory with regard to nuclear weapons (Steele 2013; Fishel 2015), and shown how important language and framing are with regard to the politics of arms control and disarmament (Mutimer 2011, 2000; Considine 2017). Following feminist insights, critical approaches to nuclear weapons have shifted towards 'the everyday' as a source of insight for understanding nuclear weapons, 'thereby demystifying the processes through which the nuclear state is maintained' (Eschle 2018, 3) through the ways it is made meaningful in our everyday lives.

In the shift towards language, representation, identities, emotions, and the everyday as legitimate sources of insight for understanding the politics of nuclear weapons, their study has been opened up. No longer are we only concerned with counting bombers, missiles, and warheads and strategising about their impact on 'strategic stability'. No longer are we only focused on the 'high politics' of presidents, militaries, and grey men in grey suits playing war games in grey buildings as if they were characters in *Dr Strangelove* (although such research continues to dominate the orthodox political science approach to nuclear weapons; see Pelopidas 2016; Braut-Hegghammer 2019). Instead, a critical approach to nuclear weapons adopted herein is concerned with these spaces and sites of study, but also with the 'low politics' of popular culture. Secrecy surrounds nuclear weapons, so it is through popular culture that people come to know about them – in the representations of nuclear weapons in films like *Dr Strangelove*, in videogames such as those in the *Fallout* series, as well as in the everyday actions, thoughts, feelings, words, and memes shared online by 'ordinary' people who may, or may not, live near nuclear weapons sites, resist them, support them, or feel ambivalent towards them. In essence, a critical approach to nuclear weapons is attentive to a broad range of sites for analysis and is concerned with the role of *nuclear culture*.

Following Stuart Hall's work that has avowedly demonstrated that 'questions of culture … are absolutely deadly political questions' (1997, 290), culture is here understood as a 'critical site of social action and intervention, where power relations are both established and potentially unsettled' (Procter 2004, 1). Nuclear culture is therefore culture 'characterised by the development of the nuclear state and the complex and varied ways in which people controlled, responded to, resisted or represented the complex influence of nuclear science and technology, the official nuclear state, and the threat of nuclear war' (Hogg 2016, 7). Nuclear culture is an intertextual site where meanings, identities, and interests are made, power is conferred, and nuclear weapons and strategies of deterrence are claimed to be legitimate, then granted legitimacy, or indeed challenged and contested by others. Understanding the role of nuclear culture in shaping the Third Nuclear Age, and understanding how it can contribute to, but perhaps also counter and prevent, impending unparalleled catastrophe, is central to a critical approach to nuclear weapons.

Building from these theoretical foundations and drawing from a broader range of less easily categorisable scholarship, we are concerned with the global harms – both potential and current – caused by nuclear weapons. These harms exist not only in the form of their threat to the lives of people directly affected by the testing and use of nuclear weapons, or the potential threat to the lives of people in cities and places targeted by nuclear weapons, but in the threats nuclear weapons pose to society, civilisation, *all life* on planet earth, alongside the planet itself. Therefore, a critical approach to nuclear weapons needs to draw upon ecological perspectives to planetary politics (Burke *et al.* 2016; Taylor 2019; Higuchi 2020; Van Munster and Sylvest 2021). If a nuclear war ever takes place, not only will it kill millions of people instantaneously, it is likely to cause a 'nuclear winter' that would blacken the skies, stop food crops from growing, and thereby starve most survivors (Sagan 1983a, 1983b; Robock, Oman, and Stenchikov 2007). It would, in short, be 'a severe assault on our civilisation and our species' (Sagan 1983b). Even with these warnings that have been prominent in popular consciousness for decades now, traditional theories of global politics have had remarkably little to say about the potential of realistic, catastrophic extinction events or of nuclear harms 'massive in their scale and moral horror' (Burke *et al.* 2016, 517).

Consequently, critical nuclear studies aims to draw attention to 'the enormity, complexity, and scale' (Burke *et al.* 2016, 517) of threats nuclear weapons pose. I contribute and further this project by applying the concept of *nuclear exterminism* – an idea first introduced by the historian and socialist peace campaigner E. P. Thompson in the early 1980s (Thompson 1982a). For Thompson, the development of nuclear weapons required a theorisation of society and politics that went beyond the concepts of militarism (understood as a characteristic of societies that privilege and build up their militaries in preparation for war) and imperialism (understood as a characteristic of societies that are built upon the exploitation of others). Whilst Thompson found value in these concepts, both of which have since become the focus of subfields of critical security studies, he developed an understanding of exterminism as a central way of making sense of the nuclear age he was living through. Despite the prominence of Thompson's thought and activism within the peace movement during the Cold War, his idea of exterminism has not gained much, if any, traction within security studies (and whilst the concepts of militarism and imperialism have generated detailed studies within IR, exterminism, when mentioned, is often only briefly discussed; see Luckham 1984, 357–8; Fehér and Agnes 1986; Walker 1986, 486; Halliday 1987, 168; Stavrianakis and Selby 2012, 6; Baker 2017).

I contribute to the burgeoning field of critical nuclear studies by drawing upon Thompson's work on exterminism to analyse the Third Nuclear Age and highlight the serious dangers brought about by recent events. Thompson recognised that nuclear weapons were not inert objects or military tools; rather, he viewed them as 'a thing of menace' that needed to be understood within their broader social, political, economic, and cultural contexts (1982b, 45). In understanding 'the Bomb' as 'a component in a weapons-*system*', Thompson suggested that

> producing, manning and supporting that system is a correspondent social system – a distinct organization of labour, research and operation, with distinctive hierarchies of command, rules of secrecy, prior access to resources and skills, and high levels of policing and discipline: a distinctive organization of production, which, while militarist in character, employs and is supported by great numbers of civilians (civil servants, scientists, academics) who are subordinated to its discipline and rules. (1982b, 45)

The existence of nuclear weapons relies upon 'an internal dynamic and reciprocal logic' that permeates modern societies in complex ways and 'requires a new category for its analysis' (Thompson 1982b, 45). 'If', Thompson went on, '"the handmill gives you society with the feudal lord; the steam-mill, society with the industrial capitalist", what are we given by those Satanic mills which are now at work, grinding out the means of human extermination?' (Thompson 1982b, 45). In Thompson's view, society was no longer feudal, nor capitalist; it was instead exterminist.

For Thompson, the concept of exterminism was needed to make sense of the world around him. He defines exterminism as 'those characteristics of a society – expressed, in differing degrees, within its economy, its polity and its ideology – which thrust it in a direction whose outcome must be the extermination of multitudes' (Thompson 1982a, 20). With the development and existence of nuclear weapons, nuclear-armed states are leading the world towards unparalleled catastrophe where the extermination of people and the planet itself 'will not happen accidentally (even if the final trigger is "accidental") but as a direct consequence of prior acts of policy, of the accumulation and perfection of the means of extermination, and of the structuring of whole societies so that these are directed towards that end' (Thompson 1982a, 20).

Following Thompson, I recognise that nuclear exterminism is a discourse – a configuration of language, representations, objects, and practices – found across a broad range of sites within modern societies, concerned with the build-up and preparation for nuclear war – and the inevitable extermination that would follow from those weapons being used. Exterminism is not confined to a nuclear-military-industrial complex, or the military, or the arms industry; rather, it extends 'through the whole societal body' (Thompson 1982a, 21) and is a 'cumulative process' (Thompson 1982a, 24) crystallised in culture, economics, and politics. Writing during the Cold War, Thompson understood exterminism to be underpinned by bilateral arms races and confrontation between the USA and the USSR. Today, with the modernisation and development of novel nuclear weapons, an increase in potentially adversarial nuclear relationships, and the resurgence of nuclear superpower confrontation – but now on a trilateral basis with the USA, Russia, and China – it is an ever more concerning prospect that 'exterminism will reach its historical destination' (Thompson 1982a, 25). However, by highlighting how exterminism is present in the Third Nuclear Age, I hope in this book to contribute to thinking about how we can break out of this 'doomed logic' (Thompson 1990, 141) and avoid the unparalleled catastrophe envisaged by Einstein.

An attention to nuclear exterminism focuses not only on the potential harms that could be caused by nuclear weapons, but also draws our attention to the very real harms already caused by nuclear weapons. As postcolonial scholarship reminds us, nuclear weapons already cause adverse harms and horrors to indigenous populations affected by testing and people in the Global South exploited in the mining of uranium (Hecht 2014). Nuclear weapons also cause untold ecological harm in the places they have been tested, where nuclear waste is stored (Pearce 2018), where there have been accidents (Sagan 1993) – and nuclear weapons have already left their mark on the atmosphere itself (Higuchi 2020). In fact, one recent study of honey produced across the USA found that it contained radioactivity from nuclear weapons tests even though some samples were taken 'thousands of kilometres' from places where nuclear testing occurred more than five decades ago (Kaste, Volante, and Elmore 2021, 1).

Nuclear weapons also cause harm to the functioning of democracy (Pelopidas 2021a). Critical scholars have drawn attention to 'the authoritarian proclivities of the nuclear state' (Biswas 2014, 190), and, according to the philosopher Elaine Scarry, nuclear weapons are at odds with the basic principles of democracy since they are monarchic: only the executive branch of government has control over their use, and legislatures and broader populations in nuclear weapons states have no say in nuclear weapons policies (Scarry 2014, 6). Nuclear weapons pose a terrifying threat to the states and populations they are aimed at, where these people have 'lost the capacity for self-preservation' and 'have ceased to be, with respect to their own survival, rights-bearing persons' (Scarry 2014, 6) because they no longer have a right to self-defence. In addition, the domestic populations of nuclear-armed states have lost any semblance of a democratic voice because even in democracies such as the USA and UK, only one person – the President and the Prime Minister – has the power to launch nuclear weapons (Kaplan 2020; Perry and Collina 2020). We therefore live in a world where we, the people, are 'disempowered, disabled ... frozen in structures of thermonuclear subjugation' (Scarry 2014, 22), as national defence in nuclear weapon states and their allies is now located 'wholly outside the social contract' (Scarry 2014, 24). With the continued potential extermination of people and the planet, alongside the harms already caused to people and our environment by nuclear weapons, as well as the extermination of democracy brought about by nuclear weapons, the concept of nuclear exterminism can help us make sense of and address the challenges of the Third Nuclear Age.

Conclusion

The following chapters of this book draw upon the aforementioned bodies of critical thought and their associated concepts – nuclear masculinity, nuclear imperialism, nuclear culture, and nuclear exterminism – to analyse the Third Nuclear Age and provide a warning about how we are heading towards unparalleled catastrophe. Given the broad theoretical and methodological insights opened up by critical nuclear studies, the following chapters do not just focus on the realm of 'high politics' and the data sources of sanitised state leader statements, obtuse military doctrine, and national security strategies. Rather, whilst these sources are drawn upon and engaged with, so too are sites that are often considered 'low politics' and irrelevant to the serious study of nuclear weapons: news media, films, TV shows, pop songs, tweets, Facebook comments, memes, and other sources of everyday insight such as my own quotidian interactions with the nuclear state in rather unexpected places.

Instead of beginning in the corridors of power of Washington, Moscow, or London, the next chapter opens on the shores of a Scottish sea loch where I was sat eating fish and chips with my fiancée Rhiannon as a nuclear submarine cut across the water and headed out to the North Atlantic. A few weeks prior, storms had gathered hundreds of miles away over this very same sea, and the hurricanes they formed were set to hit the US mainland. In a meeting with his advisers on what to do about the coming storms, Donald Trump raised his voice and exclaimed, 'I got it. I got it. Why don't we nuke them?' (Trump quoted in Swan 2019). Not only did the collapse of the INF Treaty at the start of August 2019 highlight the new threat posed to nuclear arms control, but statements such as Trump's reveal broader concerns about the efficacy of the norm around the non-use of nuclear weapons. The next chapter therefore explores the politics of arms control and the 'nuclear taboo' (Tannenwald 2007) at the start of the Third Nuclear Age.

3

'I got it. I got it. Why don't we nuke them?': August to October 2019

> I got it. I got it. Why don't we nuke them?
>
> Donald Trump, 25 August 2019

It's a warm September day in Scotland as my fiancée Rhiannon and I sit in our car waiting for a ferry to take us to the Isle of Bute. We're eating fish and chips wrapped in yesterday's newspaper as we look out over the Firth of Clyde where the sunlight glistens on the water. Across the waves we notice a submarine travelling slowly out to sea. Cutting through the Firth, the submarine could be one of the Royal Navy's nuclear-powered, self-proclaimed 'hunter-killers', designed to 'hunt out and destroy enemy nuclear missile submarines' (Royal Navy 2019). Alternatively, it could be one of four Vanguard class submarines armed with up to eight Trident missiles and forty nuclear warheads, each of which is six times more powerful than the atomic bomb dropped on Hiroshima (Futter 2021, 27). As we sit there gazing across the water, the devastating potential of Britain's nuclear arsenal is all too real. It is no longer secretly hidden away down in the depths of a distant ocean, nor is it behind the barbed wire fences of a remote naval base. It is right there, a few hundred metres away, in front of me and my pregnant fiancée as we go about our lives.

The day after we arrive on the Isle of Bute, Rhiannon and I attend a friend's wedding at the historic Mount Stewart House – a stately home built in the nineteenth century, grand in scale and ornate in decor. During the reception, drinks in hand, a friend and I walk out to a balcony to enjoy the sun and take in the view across the Clyde to the mainland. As we chat and look out over the pristine green lawn, a dark shape cuts through the blue water. Another submarine makes the journey out to sea.

For many people, the world's nuclear weapons are somewhat distant and abstract. Nuclear submarine and air force bases, as well as the missile silos that house nuclear-armed ICBMs, are placed far from population centres and prying eyes. Politicians talk about nuclear weapons and strategies of deterrence on television, journalists report on them in the papers, Hollywood films feature them, and their effects are remembered in history books, or imagined in videogames. Yet even as nuclear weapons might capture our imaginations in popular culture, the activities of the 'nuclear military industrial establishment are often unseen or unseeable' (Alexis-Martin 2019a: 69). Because of this lack of visibility, society suffers from a 'nuclear unconsciousness', where many people 'do not want to think or even know about the full extent of the nuclear threat' (Schwab 2020, 5). However, here on the shores of the Firth of Clyde, the comings and goings of nuclear armed submarines from the naval base at Faslane are a regular reminder of the destructive capabilities of Britain's nuclear arsenal. When you see submarines out in the water, you realise their proximity to the people who live in this beautiful part of the world, where the Atlantic meets the Highlands, and people go about their business in the coastal towns of Helensburgh, Dunoon, and Ayr, and on the isles of Arran and Bute. The city of Glasgow, where I and another 1.6 million people live, is only twenty-five miles away.

My brief sightings of British nuclear submarines came after a turbulent month in nuclear politics, as the United States and Russia both withdrew from the Intermediate-Range Nuclear Forces (INF) Treaty at the start of August 2019. This treaty banned both states from deploying nuclear capable missiles with a range of 500–5,500 kilometres, and it was a cornerstone of bilateral arms control. In this chapter I argue that the collapse of the INF Treaty heralds the dawn of the Third Nuclear Age. I develop this argument by analysing events that took place between the start of August 2019 and the end of October 2019. In particular I examine the significance of arms control and how the unravelling of treaties such as the INF demonstrates the precarious nature of these agreements, especially in the current context of contentious global politics. I then move beyond a narrow focus on arms control and the rather dry details of bilateral or multilateral agreements, and instead show how the broader political, social, and cultural understanding of a norm around the non-use of nuclear weapons – or what some scholars refer to as a 'nuclear taboo' (Tannenwald 2007) – is eroding and being undermined in the new nuclear age. This discussion takes in a range of sources and issues beyond the narrow focus of arms control treaties. It involves an insight into the statements of political leaders whilst also examining ideas by the likes of Elon Musk, the billionaire owner of Tesla and SpaceX who wanted to 'Nuke Mars!' around the same time that Donald Trump suggested he could stop hurricanes with nuclear weapons. Before we examine these issues, we turn to 2 August 2019 in order to understand how and why the Third Nuclear Age begins on this date.

The collapse of the INF Treaty and the start of the Third Nuclear Age

According to John W. Gardner, the former US Secretary of Health, Education and Welfare under President Lyndon B. Johnson, 'history never looks like history when you are living through it'. Yet the first days of August 2019 looked and felt like history in the making as the USA and Russia finally walked away from the INF Treaty. Originally signed in 1987 before the end of the Cold War, the INF Treaty had removed an entire class of nuclear weapons from Europe and banned the USA and Russia from possessing missiles with short to intermediate ranges between 500 and 5,500 kilometres. The BBC reported that the end of the INF Treaty raised 'fears of a new arms race' (BBC News 2019), and the UN Secretary General António Guterres warned that 'an invaluable brake on nuclear war' was lost with the demise of the treaty which, he added, would 'heighten, not reduce, the threat posed by ballistic missiles' (Guterres in Reuters 2019).

Two main issues explain the collapse of the INF Treaty. First, the United States and its allies claimed that the Russian deployment of the 9M729 missile was a 'material breach' of the treaty's conditions, and US Secretary of State Mike Pompeo stated that 'Russia is solely responsible for the treaty's demise' (Pompeo 2020). In response, Vladimir Putin placed the blame on the USA, and stated that 'the INF Treaty no longer exists. Our US colleagues sent it to the archives, making it a thing of the past' (Putin 2019). Second, US concerns about China, which was not party to the constraints of the INF Treaty and was thus able to develop missiles within the banned range, led to the USA seeking to leave the treaty. In fact, the day after the USA officially withdrew, Mark Esper (the US Secretary of Defense at the time) stated that the United States would deploy intermediate-range missiles in the Pacific within months (Ali 2019). As the INF Treaty collapsed there was no plan to replace it or to develop a trilateral treaty to include China. Instead, both the USA and Russia sought to immediately develop and deploy weapons that had been banned since 1987. The end of the INF Treaty therefore signals the true beginning of the Third Nuclear Age. It marks a distinct step backwards after decades of nuclear arms control and progress, no matter how slow, towards disarmament. It returns us to a potential arms race where we run the risk of nuclear exterminism.

If we want to understand why the collapse of the INF Treaty is so important for heralding the Third Nuclear Age, we first need to understand what nuclear arms control is and how and why it matters in global politics. Classical work on nuclear arms control emerged during the early 1960s as policy makers and academics began to grapple with the proliferation of nuclear weapons to states beyond the USA. Writing in 1961 in what would become one of the definitive texts on arms control, Thomas Schelling and Morton Halperin defined arms control as 'an effort, by some kind of reciprocity or cooperation with our potential enemies, to minimise, to offset, to compensate or to deflate some of these characteristics of modern weapons and military expectations' (Schelling and Halperin 1961, 3). That same year, the International Relations theorist Hedley Bull published another landmark book on arms control, the second edition of which stated that 'arms control in its broadest sense comprises all those acts of military policy in which antagonistic states cooperate in the pursuit of common purposes even when they are struggling in the pursuit of conflicting ones' (Bull 1965, xiv). The purpose of arms control is therefore to make war less likely between adversarial states, to reduce the economic and social costs of those states preparing for war, and to make war less destructive if it does break out (Larsen and Smith 2005, 23). Nuclear arms control agreements are designed to regulate the development, deployment, possession, and use of nuclear weapons. Traditionally, instead of serving the purpose of nuclear disarmament and the abolition of nuclear weapons, nuclear arms control aimed to manage the relations between nuclear states, enhance stability, and maintain deterrence (Futter 2021, 129). Arms control, as Hans Morgenthau put it in 1975, 'is not disarmament at all, it is a mere regulation of the arms race', where states can still 'pursue that race with certain agreed-upon limits' (Morgenthau 1975, 57).

Arms control was often criticised by conservatives on the right for giving authoritarian states such as the USSR (and its later evolution into a neo-authoritarian Russia) an advantage, because such states don't have to face public scrutiny or democratic processes, while they can also covertly breach any limits of arms control treaties. Such a view appears to have underpinned the Trump administration's reasons for leaving both the INF Treaty and the Iran nuclear deal. In contrast to this conservative view of arms control, those on the left traditionally criticised arms control as 'a sham, an example of great power condominium designed to legitimise the arms race' (Croft 1996, 1–2), because it allows states to ignore pressures for complete disarmament and a reorientation of their priorities from military security. However, with the signing of the INF Treaty in particular, the distinction between arms control and disarmament became much less stark, as the INF Treaty eliminated an entire category of nuclear weapons (Croft 1996, 3). The fact that the INF Treaty was the only arms control agreement to abolish an entire class of nuclear weapons, alongside the fact that it spurred a dramatic shift in the reduction of nuclear weapons and further arms control agreements between the USA and Russia after the end of the Cold War, demonstrates how significant the demise of the INF is.

Alongside the critiques of arms control from the right and the left of the political spectrum, there is also a broader issue concerning how academic research on the details and histories of arms control agreements has led to an oversight of the broader *politics* of arms control. In the same year that the INF Treaty entered into force, the security studies expert Lawrence Freedman wrote a short essay titled *Why is Arms Control so Boring?* (1987) where the central claim of his argument was that much policy and scholarly discussion of arms control soon descended into a mind-numbing wade through minor details about the technicalities of nuclear weapons. For Freedman, this led to scholarship focusing on the minutiae of arms control agreements at the expense of analysing the broader issues that shape the context of arms control negotiations and treaties, as well as the conceptual underpinnings, practical impact, and unexplored potentialities of how arms control could bring about 'radical change' (Freedman 1987, 5), rather than reinforcing a status quo where nuclear weapons states can generally do as they please. Indeed, the predominant orientation of arms control scholarship and practice has adopted a problem-solving approach where underlying assumptions and what is considered 'common sense' – for example about the nature of states in an anarchic international system – have rarely been critically reflected on by scholars or policy makers (Cooper and Mutimer 2011, 3). Therefore, if we are to understand the true significance of the INF Treaty's collapse, then an understanding of arms control from a critical, rather than problem-solving, perspective is needed as it broadens our understanding of how and why arms control matters.

In his historical overview of arms control, from ancient history to the early post-Cold War era, Stuart Croft points out that a critical approach to arms control recognises that it has been characterised by three features. First, arms control has been conducted by states and political entities with the assumption that 'it would be both possible and desirable to develop some form of cooperation in the military field in order to avoid war, manage crises and, should war nevertheless occur, to limit the ensuing damage' (Croft 1996, 13). Second, arms control has aimed to control certain forms of weaponry, their possession, and their means of production. Third, arms control arrangements have been implicitly or explicitly 'based on a hope ... that they would lead to an improvement in political relations between the participants' (Croft 1996, 14). Here, the hope is that improvement in state relations would arise from the expectation that security concerns could be minimised and that agreements would form 'the basis for further confidence building measures' (Croft 1996, 13; Nye 1991). Consequently, 'arms control has always been about creating and/or supporting norms of behaviour in international politics' (Croft 1996, 14). The significance of arms control is hence not simply about complex negotiations between states and how they reduce certain weapons; rather, it is about how they can have a broader societal impact by changing the behaviour of political actors.

There are several features central to a critical understanding of nuclear arms control. The first two overlap with problem-solving approaches: first, an attention to cooperation between nuclear weapons states in order to avoid war and crises; and second, a focus on how arms control limits the testing, development, deployment, and scope of nuclear weapons (Futter 2021, 180). Beyond this, we need also to recognise how arms control creates and supports norms of behaviour. This is because arms control agreements help to shape the broader relations between political actors; they enable and constraint certain behaviours, and thus have an impact beyond the specifics of what is outlined in the text of their treaties. Moreover, we need to consider how arms control agreements serve as 'the embodiment of potentially dystopian futures that need to be guarded against' (Cooper and Mutimer 2011, 5). Rather than being a scientifically rigorous field of immutable truths, scholarship and policy on arms control often doesn't 'so much resemble science as science fiction' (Cooper and Mutimer 2011, 5). This is because arms control is, just like the theory and practice of deterrence, concerned with thought experiments and fears of a future that has yet to pass, where arms control is 'an exercise in making assumptions about a form of war that had never occurred' (Cooper and Mutimer 2011, 6).

If we think in these terms about the INF Treaty it becomes apparent how and why its demise has drastic implications for global politics and security. The INF Treaty was an important step in cooperation between the United States and the Soviet Union (and then Russia) as the treaty was negotiated in response to NATO's deployment of hundreds of ground-launched ballistic and cruise missiles in Western Europe and the Soviet Union's deployment of similar weapons across its territories. The negotiations for the INF Treaty began on 23 September 1981 and took place over six years during heightened tension between the USA and the USSR in the early and mid-1980s. Despite the journey to the INF Treaty being 'a truly tortured one' (Sauer 1998, 98), it was through face-to-face diplomacy and the gradual building of trust between Reagan and Gorbachev – which led to a cooperative, friendly relationship between the two leaders (Wheeler 2018, 168) – that the INF Treaty was signed at a summit meeting in Washington on 8 December 1987. According to President Reagan himself, the INF Treaty was 'epoch-making' as it was 'the first treaty to eliminate an entire class of US and Soviet nuclear missiles' (1988). As Reagan put it at the time; 'we have walked a long way together to clear a path for peace' (1988), and the INF Treaty was truly ground-breaking in banning an entire class of nuclear weapon.

The achievements of the INF Treaty are a central aspect of why its end marks the real beginning of the Third Nuclear Age. On 11 May 1991, less than four years after the INF Treaty was signed, the USA and the USSR had eliminated a total of 2,692 nuclear missiles. The INF Treaty subsequently eliminated intermediate-range nuclear weapons, and even though both countries have accused one another of breaching the treaty since 2014, the general adherence of both parties to the treaty suggests it had a substantial impact on not only controlling nuclear arms but also on working to abolish an entire category of weapons for over two decades.

We should also be concerned about the end of the INF Treaty because it played an important role in creating a norm of cooperation between the USA and Russia in the realm of nuclear arms control and disarmament. In his memoir, Gorbachev said that with the INF Treaty, 'We had reached a new level of trust in our relations with the United States and initiated a genuine disarmament process, creating a new security system that would be based on comprehensive co-operation instead of the threat of mutual destruction' (Gorbachev quoted in Wheeler 2018, 170). This 'genuine disarmament process' involved the abolition of US and Russian tactical, non-strategic nuclear weapons in the early 1990s as well as the later START and SORT treaties which greatly reduced the number of strategic weapons that the USA and Russia could possess. Ultimately, the INF Treaty began a wave of unprecedented nuclear arms control and disarmament measures between the two largest nuclear weapon states.

The agreement of the INF Treaty also represented, in Gorbachev's words, an event of 'universal significance' that offered 'a big chance ... to get onto the road leading away from the threat of catastrophe' (in Reagan and Gorbachev 1987). In this sense, the INF Treaty embodied a fear of a dystopian future that could be avoided through cooperation and nuclear disarmament. It was, as Reagan put it, 'the beginning of a working relationship' (in Reagan and Gorbachev 1987) that would see an end to hostilities and confrontation between the two superpowers, and would instead, as Gorbachev suggested, be a step 'toward a nuclear-free world, which holds out for our children and grandchildren and for their children and grandchildren the promise of a fulfilling and happy life without fear and without a senseless waste of resources on weapons of destruction' (in Reagan and Gorbachev 1987). The INF Treaty was seen by those leaders who signed it as 'the watershed separating the era of a mounting risk of nuclear war from the era of a demilitarization of human life' (Gorbachev in Reagan and Gorbachev 1987), and on signing the INF Treaty, Gorbachev remarked that it was a 'sapling, which may one day grow into a mighty tree of peace' (Gorbachev in Reagan and Gorbachev 1987).

The formal US and Russian withdrawal from the INF Treaty in August 2019 is therefore a watershed moment where decades of progress on nuclear arms control truly began to unravel as the leaves on the tree of peace began to wither and fall. The INF Treaty's demise is the pivotal moment around which the Third Nuclear Age began, and the unravelling of the INF Treaty has had serious consequences for global politics: not only does it signal a serious deterioration of formal cooperative nuclear arms control relations between the United States and Russia, but it also marks an incredible step backwards since the USA and Russia sought to immediately deploy nuclear weapons that had previously been banned under the treaty.

Within one week of the INF Treaty's end, on 8 August 2019, a Russian test of a ground-launched nuclear-powered cruise missile capable of carrying nuclear warheads ended in disaster as it exploded and killed seven people on a test range near the White Sea. Despite the explosion, Vladimir Putin vowed to continue working on the 'unparalleled weapon' which was 'designed to ensure Russia's sovereignty and security for decades to come' and would be 'the most important reliable guarantee of peace on the planet today' (quoted in Moscow Times 2019).

Russia was not the only state that sought to develop new capabilities now that the INF Treaty had collapsed. Ten days after the failed Russian missile test, on 18 August, the US Department of Defense tested a ground-launched cruise missile, with a range of between 500 and 5,500 kilometres, on the coast of California. In a statement the Department of Defense announced that the test would inform their 'development of future intermediate-range capabilities' (Department of Defense 2019). A day later, US Defense Secretary Mark Esper announced that he was looking to deploy INF missiles in Europe and in the Asia-Pacific region (quoted in Ali 2019). In response, Matt Korda, a nuclear policy analyst at the Federation of American Scientists, stated, 'it definitely doesn't help diffuse the arms race at all. It's not really worth it just to give the corpse of the INF treaty the middle finger' (in Ploughshares Fund 2019).

The immediate steps taken by Russia and the United States clearly demonstrate the risk of exterminism brought about through a new nuclear arms race as each state seeks a military advantage by developing and testing new missiles capable of carrying nuclear warheads. With the end of the INF Treaty, the world entered an age of 'strategic instability' between the USA and Russia, where 'an accident or mishap could set off a cataclysm', where 'unlike during the Cold War, both sides seem wilfully blind to the peril' (Moniz and Nunn 2019). Significantly, whereas since the late 1980s nuclear arms control and disarmament were understood to be essential for ensuring the future survival and security of states and the planet itself, the developments since the end of the INF Treaty demonstrate that this is no longer the case. Instead, in the Third Nuclear Age, the USA and Russia now view the development of new nuclear weapons technologies as central to ensuring their own security. With the immediate testing of intermediate-range missiles, not only did the USA and Russia undermine the progress they had made in arms control and disarmament, but they created the impression that other states, such as China, should feel vindicated that they were not party to such arms control agreements.

Despite demands from the Trump administration that China should enter into trilateral arms control agreements on INF missiles and strategic nuclear weapons with the United States and Russia, it now became even easier for China to dismiss these claims. Why should they – a state with far fewer nuclear weapons than either the USA or Russia – enter into talks to limit nuclear weapons when others were so keen to develop new ones? This is exactly how China responded to the collapse of the INF Treaty, with one Chinese diplomat stating that China had 'no interest' in trilateral arms control because of these developments and 'the huge gap between [the] nuclear arsenal of China and those of the U.S. and the Russian Federation'. Therefore, China would not 'participate in any nuclear reduction negotiations at this stage' (Cong in Ministry of Foreign Affairs of the People's Republic of China 2019). The Chinese diplomat went on to note that the USA and Russia 'bear special and primary responsibilities on nuclear disarmament' and that they 'should maintain the existing arms control treaties, and on that basis, continue to further cut their huge nuclear arsenals, so as to create conditions for other countries to participate in this process' (Cong in Ministry of Foreign Affairs of the People's Republic of China 2019). Clearly, the end of the INF Treaty was not conducive to furthering international cooperation in arms control.

Soon after the end of the INF Treaty another significant event signalled the further unravelling of nuclear arms control and disarmament: the announcement that the Trump administration was seeking to leave the Open Skies Treaty. This treaty allowed the USA, Russia, and European states to fly over each other's territory for surveillance purposes; it was intended to promote openness and transparency because states could fly over military installations and verify what they saw. One US Congressman wrote to the National Security Advisor that it would be a 'reckless action' to withdraw from the Open Skies Treaty as it would 'undermine America's reliability as a stable and predictable partner when it comes to European security' (Engel 2019). Despite this call to support US allies, and other pleas from Congress, the US eventually withdrew from the treaty in May 2020. Russia followed suit in January 2021, and the incoming Biden administration announced that the United States would not seek to re-enter the treaty. Once again, in the late summer of 2019 the USA and Russia began taking backward steps that undermined progress in cooperation, openness, and measures intended to avoid tensions and crises between them.

As the INF Treaty ended, the Third Nuclear Age began. Both Russia and the United States sought to develop and deploy new missiles, other states such as China expressed that without the USA and Russia being engaged in arms control measures they would not enter into any agreements, and we saw the beginning of the end for other important international treaties. However, the dawn of the Third Nuclear Age did not simply involve the demise of formal arms control treaties, it also involved the erosion of global norms around the non-use of nuclear weapons as state leaders and public figures began to talk about using nuclear weapons for various purposes, such as stopping hurricanes, terraforming Mars, or using low-yield weapons to fight a nuclear war.

Nuclear weapons as a silver bullet: the erosion of the nuclear taboo

Nuclear weapons are often claimed to have brought about a revolution in international politics. In one sense, nuclear weapons have been revolutionary due to their sheer ability to cause such incredible levels of destruction in the blink of an eye. As the International Relations scholar Daniel Deudney has put it, nuclear weapons are revolutionary because of 'certain awesome facts that are beyond controversy: nuclear science and technology have given us the capability to wreak violence at an unprecedented scale and speed' (Deudney 1995, 210). In another sense, nuclear weapons have been understood to be revolutionary due to how 'the prospect of nuclear omnicide' (Craig and Amadae 2021, 1) dissuades states from intense competition and conflict, thereby supposedly contributing to global stability and peace (Jervis 1990). As events towards the end of the Cold War have demonstrated, this latter view of a nuclear revolution is inaccurate, as the USA did in fact seek nuclear superiority over, rather than balance with, the Soviet Union (Green 2020). Moreover, as recent events have shown, the USA is now seeking nuclear war-winning capabilities and nuclear weapon states are engaged in intense security competition (Lieber and Press 2020). The revolutionary destructive power of nuclear weapons has not brought about a revolution in the peace and security of the world. Indeed, quite the opposite is true, as the above discussion of the end of the INF Treaty and the nascent arms race has shown.

Even though nuclear weapons have not brought about an end to security competition, they have not been used in war since the USA dropped them on Japan in 1945. This seven-decade period of the non-use of nuclear weapons has provided an intriguing puzzle for scholars of International

Relations, and has been explained by the development of a 'nuclear taboo' (Tannenwald 1999, 2007). Conventional explanations for the non-use of nuclear weapons would suggest that nuclear deterrence has been effective in preventing their use. However, deterrence fails to explain how and why nuclear-armed states have not used nuclear weapons against states that don't possess nuclear weapons. Nor does deterrence explain how and why nuclear-armed states have not retaliated with nuclear weapons against non-nuclear-armed states who have attacked them. In viewing deterrence as having insufficient explanatory value for the non-use of nuclear weapons, Nina Tannenwald has argued that a powerful norm of a taboo has developed around nuclear weapons (Tannenwald 1999, 2007; see also Rublee and Cohen 2018), whereby even states that possess them are prohibited from using them as the use of nuclear weapons is understood to be just too unethical and abhorrent.

In contrast to viewing the 'nuclear taboo' as a social norm, other scholars have argued that nuclear non-use is not due to deterrence or a strong taboo around nuclear weapons, rather it is a 'tradition of non-use' (Paul 2010) where states have rationally and strategically decided not to use nuclear weapons due to the perceived consequences that breaking the tradition of non-use would bring about by setting a bad precedent, and potentially leading to further nuclear proliferation and use. In this view, nuclear non-use is not a strong norm that constitutes a taboo that can never be broken; instead it is 'fragile and contingent on the dynamics of strategic interaction' (Smetana and Wunderlich 2021, 5; see also Pauly 2018; Davis Gibbons and Lieber 2019). As Harald Müller has recently argued,

> a taboo on the use of nuclear weapons can logically not coexist with the maintenance of nuclear deterrence as a security doctrine and the existence (in physical or 'virtual' form) of nuclear weapons themselves. Deterrence ideology, paradoxically, presumes the planning, preparing, and therefore thinking and speaking about nuclear use in order to avoid nuclear use ... These institutionalized practices are a fixed part of the governmental apparatus and of national security discourse, even if it recedes occasionally into the background like in the nineties and during the early Obama Administration. With these requirements, a taboo is impossible to achieve. (Müller in Smetana and Wunderlich 2021, 13–14)

Instead, there are 'normative inhibitions against firing nuclear arms' (Müller in Smetana and Wunderlich 2021, 114) but states are still prepared to use them.

The weakness of the nuclear taboo has also been highlighted by recent research into public opinion about the use of nuclear weapons. Whereas claims about the nuclear taboo or tradition of non-use were originally based on analyses of governmental archives and elite statements, recent studies have asked the public what they think about the use of nuclear weapons. Through survey experiments and polling, scholars have found that there is 'relatively little evidence that the U.S. public strongly opposes the U.S. use of nuclear weapons' (Press, Sagan, and Valentino 2013, 189). One study has in fact found that a majority of the American public would approve using nuclear weapons that would kill millions of civilians in a non-nuclear-armed state if it would save the lives of American soldiers (Sagan and Valentino 2017, 45). Other studies of American public opinion have also found that 'the nuclear taboo, if it exists, is fragile' (Koch and Wells 2021, 16), because Americans appear to support the use of nuclear weapons unless they are presented with vivid information about 'the material or human harms that result from a nuclear detonation' (Koch and Wells 2021, 16).

Research on public opinion about nuclear weapons in Europe provides a more positive picture. Seventy-four per cent of respondents to a poll in 2019 supported the abolition of nuclear weapons, and even when citizens of Europe's two nuclear powers (the UK and France) were asked when it would be permissible to use a nuclear weapon, 79 per cent said that 'it is never acceptable to use nuclear weapons' (Pelopidas and Egeland 2020). Whilst we know much less about public opinion on nuclear weapons in other parts of the world, recent research has found that in Japan 85 per cent of the public would not support the use of a nuclear weapon on North Korea, even if they attacked Japan with a nuclear weapon, and 75 per cent of the Japanese public support a ban on nuclear weapons (Baron, Gibbons, and Herzog 2020, 301). Further research is needed to provide a more detailed insight into the nuclear taboo across different countries and cultures (Smetana and Wunderlich 2021, 5), especially when different methods of research produce such different results (Tannenwald in Smetana and Wunderlich 2021, 10). However, regardless of whether the non-use of nuclear weapons can be explained as a strong social norm of a nuclear taboo, or a weak tradition underpinned by rationalist strategic logics, or indeed regardless of whether it even matters if citizens support it or not (Rublee in Smetana and Wunderlich 2021), events in the summer of 2019 evidenced an erosion in 'atomic aversion' (Press, Sagan, and Valentino 2013).

The waning idea that nuclear weapons should not be used is evident in statements from the US President and other prominent public figures made during the months of August–October 2019. These statements proposed that nuclear weapons were a silver bullet to national and global problems. On 16 August, Elon Musk, the tech entrepreneur and billionaire owner of SpaceX, tweeted 'Nuke Mars!' to millions of his followers on the social media platform Twitter. The reason for his tweet was the theory that nuclear weapons could be used to terraform the red planet, quickly making it habitable for humans by evaporating water at the poles and releasing carbon dioxide into the atmosphere to cause a greenhouse effect to support life. Despite this theory being debunked by scientists, Musk began selling T-shirts with the slogan 'NUKE MARS' for the cost of $30 on the SpaceX website the day after sending this tweet. Not only would Musk go on to wear the 'NUKE MARS' shirt in front of an audience of 7.3 million people during his May 2021 appearance on Saturday Night Live (USA Today 2021), but he also later expanded on his idea, stating that he needed 'more than 10,000' of the biggest nuclear weapons currently available to terraform Mars (Musk quoted in Delbert 2020). Given that the earth's entire nuclear weapon stockpile currently stands at just over 13,000 nuclear weapons, Musk's plans would involve almost doubling the number of nuclear weapons in existence and actually using them, albeit on another planet.

On 25 August, another fantastical suggestion for the use of nuclear weapons was made by a prominent public figure, but this time it came from the President of the United States himself. In the midst of hurricane season in the USA, the news website Axios reported that Donald Trump had suggested 'several times' in meetings with government officials that the American government should consider using nuclear weapons to stop hurricanes reaching the US mainland. According to a source, Trump said in one hurricane briefing, 'I got it. I got it. Why don't we nuke them? … They start forming off the coast of Africa, as they're moving across the Atlantic, we drop a bomb inside the eye of the hurricane and it disrupts it. Why can't we do that?' (quoted in Swan 2019). In response, someone in the room said, 'Sir, we'll look into that' (quoted in Swan 2019).

Later that day, Trump tweeted 'The story by Axios that President Trump wanted to blow up large hurricanes with nuclear weapons prior to reaching shore is ridiculous. I never said this. Just more FAKE NEWS!' Yet despite this, a senior administration official did not deny that Trump proposed using nuclear weapons against hurricanes, and simply stated: 'His goal – to keep a catastrophic hurricane from hitting the mainland – is not bad. … His objective is not bad' (quoted in Swan 2019). However, as with the idea of nuking Mars, scientists have also proven that nuking hurricanes is a bad idea; not least because it would create nuclear fallout that would cause devastating environmental problems whilst likely having little to no impact on slowing or stopping a hurricane (Strauss 2016).

These two humorous examples reveal how nuclear exterminism becomes manifest when nuclear weapons are envisioned as a potential solution for national and global problems. These ideas should cause concern because of, not despite, their seeming ridiculousness. Musk's comments indicate a normalisation of nuclear weapons as a tool of 'space expansionism' which will dramatically shape the future of planet earth even if it all seems like science fiction (Deudney 2020, 23). Musk's desire to colonise space and to expand the human habitat by using nuclear weapons paradoxically risks a potential extinction event that he and other billionaire space expansionists, like Amazon's Jeff Bezos, are seeking to avoid. Similarly, Trump's calls to nuke a hurricane pose an even greater danger than the threat of hurricanes themselves. Both of these ideas for using nuclear weapons make them appear as a simple silver bullet and a solution to complex problems. Despite evidence suggesting that nuclear weapons are not, and will never be, effective solutions for those problems, the mere suggestion from prominent figures like Musk and Trump that nuclear weapons can and should be used serves to undermine the idea of nuclear non-use whilst also distracting from the inherent violent and destructive potential of such weapons.

The fact that these ideas are funny – perhaps even jokes – doesn't mean that we should think them insignificant. Humour serves to obfuscate and make light of whatever is being joked about, and by eliciting a positive emotional response in the audience, a joke can serve to normalise an idea and legitimise it in global politics (Crilley and Chatterje-Doody 2021; Crilley and Pears 2021; Chernobrov 2022; Saunders, Crilley, and Chatterje-Doody 2022). Some of us might laugh at the idea of nuking Mars or hurricanes, but others will not, and given the large, cult-like followings that Musk and Trump both have, these ideas could gain popular support. Musk's 'Nuke Mars!' tweet, for example, received over 26,000 retweets and 222,000 likes. As nuclear weapons become tools to terraform a planet or stop a hurricane, they become disassociated with their use in war, and by distracting the public from this, elite figures erode whatever is left of the taboo or tradition of non-use around nuclear weapons. Whilst Musk's idea also causes concern as it proposes a future where wealthy individuals and private companies should possess nuclear weapons, it currently remains fantastical. Yet, not too long ago, Musk's ambition to make self-driving cars or send astronauts into space via rockets made by his own private company also seemed like impossible dreams. Trump's comments are even more concerning given that the US President has sole authority over America's nuclear arsenal and there is nothing in place institutionally to stop him from using nuclear weapons however he pleases. Simply by uttering these ideas, Musk and Trump have spoken an erosion of the nuclear taboo into existence, and later developments that we will examine in subsequent chapters add further weight to the argument that in the Third Nuclear Age we are seeing serious steps towards nuclear weapons being used again.

Conclusion: why we need arms control and the nuclear taboo

The development of nuclear arms control agreements, viewed as part of a broader global nuclear non-proliferation regime, have been criticised due to how they are an insubstantial solution to the problem of potential nuclear catastrophe that requires more radical solutions which are often overlooked or silenced by the sustainment of a 'nuclear order' that serves the interest of the nuclear weapon states (see Craig and Ruzicka 2013; Biswas 2014; Pelopidas 2016; Considine 2017; Meyn 2018; Ruzicka 2018; Ritchie 2019; Egeland 2021). Nuclear arms control measures such as the NPT may aim to prevent the spread of nuclear weapons to other states, but they enshrine the possessors of nuclear weapons with legitimacy and make hollow commitments to nuclear disarmament. The failure of nuclear weapons states to uphold or to make substantial progress in their commitments to nuclear disarmament has led to the entry into force of the Treaty on the Prohibition of Nuclear Weapons (TPNW/Ban Treaty). The TPNW aims to globally ban nuclear weapons, and it challenges the idea that a handful of nuclear weapons states have special rights and are guardians of order by highlighting how the status quo is a system 'in which certain states possess indiscriminate weapons in defiance of international legal norms' (Egeland 2021, 21). The TPNW, then, is an instrument of disarmament as it aims to abolish nuclear weapons in their entirety. However, whilst we need radical developments such as the Ban Treaty to move towards a world without nuclear weapons, given that no nuclear weapons states have signed the Ban Treaty (and are unlikely to sign it anytime soon), if we hope to temper the nuclear exterminism of the Third Nuclear Age then we also need arms control measures and agreements between nuclear weapon states.

The INF Treaty was ground-breaking as it was an arms control agreement that worked towards nuclear disarmament by banning nuclear-capable missiles of a certain range. Its demise is a dangerous portent of exterminism as states have immediately sought to develop and deploy previously banned nuclear weapons and have brought us as into a new nuclear arms race. Because of this, we need nuclear arms control agreements. Not only do treaties such as the INF place limitations on the arsenals of nuclear weapons states and help to avoid arms races, they also contribute to the development of international norms of cooperation, trust, verification, and nuclear non-use, all of which help to provide a platform from which we can work towards further disarmament.

The norm of nuclear non-use is also integral to avoiding nuclear catastrophe, yet we have seen its erosion at the outset of the Third Nuclear Age. Regardless of whether this norm is a strong taboo or a tradition of rational strategic behaviour, it has played a role in ensuring that nuclear weapons have not been used since 1945. As we saw in this chapter, the ideas of prominent global figures to use nuclear weapons as a silver bullet to fix problems such as hurricanes or terraforming Mars are funny because they are so utterly stupid, but they work to undermine the notion that nuclear weapons should not be used. Significantly, even in their ridiculousness, these ideas are dangerous because they make light of the very real harms that nuclear weapons cause.

This chapter has argued that the Third Nuclear Age began with the collapse of the INF Treaty in August 2019. In doing so I explained how and why arms control can help to avoid nuclear exterminism whilst demonstrating how dangerous the end of the INF Treaty is. Beyond this, I highlighted how a norm around the non-use of nuclear weapons also helps to prevent catastrophe, and I drew attention to the dangers of this norm eroding in the new nuclear age. In the next chapter we build upon this argument and explore how the development of new nuclear weapons technologies, such as low-yield weapons and hypersonic missiles, signals a further step away from the 'atomic aversion' that has been prominent in global politics since the late 1980s. At the same time, we also examine the role of popular culture in shaping how we come to know and think about nuclear weapons, their most recent technological developments, and the unparalleled catastrophe they threaten us with.

4

'This is a high time for hypersonic missiles': November 2019 to January 2020

> When the bombs drop darling, can you say that you've lived your life?
> Oh, this is a high time for hypersonic missiles
>
> Sam Fender, 2019

On a dark December evening a few days before Christmas, I'm driving to a friend's house with Rhiannon who is heavily pregnant as we await the imminent arrival of our first child. The traffic is heavy, but we're in a good mood listening to one of our favourite DJs on the radio where Annie Mac is playing an eclectic mix of new music on BBC Radio 1. As it's nearly the end of the year, Annie announces the results of a listener vote for the 'Hottest Record of the Year'. The award goes to Sam Fender – a young indie artist from Newcastle – for his record 'Hypersonic Missiles'.

As we slowly make our way through the city, 'Hypersonic Missiles' channels the sound of Bruce Springsteen and opens with the muted strumming of a guitar as Fender lyrically paints a bleak picture of modern life for the disaffected youth of today. Fender begins by singing about consuming goods from American corporations, watching American movies, and living with wool over his eyes. As Fender mocks his own participation in American corporate and popular culture, we continue to drive. The drums kick in and the music gradually builds as Fender points out how we're distracted from war and conflict. Sardonically highlighting his own ignorance, Fender sings about how he is blissfully unaware of what goes on in the world as children are bombed and global tensions are rising.

The song crescendos as the chorus kicks in, and in his Geordie-accented Springsteen-esque tenor Fender sings:

> All the silver-tongued suits and cartoons that rule my world
> Are saying it's a high time for hypersonic missiles
> When the bombs drop darling, can you say that you've lived your life?
> Oh, this is a high time for hypersonic missiles

I turn the radio up, and as I nod along I think how weird it is that the 'Hottest Record of the Year' as decided by listeners of the UK's most popular radio station is a critique of new nuclear weapons technology. I guess it's a sign of the times.

According to Annie Mac, the 'Hottest Record of the Year' is a chance to 'celebrate the state of play when it comes to our music landscape and the culture around it', and Fender's song was so popular because 'something about his art touches people and connects them in a way that doesn't come around that often … he's not afraid to sing about the scary stuff in life' (Mac 2019). The popularity of 'Hypersonic Missiles' reveals how popular culture is not separate from world politics; rather, the two issues are inextricably linked and constitutive of each other (Grayson, Davies, and Philpott 2009). As Fender stated in an interview:

> I write songs about what I see; that could be about anything, from my hometown to the stuff that I see online in the news or on the telly … I just grew up and saw the world for what it was. So I started to write about these broader subjects. (In Mitchinson 2019)

Here, Fender's engagement with politics through what he saw in the media shaped the music he made. Then, his music engaged a popular audience who are more likely to have learnt about hypersonic missiles through his songs than through reading policy briefings about new nuclear weapons technologies. Fender's first album went to number one in the UK charts and his tours have sold out stadium venues throughout the country. He is, I would hazard a guess, the first artist to sing about hypersonic missiles to a packed-out Wembley Stadium. This development is indicative of the salience that nuclear weapons are once again gaining in the public imagination. In the context of hypersonic missiles becoming infamous through a pop song, this chapter explores the issue of new technologies and popular culture in the Third Nuclear Age. It documents events between November 2019 and January 2020, beginning with a focus on hypersonic missiles and the role of new nuclear weapons technologies. Then I explore the significance of popular culture and the media in shaping how the world comes to know, think about, and act towards nuclear weapons.

New technologies and the Third Nuclear Age

One week after 'Hypersonic Missiles' was announced as the hottest record of the year on British radio, in the Orenburg region of the southern Ural Mountains, Russia became the first country to deploy hypersonic missiles. On 27 December 2019 Russia announced that the Avangard hypersonic missile system was now in military service, capable of travelling twenty-seven times faster than the speed of sound and able to avoid the missile defences of potential adversaries. When Vladimir Putin originally announced the development of this weapon in March 2018, he bragged that it was 'absolutely invulnerable ... it flies to its target like a meteorite, like a ball of fire' (quoted in O'Connor 2018). In a speech after the deployment of the Avangard missile, Putin said that the West was now 'playing catch up'. As if to prove Putin's point, in December 2019 the US Congress approved the largest military budget since the Second World War (with the exception of during the Iraq War), funding the Pentagon with $738 billion. Not only did this military budget fund a low-yield nuclear warhead for US Navy submarines, it also ramped up the Pentagon's research into hypersonic technology by requesting $2.6 billion to develop these new weapons. In the previous year, the Pentagon's spending on hypersonics had increased by an incredible 136 per cent, and since 2019 spending on hypersonic missiles and associated technologies has continued to increase, with the Pentagon requesting $3.8 billion for hypersonic missile research and development in their 2022 budget proposal.

So, what exactly is a hypersonic missile? Unlike conventional intercontinental ballistic missiles that launch nuclear warheads on fixed and therefore predictable trajectories, hypersonic missiles can potentially be steered on unpredictable trajectories once they have been launched. Hypersonics are launched by 'booster' missiles which they then separate from in order to glide towards their target whilst also being manoeuvrable so as to avoid any missile defence measures. Capable of travelling many times faster than the speed of sound (hence the name 'hypersonic'), carrying heavy payloads, and potentially having intercontinental reach, hypersonic missiles are attractive technologies to states who possess nuclear weapons, yet hypersonics pose challenges for global security and the relations between the nuclear weapons states that seek them (Williams 2019; Futter and Zala 2021). This is because hypersonic missiles cause a high level of uncertainty that undermines what some analysts refer to as 'strategic stability' – the notion that nuclear weapons states have a level of predictability and transparency in their interactions with each other – whilst also contributing to a new arms race.

Hypersonic missiles pose several major risks to undermining stability and global security. First, because hypersonic missiles can carry conventional or nuclear warheads, they have a dual-use capability that blurs the boundaries between nuclear and non-nuclear military forces. As these two distinct areas become 'entangled' (Acton 2018), we are presented with ambiguity with regard to what type of warheads missiles are carrying, alongside ambiguity in where they might be targeted. This dual capability increases the potential risk of 'inadvertent or unintentional escalation' at times of crisis (Williams 2019, 797). Second, the development of advanced conventional hypersonic weapons may lead to states believing that they can conduct a non-nuclear first strike that would destroy an adversary's nuclear arsenal (Williams 2019, 798). By making states uncertain about the survivability of their nuclear weapons, states may come to believe that the best course of action is for them to strike first, therefore making conflict and a potential nuclear war more likely. Third, the deployment of hypersonic missiles in Russia has led to dramatic increases in the development of hypersonic missiles and related missile defence systems in the United States, as a hypersonic arms race has fast become a reality. Not only has the rush to develop and deploy hypersonics outpaced much consideration of their 'potential perils' (Smith 2019), but there are still no arms control measures in place – nor serious discussions to implement them on a bilateral or multilateral basis – to limit their development and use.

If the December 2019 deployment of Russian hypersonic missiles and the ensuing arms race wasn't enough to demonstrate the onslaught of a dangerous new nuclear era, other developments in nuclear weapons technology during these winter months also illustrate how the world is edging towards potential catastrophe. In January 2020 the US Navy confirmed that they had deployed a new low-yield nuclear warhead on the Trident missile submarine *USS Tennessee*. With the explosive power of six kilotons, the new W76-2 warhead is described as 'low yield' because its explosive yield is lower than the 90–450 kilotons of other Trident missile warheads deployed on US Navy submarines. However, the 'low yield' warhead is still more than 500 times as powerful as the most powerful conventional explosive in the US arsenal (Facini 2020) and a third as powerful as the atomic bomb that destroyed Hiroshima in 1945.

The decision to deploy this new warhead was originally set out in the Trump administration's 2018 Nuclear Posture Review which claimed that a new low-yield warhead was needed 'for the preservation of credible deterrence against regional aggression' (Department of Defense 2018, xii). Seen as a 'low cost and near term modification', the new low-yield nuclear warhead was intended to 'counter any mistaken perception of an exploitable "gap" in US regional deterrence capabilities' (Department of Defense 2018, xii). Here, the US made presumptions about a Russian strategy of 'escalate to de-escalate' where the thinking was that if conventional war broke out in Europe, Russia could use a low-yield nuclear weapon against NATO and US forces, who would supposedly have to surrender if they could not retaliate with their own low-yield nuke. The USA therefore proposed that by deploying its own low-yield weapon it could deter the Russians from ever using theirs. According to the 2018 NPR, deploying a new nuclear weapon was justified as it would 'raise the nuclear threshold and help ensure that potential adversaries perceive no possible advantage in limited nuclear escalation, making nuclear employment less likely' (Department of Defense 2018, xii).

Ironically, the deployment of the 'low yield' warhead is intended to signal that the USA is *more* willing to use a nuclear weapon in a potential warfighting scenario, yet it claims that it will make nuclear conflict *less* likely. This is a dangerous leap of (il)logic, as low-yield nuclear weapons are designed to be 'more usable as weapons of war' (Kaplan 2020, 284) and are therefore more likely to actually be used, especially by an erratic state leader in a crisis. Indeed, even one Republican senator referred to the White House as an 'adult day care centre' and thought Trump's threats and nuclear policies – such as the 'low yield' warhead – paved a 'path to World War III' (Bob Corker quoted in Kaplan 2020, 285).

Fears that an American president would do something rash and dangerous were brought to the fore in January 2020 when an American drone strike at Baghdad airport in Iraq killed Iran's most prominent military commander, General Qasem Soleimani. The Pentagon stated that the strike 'was aimed at deterring future Iranian attack plans' (Department of Defense 2020), since Soleimani was viewed as a dangerous figure responsible for orchestrating Bashar al-Assad's brutal war in Syria as well as organising covert operations and supporting militias in Iraq, Lebanon, and Palestine. Viewed by the United States as an act of deterrence, other actors such as the UN were quick to point out that the assassination of a military leader in a foreign country was an unlawful, extrajudicial killing. Due to a distinct lack of evidence that there was 'an actual imminent threat to life, the course of action taken by the US was unlawful' (Callamard 2020, 40). The killing was, in the words of one UN report, an 'arbitrary killing for which the US is responsible' (Callamard 2020, 39).

The assassination of adversaries through drone strikes in foreign countries became a regular occurrence during the War on Terror, and under Barack Obama's presidency there were ten times as many drone strikes as under George W. Bush. Under the presidency of Donald Trump, America's assassination programme ramped up. Trump relaxed the rules of engagement for authorising drone strikes and removed transparency measures such as the reporting requirement for casualties outside of designated battlefields. Despite these measures to avoid scrutiny, research shows that, for example, in the first few months of 2020 Trump launched forty airstrikes in Somalia – whereas between 2007 and 2016 Bush and Obama launched a combined total of forty-one airstrikes (Atherton 2020). In Afghanistan, between 2017 and 2019 civilian deaths from drone strikes 'dramatically increased' (Crawford 2020, 1), and in 2019, 700 Afghan civilians were killed by airstrikes – more than in any other year since 2002 and the start of the American-led war in Afghanistan. Trump's escalation of American drone strikes and the subsequent increase in civilian casualties – as well as the targeting of Iranian military figures such as Soleimani rather than terrorist figures from al-Qaeda or ISIS

– indicate that earlier beliefs that Trump was 'Donald the Dove' (Dowd 2016) were embarrassingly misplaced.

Trump's hawkish, feverishly erratic, and dangerous actions were brought to the fore in the days after the assassination of Soleimani. On 4 January 2020 Trump tweeted:

> Let this serve as a WARNING that if Iran strikes any Americans, or American assets, we have … targeted 52 Iranian sites (representing the 52 American hostages taken by Iran many years ago), some at a very high level & important to Iran & the Iranian culture, and those targets, and Iran itself WILL BE HIT VERY FAST AND VERY HARD.

In response, the Iranian foreign minister Javad Zarif pointed out that, 'having committed grave breaches of [international] law in Friday's cowardly assassinations, [Donald Trump] threatens to commit new breaches … targeting cultural sites is a WAR CRIME'. Since Trump withdrew the United States from the JCPOA with the intention of negotiating a better deal (spoiler alert: he never did), relations between the USA and Iran deteriorated to a worrying new low after the assassination of Soleimani.

The strike against Soleimani and the following threat to strike fifty-two Iranian sites – a figure chosen because of petty nostalgia for the Iranian taking of American hostages in 1979 – were the latest aspects of an American 'maximum pressure' campaign that had involved economic sanctions and increasingly hawkish actions from the Trump administration. Rather than bringing Iran to heel, Trump's 'diplomacy' was a disaster that served to alienate Iran further and edge it closer to developing a nuclear weapon. In response to the assassination of Soleimani, Iran announced it would cease to adhere to any operational restrictions that had been imposed by the JCPOA. The terms of this deal had restricted Iran from enriching uranium to weapons-grade level and drastically cut back its nuclear centrifuges, nuclear stockpile of uranium, and its ability to produce plutonium that could be used in a bomb. Now, after Soleimani's assassination, Iran had finally walked away from the terms of the deal. As two commentators in the *New York Times* put it, because of Trump's actions, 'the Trump administration could soon find itself facing a choice between allowing Iran to get nuclear weapons or to bomb Iran' (Tabatabai and Gordon 2020).

With scant regard for international law and with an indication that he was revelling in the prospect of bombing Iran, on 5 January Trump tweeted that 'the United States just spent Two Trillion Dollars on Military Equipment. We are the biggest and by far the BEST in the World! If Iran attacks an American Base, or any American, we will be sending some of that brand new beautiful equipment their way … and without hesitation!' Trump's comments echo General Groves's 1946 claims about needing 'the best, the biggest and the most' atomic weapons, and indicate a bloodthirsty attraction to weapons as fetishised 'beautiful' objects.

Together, the development of hypersonic missiles, the deployment of a new 'low yield' nuclear warhead, and the Trump administration's acceleration of drone strikes to target foreign military leaders like Soleimani indicate that in the winter months following the collapse of the INF Treaty the Third Nuclear Age was taken beyond the confines of an arms race around nuclear armed missiles of a certain range. As hypersonic missiles were deployed by Russia, and the United States rushed to catch up, the arms race took on a new technological edge which blurred the boundaries between nuclear and conventional technologies and added a dangerous level of uncertainty into the equation. The placement of new, low-yield nukes on US submarines suggested that the USA was willing to match Russia warhead for warhead, and indicated that the Trump administration was more willing to use a nuclear weapon than any administration since the Cold War. Alongside this, the American assassination of an Iranian military leader not only broke international law but also directly led to Iran leaving the constraints of the nuclear deal that had previously halted their development of nuclear weapons. Trump's actions also indicated he was willing to risk a potential war with Iran. This toxic combination of events that occurred during November 2019 and January 2020 all involved a novel technological aspect – newer, faster missiles; newer, smaller nukes; and the continuation of drone strikes against new enemies – yet over this same period, culture would also play a prominent role in demonstrating how the Third Nuclear Age manifested in people's lives.

Nukes go pop: how popular culture shapes the Third Nuclear Age

The dichotomy between nuclear weapons technology on one hand and nuclear culture on the other is a false one. This is because the technologies used to threaten and wage war are 'a historical product and a social creation' (MacKenzie 1993, 2). There is nothing natural or inevitable about the development of nuclear weapons technology such as hypersonic missiles, low-yield warheads, and the turn to relying on drones as a central tool of modern warfare. Nor is it a case that these things simply happen because rational actors make cost–benefit decisions and simply determine that they must. Technological developments are the result of complex interactions and processes 'between a range of social actors' (MacKenzie 1993, 3) that include political leaders, militaries, scientists, corporations, and broader publics (MacKenzie 1993; Peoples 2010). Pointing out that we – people like you and me who don't have any nuclear decision-making power or access to the nuclear launch codes – are implicated in shaping the Third Nuclear Age is not to burden ourselves with an equal share of the blame with the likes of Presidents Trump, Putin, and Xi. Rather, it is to challenge the idea that we are simply pessimistic, passive actors who can do nothing to change the current dire state of affairs in the Third Nuclear Age. As Donald MacKenzie has put it, 'to see the mundane social processes that form the nuclear world is to see simultaneously the possibility of intervening in them, of reshaping the world' (MacKenzie 1993, 4). Subsequently, this section of this chapter illuminates how the high technology of the Third Nuclear Age is manifested in, and can potentially be shaped by, the 'low' politics of popular culture. In his historical overview of British nuclear culture, Jonathan Hogg points out that 'for the vast majority of people nuclear weapons or nuclear reactors remained alien and distant ... [they] would have a purely imagined connection to nuclear technology' (2016, 7), therefore the media and other forms of popular culture such as Sam Fender's 'Hypersonic Missiles' are significant in the Third Nuclear Age as they play in role in determining how people come to make sense of it.

The significance of news media in shaping nuclear politics has a long history. John Hershey's investigative journalism documenting the Hiroshima bombing is widely viewed as playing a pivotal role in bringing the horrors of nuclear weapons to the public's attention (Hershey 1946; Blume 2020). The importance of news media in the Third Nuclear Age is illustrated during the run-up to the 2019 UK general election that took place on 12 December 2019. A key issue of national debate during this time centred around Jeremy Corbyn – the leader of the UK Labour Party and the leader of the opposition in the Houses of Parliament – and his historical membership of CND that brought with it an opposition to nuclear weapons. Despite their leader's opposition to nuclear weapons, the Labour Party supported the renewal of Trident nuclear weapons, and their 2019 manifesto contained the rather contradictory position of committing a Labour government to the renewal of Trident as well as an 'obligation ... to create a nuclear-free world' (Labour Party 2019). Jeremy Corbyn subsequently became an object of ridicule for much of the right-wing media who referred to him on their front pages as 'the most dangerous chicken in Britain' and a 'security risk'. Yet those on the left also scrutinised him for not doing more to oppose his party's pro-nuclear position.

Either way, nuclear weapons and the potential prime minister's willingness to use them came to be a key topic of contention in the run-up to election day. On 19 November, Jo Swinson – the leader of the Liberal Democrats – was interviewed by a journalist on primetime British TV. Swinson was asked, 'Would you ever be prepared to use a nuclear weapon?' and, without missing a beat, in an enthusiastic, jovial tone of reckless abandon she replied 'yes'. In response, the interviewer replied, 'that was a brilliant short answer. Thank you very much'. Perhaps there is something appealing about a politician providing a brief, simple, and truthful answer to a journalist's question – especially in the post-Brexit, post-truth age of Boris Johnson's obfuscating language. However, it is symptomatic of the ills of the Third Nuclear Age that when a politician jumps at the opportunity to admit they are willing to incinerate hundreds of thousands of people, and to potentially initiate a nuclear war that would wipe out the entire planet, they are thanked for their answer and lauded as 'brilliant'.

Swinson's enthusiastic declaration that she was prepared to use nuclear weapons was described as 'sickening' by the Scottish First Minister Nicola Sturgeon who tweeted that the question should not be asked 'as if it's some kind of virility test and without any context'. Sturgeon went on to pen an article in *The Guardian* under the headline 'Why I'd never press the nuclear button' (2019), and she presented her case by stating:

> [E]ven those who buy into the idea of mutually assured destruction should balk at the casual way in which political discourse on this topic has developed. If a mainstream politician unblinkingly said that they would use a chemical weapon against civilians there would be uproar. If a self-proclaimed candidate for prime minister boasted that they would commit war crimes, it would be seen as a national scandal. Nuclear weapons should be seen no differently – but a dated Cold War mentality is used to cloak these weapons of mass destruction in respectability. (2019)

Whilst Swinson's nuclear decisiveness was criticised by Sturgeon, it was lauded by mainstream media journalists. Alternative news outlets were, however, quick to ridicule her stance. 'Want to be prime minister? Hope you're ready to nuke millions' (Whyman 2019) ran the headline to one *VICE News* article. Yet it was a meme created by one social media user that provided one of the most cutting, satirical critiques of Swinson's views. On Twitter, at the start of November, a user named @groovyguyzone – with a reputation for making up satirical 'shitposting' content – shared a faked news article reporting that footage had emerged of Jo Swinson killing squirrels with a slingshot. The faked screenshots eventually gained thousands of likes and shares across Twitter and Facebook, so much so that in an LBC interview on 19 November – the same day she enthusiastically stated she was willing to use nuclear weapons – Swinson had to deny that she was a #squirrelkiller. 'I like squirrels', she said, describing the story as 'very fake news' (quoted in LBC News 2019). Eventually, on the night of the election, Swinson lost her seat in East Dunbartonshire by 149 votes as Nicola Sturgeon's SNP

(Scottish National Party) colleague Amy Callaghan took the seat after being avowedly anti-nuclear throughout her campaign.

This episode reveals that in the Third Nuclear Age it has become common sense for political leaders in the United Kingdom and other nuclear-armed states to view the possibility of using nuclear weapons as a necessity that must unequivocally and immediately be defended. On the same day that Swinson stated with a one-word answer that she would be happy to potentially cause the deaths of millions of people, she derided how deplorable it was that social media users were making memes about her killing squirrels. This privileging of the lives of rodent pests over people presents a bitter irony that illuminates how norms against the non-use of nuclear weapons are facsimile when politicians are so quick to appear strong and masculine by expressing their 'virility' to use them. Whilst we can take solace in the fact that Swinson was beaten at the polls, it is telling that 19,523 voters in her constituency still supported her despite her unbridled enthusiasm for launching nuclear weapons if she had to.

Alongside debates around Britain's nuclear weapons becoming prominent in the British press and on social media during the run-up to the 2019 UK general election, other forms of popular culture at this time gave further meaning to nuclear weapons and the contours of the Third Nuclear Age. Sam Fender's 'Hypersonic Missiles' was awarded the accolade of Britain's 'Hottest Record of the Year' only a few days after the general election, and it captures the contemporary zeitgeist of nuclear anxieties and fears of an apocalypse. As Fender sings,

> All the silver-tongued suits and cartoons that rule my world
> Are saying it's a high time for hypersonic missiles
> When the bombs drop darling, can you say that you've lived your life?
> Oh, this is a high time for hypersonic missiles

Not only does Fender's chorus highlight how politicians and talking heads on TV, alongside fictional characters in cartoon shows, are proposing the development and use of hypersonic missiles, but it also implies an overriding sense of doom. For Fender, it's not a case of *if* but *when* the bombs drop. This sense of futile disaster appears in a broad range of modern indie-infused popular music that captures, projects, and shapes the circulation of a sense of exterminism with millennials and generation Z.

Popular songs about nuclear holocaust and the end of the world are not just a phenomenon of the new nuclear age, but the current popularity of alternative, downbeat, indie records suggests that they tap into the broader feelings of today's disaffected youth. Take, for example, the rise of Sam Fender, and other indie artists like Phoebe Bridgers who describes her 2018 breakout single 'Smoke Signals' as 'a post-apocalyptic love song' (quoted in Jordan 2018). Bridgers' music has been described as 'music for the end of the world' (Pym 2020), and she has been called 'the spooky prophet of End Times America' (Kim 2020) and 'the undisputed queen of pandemic-era pop' (Williams 2021) due to the success of her 2020 album *Punisher*. 'I Know the End', the closing song to this album, is another song about the apocalypse, and the record as a whole is, according to Bridgers, 'about having a personal life with a background of doom' (Bridgers quoted in Pym 2020). The millennial doom-laden fear of exterminism that permeates the music of Sam Fender and Phoebe Bridgers is also apparent in the music of other popular indie artists. Bon Iver's 2019 single 'Jelmore' alludes to the near apocalypse of today where 'we'll all be gone by the falling light', and The 1975's 2018 single 'Love It If We Made It' attempts to capture the 'political and socially volatile period' of the modern moment and reached number 10 in the US rock chart. Containing the lyrics 'the war has been incited and guess what? You're all invited', the song is but another example of popular music reflecting the potential – and seemingly near – prospect of annihilation in an age where it feels like we might not 'make it'.

The cultural manifestation of exterminism in the Third Nuclear Age was also brought into stark relief in January 2020 by the setting of the Doomsday Clock to 100 seconds to midnight. The doomsday clock is a symbol used by scientists to warn the public of 'how close we are to destroying our own world with dangerous technologies of our own making' (Bulletin of the Atomic Scientists 2021). With midnight as a metaphor for the end of the world, and the countdown of a clock symbolising our proximity to destruction, the Doomsday Clock is 'a universally recognised indicator of the world's vulnerability to catastrophe from nuclear weapons, climate change, and disruptive technologies in other domains' (Bulletin of the Atomic Scientists 2021).

Originally created by former workers on the Manhattan Project who founded the Bulletin of the Atomic Scientists, the Doomsday Clock was first set in 1947 at seven minutes to midnight to warn of impending nuclear catastrophe. Then in 1949 it was moved forward to three minutes to midnight after the Soviet Union tested its first nuclear bomb. When the Soviet Union tested a thermonuclear weapon in 1953, the Doomsday Clock was again moved forward to two minutes to midnight, where, 'with only a few more swings of the pendulum … atomic explosions will strike midnight for civilisation' (Rabinowitch 1953, 294). Until January 2020, this was the closest the world had been to midnight (in 2018 and 2019 the Doomsday Clock was also set at two minutes to midnight). But due to the existential threats of nuclear weapons and climate change 'that are compounded by a threat multiplier, cyber-enabled information warfare, that undercuts society's ability to respond', as well as the fact that 'world leaders have allowed the international political infrastructure for managing them to erode', the hands of the Doomsday Clock were moved forward to 100 seconds to midnight in 2020 (Bulletin of the Atomic Scientists 2020). Pointing out that the actions of world leaders have been 'counterproductive', the Bulletin of the Atomic Scientists said that by unravelling arms control treaties alongside developing new technologies such as hypersonic weapons, world leaders have undermined the management of 'the most urgent global threats to humanity' and 'helped to create a situation that will, if unaddressed, lead to catastrophe, sooner rather than later' (2020). In January 2023, due to Russia's invasion of Ukraine and Putin's nuclear threats, the Doomsday Clock was set at 90 seconds – the closest it has ever been – to midnight.

Conclusion: why we need to rethink what matters in nuclear politics

Addressed to 'leaders and citizens of the world', the setting of the Doomsday Clock closer to midnight than ever before shows how a cultural symbol can draw attention to the exterminism of the Third Nuclear Age (Bulletin of the Atomic Scientists 2020). As with Fender's 'Hypersonic Missiles' and Phoebe Bridgers' post-apocalyptic sad girl oeuvre, the Doomsday Clock is a part of the cultural landscape by which the world makes sense of nuclear weapons. By drawing attention to the potential exterminism nuclear weapons pose for the planet, such cultural objects can work to resist the dominant ways of thinking and practice around nuclear weapons in nuclear-armed states. Yet despite this possibility of resistance, as we can see from Jo Swinson's unhesitant enthusiasm for being willing to use nuclear weapons, alongside the broader media reportage that was critical of those like Corbyn and Sturgeon who support nuclear abolition, the logic of deterrence and the belief that nuclear weapons are a necessity to ensure our security is entrenched within the mainstream of political culture. It is difficult to evaluate the efficacy of popular culture and sad songs about the end of the world in changing nuclear policy directly. Yet such artefacts and their consumption by members of the public contribute to a broader social milieu of the Third Nuclear Age, where the value of nuclear weapons is contested and their effects are imagined. This contestation of meaning can open up a space for reimagining our world and the place of nuclear weapons in it.

Ultimately, whilst the technological developments of hypersonic missiles and low-yield nuclear weapons, and an increasing reliance on drone strikes as a tool of foreign policy, characterise the Third Nuclear Age, these technologies are made possible, meaningful, and are contested and challenged through popular culture. If the British public voted for a song called 'Hypersonic Missiles' as the hottest record of 2019 then we can clearly see that popular culture and world politics are intersecting, making each other meaningful, and shaping the public consciousness and lived experience of the Third Nuclear Age. It is indeed 'a high time for hypersonic missiles'. Even so, as January 2020 ended and February began, a new global threat began to emerge. In the next chapter we explore the onset of the COVID-19 pandemic, its significance in global politics, and how the events of February, March, and April 2020 shaped the Third Nuclear Age.

5

'The world of post-apocalypse movies': February to April 2020

> The virus had an unusually high infectivity rate ... and belonged to the world of post-apocalypse movies.
> Jonathan Calvert, George Abuthnott, and Joanthan Leake, 19 April 2020

In early 2020, reports began to reach the UK that there was a deadly and mysterious respiratory disease breaking out in the Chinese city of Wuhan. I, like many other British citizens, paid these reports little attention. Previous outbreaks of bird flu, swine flu, SARS, MERS, and Ebola happened in seemingly far away parts of the world like Asia, Africa, and the Middle East. These outbreaks were often contained locally, and the idea that a highly transmissible, fast-spreading, lethal pandemic could spread around the globe felt largely fictitious, and to many 'Western' policy makers it also felt like 'a distant problem' (Calvert and Arbuthnott 2021, 15). Global pandemics were a thing of post-apocalypse movies, videogames, and novels, or they were associated with history books: the Black Death of the mid-1300s, the Spanish flu of 1918, and the onset of HIV/AIDS in the 1980s.

Despite the UK National Security Risk Assessment of 2019 placing 'an influenza-type pandemic' (Hopkins 2020) at the top of the threats facing the UK, politicians in seats of power – responsible for the safety of their citizens – felt a false sense of security. The UK was, according to the 2019 Global Health Security Index, the second-best prepared country in the world to face biological threats such as an epidemic or pandemic. Only the United States was supposedly better equipped for a pandemic public health disaster. These predictions now seem tragically absurd. At the time of writing, the USA has the highest COVID-19 death toll in the entire world, and the UK has the seventh highest number of COVID deaths (only in Brazil, India, Russia, Mexico, and Peru have more people died).

It was in early February that I began to worry about the COVID-19 outbreak. I was with Rhiannon and our newborn baby in a DIY store, located in a nondescript retail park outside of Glasgow. We were on the hunt for masks to wear as we scraped paint from the window surrounds in our house. We had recently found that the paint contained lead and was therefore poisonous if you inhaled the dust or fumes that would inevitably be created by our amateur home improvement efforts. Because of this risk we had to buy a certain type of mask that was able to filter out dangerous particles. Yet when we found the aisle where masks should have been located, the shelves were bare. We asked a member of staff where the masks had gone, and he replied that people had bought them to ship to friends and family in China. We asked when they might be getting more masks delivered, and he said that he had no idea because there were no masks in any DIY store in the country.

Whilst I was mildly annoyed that there were no masks in my local DIY store, I would have been horrified if I had known that there were also hardly any masks available to the medical personnel that would soon need them most. Not only were NHS staff also having to scour DIY stores themselves to obtain masks and personal protective equipment (PPE) as COVID began to spread across the UK in February (Calvert and Arbuthnott 2021, 232), but the British government's pandemic preparation stockpile was also desperately empty. Despite a pandemic being identified as the number one threat to Britain, the government had actively gutted the national pandemic stockpile through years of austerity cuts. A study by *The Guardian* found that the value of equipment stored for a health emergency fell by £325 million over a period of six years leading up to the start of the COVID-19 pandemic (Davies, Pegg, and Lawrence 2020). Almost half of the boxes in storage contained PPE equipment that was past its use-by date and 80 per cent of respirators were out of date by the time the pandemic hit the UK (Channel 4 News 2020).

Across the Atlantic, public health preparedness was in a similarly dire state. The US Strategic National Stockpile was originally created to stockpile drugs, vaccines, medical supplies, and pharmaceutical equipment to be used in the event of a bioterrorism event, but has since been expanded to prepare the USA for a chemical, biological, radiological, and nuclear (CBRN) threat, an influenza outbreak, and natural disasters. Once COVID-19 reached the United States, 'the quantities of material in the stockpile were not nearly enough' (Gerstein 2020, 3), and the American pandemic response was further hindered by the fact that in 2018 President Trump had disbanded the Global Health Security and Biodefense unit which was responsible for pandemic preparedness. In February 2020, the USA and the UK were held up as bastions of global public health, and were supposedly the states most ready to take on the threat of a pandemic even though both had actively undermined their own preparations for such a threat. The tragedy of this misguided and illusory ability to deal with major security threats would become apparent over the course of the next few months.

This chapter documents the unfolding of the COVID-19 pandemic during February, March, and April 2020. I argue that COVID-19 is relevant to understanding the Third Nuclear Age, as the response to the pandemic reveals a damning indictment of how nuclear weapons states conceptualise security. I focus on the issues of mass deaths caused by COVID-19 in the UK, the failure of the British government to prepare properly for what was supposedly *the* major security threat to the UK, or to take COVID-19 seriously once it began to take hold. Alongside this I draw attention to the British government's delay in enacting measures to address the threat of COVID-19, the role of the state in sharing disinformation and erasing transparency around the handling of COVID-19, as well as exploring how the pandemic response was marked by corruption. In drawing attention to these issues I explore how we run the risk of unparalleled catastrophe in the Third Nuclear Age as all of these factors are relevant to the sphere of nuclear weapons: the risk of a mass casualty event, a widespread ignorance of this risk and a belief that it can be controlled, a delay in implementing measures that will mitigate the risk, a plethora of lies, disinformation, and an increasing lack of transparency, as well as procurement practices and industry–government relations that are problematic at best and corrupt at worst. In the face of this state of affairs, this chapter argues that these issues can be addressed through a reimagining of security that focuses on people and planet rather than states and militaries. Only by rethinking and reimagining a fundamentally flawed understanding of security can we overcome the challenges of the new nuclear age.

'The coronavirus can't stop America's nukes!'

After the collapse of the INF Treaty and the development of hypersonic missiles in preceding months, the global spread of COVID-19 in February 2020 added a new layer of complexity and tragedy to the Third Nuclear Age. In the United States, headlines would soon ask 'How COVID-19 might affect US nuclear weapons and planning' (Pifer 2020), and others would proclaim that 'The coronavirus can't stop America's nukes!' (Pappalardo 2020). The former article noted that COVID-19 might lead to reductions in defence spending (surprise! It didn't) and argued that the Pentagon needed to get the balance right between spending on nuclear capabilities and conventional forces in an age of 'great power competition'. The latter piece claimed that 'humanity's most lethal weapons could be nullified by an organism that can't even be seen', but then assured us that the military officials responsible for America's nuclear arsenal were staying COVID secure. One Air Force general pointed out that the rural location of ICBM bases helped with keeping personnel isolated: 'the ICBM fields in Montana are just vast … North Dakota is not the same as New York city. We're taking advantage of that' (quoted in Pappalardo 2020), whilst also seeming pleased with the fact that the Air Force had devised new ways to prepare laptops for service personnel so that they could work from home and maintain 'the same launch-on-command level of readiness' (Pappalardo 2020). For most of the nuclear-military-industrial complex, it was business as usual as COVID-19 began to tear across the planet. Those responsible for the world's nuclear weapons followed social distancing measures, worked remotely when they could, and despite concerns that nuclear budgets would be cut, defence spending in all but one of the nuclear weapons states actually increased during the pandemic (Pakistan was the only nuclear-armed state to spend less on its military than in previous years). In 2020, the US military budget increased by 4.4 per cent and accounted for 39 per cent of global military spending (Silva, Tian, and Marksteiner 2021). Coronavirus didn't stop America's nukes, nor those of anyone else.

Even though the world's nuclear forces were not disrupted by COVID-19, the pandemic did reveal a worrying aspect of nuclear weapons policy for those states where a single leader has sole authority over the use of nuclear weapons. In the UK and the USA, the decision to launch nuclear weapons lies solely with the head of state, as it does in authoritarian nuclear weapons states led by the likes of Vladimir Putin and Xi Jinping who have sole authority over their nuclear launch decisions. In April 2020, as the British prime minister Boris Johnson suffered from COVID-19 and was taken to hospital and then intensive care, the flaws of sole authority over nuclear weapons became clear. When asked by the BBC if the foreign secretary, Dominic Raab – a man who was once described by a journalist as 'the idiot's idiot' and is apparently referred to by colleagues as 'dim Dom' – was now authorised to launch Britain's nuclear weapons, cabinet minister Michael Gove swerved the question and replied that 'Dominic Raab is in charge … There are well developed protocols which are in place … I just really cannot talk about national security issues' (quoted in Reuters 2020b).

In the United States, similar concerns were raised when Donald Trump was later admitted to hospital with COVID-19 in October of 2020. Part of his treatment included experimental, mood-altering drugs, the side effects of which include mania, paranoia, and delusions. With an already erratic temperament and a history of behaviour evident of a 'baseline of batshit crazy' (Levin 2020) the last thing the world needed was a state leader suffering from steroid-induced psychosis in charge of nuclear weapons. Yet that's what happened during the COVID-19 pandemic. As Hans Kristensen, a nuclear expert based at the Federation of American Scientists, put it, 'the last finger I would want on the nuclear button is that of a president on drugs' (quoted in Sanger and Broad 2020). However, with predictions that we are now entering a period where deadly global pandemics are increasingly likely (Marani *et al.* 2021), it's also probable that we may once again see ill, incapacitated leaders in charge of nuclear weapons.

The issue of state leaders suffering from serious illnesses that affect their decision making and hinder their ability to make rational decisions about nuclear weapons was not the only risk to security brought about by the COVID-19 pandemic. At a broader level, in causing such a devastating number of deaths across the globe, COVID-19 is a serious security risk in itself. However, it poses a threat to human security rather than threatening the military or state security apparatus, which were left relatively unscathed by COVID-19. In a recent paper written by Beatrice Fihn and Alicia Sanders-Zakre from the International Campaign to Abolish Nuclear Weapons – the 2017 winner of the Nobel Peace Prize – the authors point out that 'a virus doesn't care how many nuclear weapons your country has. Every dime wasted on nuclear weapons could be better spent giving citizens a fighting chance against Covid-19' (Fihn and Sanders-Zakre 2020, 126). In support of this claim, Fihn and Sanders-Zakre have found that 'diverting nuclear-armed state spending on nuclear weapons for only one year would meet reported gaps in health care supplies and save lives' (Fihn and Sanders-Zakre 2020, 126). If the USA was to spend the $35 billion it spent on nuclear weapons in 2019 on healthcare, the country 'could hire 150,000 nurses at an average salary of $75,000 and 75,000 doctors at an average salary of $200,000' (Fihn and Sanders-Zakre 2020, 126). Instead, the country invested in a complex infrastructure to pay for nuclear weapons that they hope never to use.

The COVID-19 pandemic reveals the high risks of sole authority in the Third Nuclear Age as well as the risks of a state-centric understanding of security that leads to the prioritisation of military spending and nuclear weapons over healthcare and measures to keep people safe from deadly pandemics. If we want to fully understand how the Third Nuclear Age has a negative impact on global security then we need to take a deeper look at the COVID-19 pandemic, the importance of public health, and how the unfolding of the pandemic stands as a dark omen of the apocalyptic horrors that would unfold should nuclear weapons ever actually be detonated again.

Public health and the Third Nuclear Age

More than 6.8 million people across the globe have now died of COVID-19. In spite of allegedly being the most prepared nation for a global pandemic, the USA has had the highest number of COVID-19 cases and deaths. In the UK, more than twice as many civilians (219,449 at the time of going to print in March 2023) have died than died during the horrors of the Blitz and the entire Second World War (70,000). This immense loss of life has since been described as 'an unparalleled crisis' (Calvert and Arbuthnott 2021, 10) that has felt for those who have lost loved ones or suffered through lockdowns like 'an all too real doomsday film' (Calvert and Arbuthnott 2021, 1).

COVID-19 is one of the most pressing security crises of our lives. Twenty years of the War on Terror cost an estimated 900,000 lives, yet in the space of three years COVID-19 killed over six million people. Yet the human, social, and economic cost of the pandemic – as well as what was required to respond to it – is trivial when compared to the prospect of a nuclear war which would 'dwarf the effect of Covid-19' (Futter et al. 2020, 271). If we want to know the immediate effect of a nuclear bomb going off, we can use the NUKEMAP – a free online tool created by the history of science researcher Alex Wellerstein – to virtually detonate a nuclear weapon of our choice over any location on earth. If we select the Dong Feng 5, the largest nuclear ICBM warhead in the Chinese arsenal, with a yield of 5 megatons, and detonate it over the Palace of Westminster in central London, we can calculate the effects with a click of a button. Within a 2 kilometre radius a nuclear fireball would effectively vaporise everything and everyone in it. The Houses of Parliament, Big Ben, 10 Downing Street, Trafalgar Square, and Buckingham Palace would turn to dust.

Within a 12 kilometre radius, 'most residential buildings collapse, injuries are universal, fatalities are widespread' (Wellerstein 2022) and fires would likely break out, causing further damage all across the capital. Third-degree burns from the blast would affect people within a 25 kilometre radius, leaving them with severe scarring and injuries potentially requiring amputation – anywhere as far away as Heathrow airport in the west and Dartford to the east. There would be further 'light' blast damage over a 34 kilometre radius. Anyone who had come to a window after seeing the nuclear flash would potentially be injured by flying glass once the pressure wave caught up and broke the windows. An estimated 2,270,430 people would die, and a further 3,630,850 people would be injured. Those injured would then face unprecedented challenges in accessing appropriate healthcare as all four of London's hospitals that serve as major trauma centres would be affected by severe blast damage, as too would most other smaller hospitals across the capital. Public transport would be unable to function, roads would be damaged and clogged, supply chains for food and medicine would collapse, as would law and order. Radioactive fallout would also affect the city and those left in it, though it is difficult to estimate the extent of this as it would depend on variables such as the weather and wind. All of this from one nuclear bomb. The detonation of a nuclear weapon would make the doomsday film of COVID-19 look like a children's TV show. By thinking through the challenges raised by the pandemic and the flaws in how it was handled, we can develop further insights into the risks of the Third Nuclear Age.

One of the most concerning aspects of the COVID-19 pandemic was how ill prepared those states that claimed to be the most prepared for the security threat of a pandemic actually were. In the UK, a 2016 public health simulation exercise named Operation Cygnus tested the British response to an influenza pandemic and demonstrated that Britain was not prepared for the demands that would be placed on the National Health Service (NHS). A report of the exercise's key findings found that 'the UK's preparedness and response, in terms of its plans, policies and capability, is currently not sufficient to cope with the extreme demands of a severe pandemic that will have a nation-wide impact' (Public Health England 2017, 6). Despite – or even perhaps because of – this worrying verdict, the report was not published by the government until October 2020. By then the British public didn't need to read fifty-seven pages of a government report to tell them that the UK couldn't effectively handle a pandemic. Thousands had already died, the country had experienced months of lockdown, and the second wave of cases and deaths was beginning to rise.

The failure to take the threat of a pandemic seriously was evident in the actions of prime minister Boris Johnson during the early months of 2020. The prime minister is usually responsible for chairing COBRA (Cabinet Office Briefing Rooms) meetings to discuss national emergencies, yet Johnson missed the first five emergency meetings discussing COVID-19. The first cases of COVID-19 were detected on British soil when two Chinese citizens tested positive on 29 January 2020, yet Johnson was preoccupied with preparations for 'Brexit day' – 31 January, when Johnson would finally 'get Brexit done' by formally leaving the European Union. A few days later, Johnson gave an upbeat speech full of optimism in the wake of Brexit, proclaiming his desire to sell Scottish haggis to the Americans, and Welsh lamb to the Chinese, whilst dismissing fears of 'new diseases such as coronavirus [that] will trigger a panic and a desire for market segregation that go beyond what is medically rational to the point of doing real and unnecessary economic damage' (Johnson 2020). That same day, the British health secretary, Matt Hancock, was asked in parliament what measures he was taking to protect the country and NHS staff from the spread of COVID-19. He replied that, 'in the case that the epidemic here gets much more serious, we have 50 highly specialist beds, and a further 500 beds are available in order to isolate people' (Hancock quoted in Hansard 2020). Such slim measures – 50 beds! – would of course prove feeble, but when poor planning combined with the cavalier attitude of government leaders (on 14 February, as COVID-19 began to grip Europe, Boris Johnson took a two-week holiday at a palatial house in the English countryside), the results would be catastrophic.

The major mishandling of COVID-19 in the United Kingdom and elsewhere concerns the delays in implementing lockdown measures that would stop the spread of the virus. Despite the Chinese government's lockdown in Wuhan, showing that lockdowns worked in reducing case numbers and deaths, the British government refused to even model the effects of a lockdown due to fears of the economic and social costs. One academic involved in the team responsible for modelling the spread of the virus in February 2020 explained that the failure to consider lockdown as a viable option was driven by a sense in the upper echelons of government that 'it can't really be that bad' (quoted in Calvert and Arbuthnott 2021, 160). On 3 March, Boris Johnson boasted, 'I was at a hospital the other night where I think a few there were actually coronavirus patients and I shook hands with everybody, you'll be pleased to know, and I continue to shake hands' (quoted in Reuters 2020a). By the end of the month, Johnson would test positive for COVID-19 and would eventually be admitted to hospital in April, only leaving hospital on 12 April after a stay in intensive care. On that day, Mary Agyapong, a pregnant 28-year-old nurse, died of COVID-19 shortly after her baby was delivered by an emergency caesarean. She would be just one of a total 886 front-line health and social care workers in England and Wales to lose their lives from COVID-19 by the end of the year.

Prior to being incapacitated in hospital, Johnson's inability to take COVID seriously was plainly evident in his referral to his government's attempts to obtain ventilators as 'Operation Last Gasp'. Yet this comment belies a broader failure of the British government to obtain appropriate equipment to deal with the pandemic. PPE stockpiles had dwindled due to the government's austerity measures, and on 19 March 2020, when the government realised there was not enough equipment to support NHS staff, they downgraded COVID-19 from a 'high consequence infectious disease' so that NHS staff wouldn't be required to wear as much PPE (Calvert and Arbuthnott 2021, 207). In March 2020 the government also stopped publishing critical care bed capacity figures because there was no critical care bed capacity left as hospitals were inundated by people with COVID-19 requiring critical care. Furthermore, after the *Sunday Times* reported the government's failings in handling the start of the COVID-19 crisis in an explosive article on 19 April, the government responded with a 2,000-word blog that claimed they were 'following the science'. In response, Richard Horton, the scientist who edits the medical journal *The Lancet*, pointed out how the government were misquoting him, and he highlighted that they had done anything but follow the science. He said that 'the UK government is deliberately rewriting history in its ongoing COVID-19 disinformation campaign' (Horton 2020), and he went on to say that the government twisted his words 'in a Kremlinesque way' and that 'there was international scientific consensus. The government had simply chosen to ignore it' (quoted in Calvert and Arbuthnott 2021, 102).

The only thing worse than the government's poor preparation for the serious threat of a pandemic was the same politicians' attempts to get rich off the back of it (Abbasi 2020, 2021). In Britain, the government set up a high priority contract scheme in order to procure PPE equipment, and companies that were referred to this scheme were ten times more likely than those who were not to secure business (Calvert and Arbuthnott 2021, 288). A national audit of these contracts found that almost five hundred suppliers had links to politicians and senior government officials, and another report found that one in five of all British government PPE contracts made between February and November 2020 'raise red flags for possible corruption' (Transparency International 2021). For example, one pest-control company that had no experience in supplying medical equipment and had been valued at £19,000 was awarded a £108 million contract to supply PPE, and another small firm, run by a Conservative councillor, was given £120 million without any competition (Calvert and Arbuthnott 2021, 288).

Whilst the NHS was stretched above and beyond capacity, thousands were dying on a daily basis and the British government was granting contracts for PPE to 'those with connections to the party of government' (Transparency International 2021). In total, almost one billion pounds was awarded to just fifteen companies with directors or individuals in control who had previously donated to the Conservative Party (Bright *et al.* 2021) and over the course of the pandemic these companies saw their profits increase by more than 57 per cent (Byline Times and the Citizens 2021). As doctors and nurses sought to save lives during a crisis they compared to 'a war zone' (Calvert and Arbuthnott 2021, 391), Conservative Party officials lined their coffers and made a tidy profit. Similarly, in the United States, Republican law makers who were privy to briefings on the potential seriousness of COVID-19 in early February went on to immediately sell stocks in companies that were set to be affected by the pandemic such as restaurants and hotels. One of the politicians who sat on the Senate Health Panel made an estimated $3.1 million by pre-emptively selling shares, and went on to invest some of that money in a company that sells home working software (Wagner and Lee 2020).

The issues that hindered the response to the COVID-19 pandemic and led to two of the highest death tolls in the world in the USA and UK are scarily relevant to the realm of nuclear weapons. We know that the use of nuclear weapons – whether by accident or on purpose – would lead to mass deaths. One recent study estimated that there is a 50 per cent chance that a nuclear strike would cause at least one million deaths, but that, on average, if a nuclear strike was to occur in the next fifty years, it is expected that at least 29 million people would die (Futter *et al.* 2020, 273). If only 1 per cent of the current global stockpile of 13,000 nuclear weapons were to be used, not only would millions die, but the climate would change catastrophically, and global food supplies would be affected (Witze 2020; Ray 2022; Xia *et al.* 2022). State leaders know this. The terrifying risk of unparalleled catastrophe has not simply come from nowhere, and the risk of mass deaths and nuclear winter have been prominent in public as well as political conciseness for decades (Sagan 1983b). However, much like with COVID-19, state leaders have failed to effectively prepare for this risk or to take it seriously. Indeed, if you take the risk of nuclear weapons being used seriously, it becomes clear that the only way to prepare for such an event is to prevent that event from ever happening. And the only way to ensure that is by reducing and eliminating nuclear weapons altogether. No state in the world has built, or could ever build, the required infrastructure to survive or effectively respond to the health and care needs of its own population in the event of a nuclear war. One nuclear weapon detonated in London would kill over two million people and leave more than three million people injured. There are only 141,000 hospital beds in the entirety of the UK (Ewbank *et al.* 2021), so the overwhelming majority of the injured would not receive the treatment they would need.

Just as with COVID-19, state leaders in nuclear weapons states are aware of the risks of nuclear weapons, yet they suggest that their strategies of nuclear deterrence ensure that we are safe. This is a dangerous ignorance that mirrors how the USA and UK were supposedly the most prepared nations to handle a pandemic. As research suggests, it is not deterrence, or effective command and control systems that have prevented nuclear weapons from being used or detonated since 1945; rather it is by sheer luck that we have avoided disaster in many instances (Pelopidas 2020). Again, as with COVID-19, state leaders in nuclear weapons states know the risks yet are constantly delaying implementing measures to effectively deal with the threat of extermination posed by nuclear weapons. The USA, Russia, and the UK have been legally obliged to work towards nuclear disarmament since they signed the Non-Proliferation Treaty in 1968, as have France and China since they acceded to it in 1992. But although there have been reductions in nuclear arsenals, nuclear weapons states have failed to seriously work towards 'general and complete disarmament' as Article VI of the NPT obligates them to.

The poor preparedness for the threat of nuclear war or accident, failure to take the threat seriously, and the delays in tackling the threat once its severity is apparent are all exacerbated by two further issues: a lack of transparency around the issue, as well as corruption and ineptitude in procuring a response to the threat. The realm of nuclear politics is shrouded in secrecy and a lack of transparency (Wellerstein 2021), and, as we shall see in Chapter 8, there is a democratic deficit in the area of nuclear policy where accountability and transparency are lacking. Related to this issue, the handling of nuclear weapon procurement is often opaque, flawed, and appallingly expensive. For example, Britain's £31 billion project to replace nuclear-armed submarines has been delayed by seven years, and the National Audit Office has found that none of the nuclear weapons projects within its purview will be 'delivered to their original timeframe' or to their original budget (National Audit Office 2020, 7). Instead, projects such as those to deliver new nuclear warheads will be delayed by up to six years and will cost an additional £1.35 billion. A 2021 parliamentary report into procurement at the Ministry of Defence stated that the House of Commons Committee of Public Accounts was 'extremely disappointed and frustrated by the continued poor track record of the Department and its suppliers – including significant net delays of twenty-one years across the programmes most recently examined by the National Audit Office – and by wastage of taxpayers' money running into the billions' (House of Commons Committee of Public Accounts 2021, 3). Oversight of the Ministry of Defence's spending was found to be so poor that it was unable to explain how an extra £16.5 billion awarded to it by the prime minister would be spent (Sabbagh 2021). Given the abundance of contracts for PPE during the COVID-19 pandemic that appear to indicate some level of corruption, the opacity and poor quality of military procurement contracts should concern us all – especially when they relate to the most dangerous weapons systems in the world. People are profiting from the potential annihilation of all life on our planet. The absurdity of this exterminist situation is succinctly highlighted by a viral cartoon by the artist Tom Toro that features a man in a bedraggled suit lecturing children around a campfire: 'Yes, the planet got destroyed. But for a beautiful moment in time we created a lot of value for shareholders.' To avoid this grim future and to address the challenges wrought by the confluence of a global pandemic with the Third Nuclear Age, we need to rethink security.

Conclusion: why we need to rethink security to make us safe

In the Third Nuclear Age, the logic of exterminism permeates how states respond to pandemics as well as how they strategise, make policy about, and then develop and deploy nuclear weapons. Both of these global ills are underpinned by problematic understandings and practices of security that dominate how states think and act in response to threats, as well as how they conceptualise what a threat is in the first place. In the study of International Relations, critical approaches to security have sought to challenge orthodox ways of conceptualising and practising security (for an introduction see Shepherd 2013; Peoples and Vaughan-Williams 2020). In doing so, this body of scholarship argues that the referent object of security – what we should be concerned about keeping safe and secure – is human life and the planet that we live on. Our approach to security therefore needs to be ethically inclusive and progressive, with the aim of emancipating people from contingent and structural harms by adopting a broader agenda than traditional approaches to security that have often served to legitimise state actions such as war and the build-up of nuclear arms (Booth 2005, 12). Essentially, as an academic project, critical approaches to security are concerned with rethinking security from the bottom up, moving beyond a fixed understanding of human nature, a focus on states and war in a supposedly anarchic international system, with the hope of developing ideas and practices that can make the world a better place for all who live here.

The need for critical approaches to security has never been clearer. As earlier chapters of this book have shown, a critical approach can help understand the collapse of arms control and the erosion of the nuclear taboo, and it can help make sense of how popular culture influences how the public understand new nuclear weapons technologies. The COVID-19 pandemic illustrates how we need critical approaches to security to extend beyond the academy and into the wider world. The exterminism of state policy that has caused millions of deaths across the globe stems from a flawed understanding of security that leads states to invest billions in militaries and nuclear weapons whilst their healthcare services struggle to function. Because security is understood to be something that can only be achieved through military might, COVID-19 has caused millions of deaths. A lethal combination of poor preparedness, a failure to take the threat seriously, and a delay in implementing measures that would address the threat and make people safe have all been exacerbated by a lack of transparency around the threat and its handling, as well as a corrupt and flawed response to the threat. These aspects of exterminism were made evident throughout the COVID-19 pandemic, yet they also apply to how nuclear weapon states are dealing with the threat of nuclear catastrophe. To wake up from the nuclear nightmare we are sleepwalking towards, we need not only to end the sole authority invested in state leaders to launch nuclear weapons, but to fundamentally rethink security, what we hope to secure, as well as how we achieve it: where people, planet, and global health measures take precedence over states and the militaries used to wage war in the name of security.

The need to rethink how we keep each other safe was given further urgency in May 2020, when George Floyd – a Black American man – was murdered by Derek Chauvin, a white police officer from the Minneapolis Police Department whose motto is 'to protect with courage, to serve with compassion'. Whilst Chauvin knelt on Floyd's neck for more than nine minutes, Floyd repeatedly said 'I can't breathe', called out for his 'mama', and said 'please' before eventually losing his life. Three other police officers were involved in pinning him down and attempting to arrest him. On that day in May, none of them protected anyone or showed an ounce of compassion. In the next chapter we explore how the police murder of George Floyd illuminates the crisis of structural racism that permeates state institutions designed to protect us, from the police on the streets of Minnesota to the armed forces responsible for nuclear weapons. As events over the next three-month period make clear, any serious analysis of the Third Nuclear Age needs to reckon with the role of racism and white supremacy in shaping our current crisis.

6

'I can't breathe': May to July 2020

'I can't breathe'

George Floyd, 25 May 2020

On 26 May 2020, as lockdown dragged on, I started my day by scrolling through Twitter. I came across a video of a white woman walking a dog in New York's Central Park, and when the man recording the video politely asks her if she can put the dog on a leash, she says she will call the police. 'I'm going to tell them there's an African American man threatening my life', she says, before picking her phone up and reaching the operator. 'There is a man, African American, he has a bicycle helmet, he is recording me and threatening me and my dog ... please send the cops immediately.' As she places this call, she grabs her dog and fixes the leash around its neck. The man recording the video stays calm and composed, as the woman continues to cry wolf to the police, becoming more and more exasperated and dragging her dog by its neck. The video is a damning indictment of racism in America, and I watched it with a sense of frustration as to how someone could use their privilege as a white person to call the police to respond to a person of colour simply (and politely) asking them to put a leash on their dog.

Later that day I came across another video on my Twitter feed. I watched in horror as, over the course of eight minutes, a white police officer knelt on the neck of a Black man and slowly killed him as he cried for help. George Floyd was accused of stealing $20 worth of groceries from a store in Minneapolis, and after returning to his parked car the police were called. The video of the incident was filmed by a passer-by on their mobile phone, and it starts as the officers take Mr Floyd from his car. Despite Mr Floyd not being aggressive and posing no threat to the four police officers at the scene, they wrestle him to the ground. One of them, an officer named Derek Chauvin, begins kneeling on his neck. He refuses to move as George Floyd spends the last minutes of his life pleading for his mother, asking for water, and telling the police officers multiple times that 'I can't breathe'. By the end of the video George Floyd lies dead, murdered by the very same people who are there to protect and serve him as a citizen of the United States.

This documented act of blatant institutional racism manifested in excessive, lethal violence acted out upon a Black man soon went viral. In doing so it sparked protests in Minneapolis that spread to cities across the globe as George Floyd's last words became a rallying cry for the Black Lives Matter movement and a global public who were now reckoning with racism and the legacies of colonialism in their own countries and everyday lives. Books on anti-racism, the history of slavery, and the ever-present legacies of colonialism soon became global bestsellers, and there seemed to be a serious conversation taking place about racism and police violence in Western societies. But what does this have to do with nuclear weapons?

This chapter argues that the police murder of George Floyd and other events occurring during May–July 2020 demonstrate the significant role that race, racism, colonialism, and white supremacy play in the Third Nuclear Age. These issues have been important in earlier nuclear ages (Gusterson 1999; Biswas, 2001, 2014; Williams 2011; Intondi 2015), but the increased visibility of racism and the reckoning with colonialism and racism that occurred after George Floyd's death make them significant today. Just as George Floyd was murdered by agents of a state institution that has proven to be consistently racist and a source of insecurity rather than security for people of colour, nuclear weapons have their genesis in the racism of the American state during the Second World War, and they continue to both pose a threat to people of colour and disproportionately affect them. This chapter therefore begins by exploring the racialised history of nuclear weapons, or what the Indian author Arundhati Roy has called the 'the ultimate colonizer' (Roy 2016, 59) – and examining, first, the context in which the United States developed and then tested the first nuclear weapon, before exploring the development of 'nuclear apartheid' (Biswas 2001; Maddock 2010) during the Cold War, and then examining the significant role that African Americans and people of colour have played in the disarmament movement.

By analysing the interconnected histories of colonialism, racism, and nuclear weapons we can then begin to understand how race and racism configure the contemporary politics of the Third Nuclear Age. To do so, the second section of this chapter reflects on the institutional racism of state security – as was so apparent in the police murder of George Floyd – and how this is also present in the realm of current nuclear strategy and politics. I then discuss the Trump administration's declaration in May 2020 that they intended to test a nuclear weapon for the first time in twenty-eight years. Here I also engage with the two-year anniversary of the collapse of the Iran deal and how racism underpinned the Trump administration's approach to nuclear non-proliferation and the rise of China. I conclude that the ills of the Third Nuclear Age can only be comprehended and addressed with a recognition of the racist and colonial history of nuclear weapons, and an anti-racist reckoning with how this legacy configures the contemporary moment.

The ultimate coloniser: racism and nuclear weapons

In July 1998, after India tested its first thermonuclear weapon, the Indian writer Arundhati Roy referred to nuclear weapons as 'the ultimate colonizer' (Roy 2016, 59). For Roy, this is because 'nuclear weapons pervade our thinking. Control our behaviour. Administer our societies. Inform our dreams. They bury themselves like meat hooks deep in the base of our brains. They are purveyors of madness' (Roy 2016, 59). They are, as Roy puts it, 'Whiter than any white man who ever lived. The very heart of whiteness.' In referring to nuclear weapons in this way and stating that they are 'the most antidemocratic, antinational, antihuman, outright evil thing that man has ever made', Roy is arguing that nuclear weapons were born out of colonialism, developed and deployed in racist ways, and manifest as the ultimate symbol of white supremacy (Roy 2016, 58). Whether the development and first use of nuclear weapons is read as 'an act of genocidal racist violence' against the Japanese, or as 'the apex of Western civilisation's scientific achievement' (Williams 2011, 1), the history of nuclear weapons is shaped by an approach to national security that is underpinned by a conception of exclusion and belonging that is bound up with race (Cooper 1995; Biswas 2001; Williams 2011). Race plays an important role in the history and present of nuclear weapons for two main reasons. First, because nuclear weapons symbolise 'the achievements, atrocities, and attitudes' of modern white, Western civilisation (Williams 2011, 15), and second, because state nuclear strategies 'reproduce a (European) colonial or (American) frontier dynamic in which white Europeans and their descendants defend and enlarge their societies at the expense of non-white peoples' (Williams 2011, 15–16). This chapter demonstrates how this is so and why this matters in the Third Nuclear Age.

To understand how race and racism shape nuclear politics, we need to turn to the context in which the first nuclear weapons were developed, tested, and then used by the United States against Japan. Whilst the Manhattan Project originally came into being because of concerns about the Nazis developing a nuclear weapon, after the Japanese attack on Pearl Harbor the American development of the atomic bomb took on a new urgency as the USA joined the war. American and Allied policy makers, military figures, and media commentators viewed Japan with contempt, and the attack on Pearl Harbor 'aroused a national bloodthirstiness that seemed unquenchable until the enemy had been totally vanquished' (Takaki cited in Intondi 2015, 11). At the time, racism towards Japanese people was prevalent across American society, with military and political leaders frequently expressing racist, dehumanising ideas and conducting racist actions. For example, in the Pacific theatre of war, US policy was seemingly to kill as many Japanese people as possible (Lawrence Wittner quoted in Intondi 2015, 11), and domestically, 120,000 American citizens of Japanese descent were detained in internment camps during the war. The Manhattan Project soon came to be focused on preparing a weapon to force Japan to surrender, and whilst policy makers considered detonating a nuclear weapon as a display of force rather than dropping it on Japan itself, Truman made the decision to target Japanese cities. The decision to drop the bomb on Hiroshima and Nagasaki was supported by 85 per cent of Americans polled at the time (Intondi 2015, 11), thereby demonstrating how the American public at large were in favour of using nuclear weapons against the Japanese people.

Anti-Japanese racism is not the only form of racism that is present at the dawn of the First Nuclear Age. As Gabriele Schwab points out in her articulation of critical nuclear race theory, the fact that uranium for the first atomic weapons was mined in Africa positions colonialism 'at the very origins' (Schwab 2020, 85) of nuclear politics. Indeed, Einstein and Szilard's 1939 letter to Roosevelt pointed out that 'the most important source of uranium is in the Belgian Congo' (Einstein and Szilard 1939). The colonisation of the Congo, and its subsequent exploitation by the Americans and other nuclear weapons states, highlights how exploitative colonial practices facilitated the development of nuclear weapons, and how nuclear weapons are inseparable from colonialism, imperialism, and racism (Alexis-Martin 2019b; Maurer and Hogue 2020).

At the same time as exploiting African uranium resources, the Manhattan Project colonised Native American lands. Uranium was mined domestically within the USA on swathes of land belonging to Native Americans, and parts of the nuclear-industrial complex – such as the Hanford processing plant – were situated on Native American reservations. These places are now some of the most toxic places on earth, and Native Americans are some of the biggest victims of the harms of radiation. The first detonation of a nuclear weapon – the Trinity test – conducted at dawn on 16 July 1945, took place on land bordering the Mescalero Apache Reservation in New Mexico, and whilst white down-winders have been compensated for suffering the effects of nuclear testing, their Native American counterparts have not. The worst radioactive accident in the USA – the Church Rock uranium spill on Navajo land, New Mexico – saw over a thousand tonnes of uranium tailings and almost a hundred million gallons of radioactive wastewater pour into Navajo water supplies in 1979, poisoning the water supply and causing cancers and adverse health effects for Navajo people that continue to this day. Yet the event largely goes unknown in accounts of nuclear history. Studies have found that 'low-income communities and communities of color bear the disproportionate burden of nuclear pollution in the United States' (Jantz 2018, 247), and according to one environmental expert, the desecration of Native American land into toxic, radioactive wastelands due to the development and testing of nuclear weapons amounts to 'a form of twentieth century genocide' (Valerie Kultez quoted in Schwab 2020, 71). Further developments in nuclear testing also affected indigenous peoples in colonised places across the Pacific (Teaiwa 1994), Africa (Jacobs 2013), and Asia (Alexis-Martin 2019b; Kassenova 2022). These tests had very real impacts on the people who were subjected to displacement and/or radiation from them that caused cancers, developmental abnormalities, as well as genetic and degenerative diseases (Jacobs 2022, 61). These health effects have been found to be far more widespread across affected populations than was originally thought. For example, one recent study of French nuclear weapons testing in French Polynesia has found that 90 per cent of the population was affected by dangerous levels of radiation exposure. Since 1974, this exposure to radiation has caused approximately 10,000 cases of cancer for a population that was at the time only 110,000 people (Philippe, Schoenberger, and Ahmed 2022, 75). Despite this, the French government has only paid out compensation to thirty-one people (Philippe, Schoenberger, and Ahmed 2022, 65).

Racism was not only apparent in the development, testing, and use of nuclear weapons but also in popular culture about nuclear weapons that proliferated throughout the Cold War. For example, the literary scholar Paul Williams has found that popular novels from the early Cold War period – such as Neville Shute's *On The Beach* (1957) – served to popularise the idea that the risk of nuclear war and apocalypse arose not from the nuclear weapons states themselves but from 'the irresponsibles' (Williams 2011, 226): states in the Global South who might eventually acquire them. In Shute's *On The Beach*, the end of the world and the fallout that is soon to reach Australia stems from a nuclear war started by, of all places, Albania. Such science fiction stories have long served to construct what the IR scholar Duncan Bell calls 'dreamworlds of race' (Bell 2022) that facilitated and enabled colonial expansion and the exploitation of people of colour in the Global South by white, 'Western' empires. In the Cold War, not only did science fiction perform this function, but so too did other modes and mediums of popular culture.

In a 1994 article, the feminist Pacific studies scholar Teresia Teaiwa highlights how the bikini bathing suit has its origins in nuclear testing. 'What does the word *bikini* evoke for you? A woman in a two-piece bathing suit, or a site for nuclear-weapons testing? A bikini-clad woman invigorated by solar radiation, or Bikini islanders cancer-ridden from nuclear radiation?' Teaiwa asks, before pointing out that 'the sensational bathing suit was named for Bikini Atoll ... the site in the Marshall Islands for the testing of twenty-five nuclear bombs between 1946 and 1958' (Teaiwa 1994, 87). She goes on to argue that 'by drawing attention to a sexualized and supposedly depoliticized female body', the bikini bathing suit, launched by a French designer in 1946 to celebrate the Allied efforts in the Second World War,

> distracts from the colonial and highly political origins of its name. The sexist dynamic the bikini performs – objectification through excessive visibility – inverts the colonial dynamics that have occurred during testing in the Pacific, objectification by rendering invisible. The bikini bathing suit manifests both a celebration and a forgetting of the nuclear power that strategically and materially marginalizes and erases the living history of Pacific Islanders. (Teaiwa 1994, 87)

The people of the Bikini Atoll were forcibly displaced by the Americans who tested nuclear weapons on their former homeland. Racism shaped this decision as policy makers viewed these people as disposable, displaceable, and irrelevant. When asked about the future of the Pacific islands in 1969, Henry Kissinger responded, 'There are only 90,000 people out there. Who gives a damn?' (quoted in Teaiwa 1994, 101).

These racist views of indigenous people and people of colour in the Global South became further entrenched in the realm of high politics as the Cold War progressed. Measures designed to limit nuclear proliferation came to support and reify a global nuclear order that privileges majority white, Western nuclear weapons states whilst denying the rest of the world the same rights. This structure of the global nuclear order has been referred to by some experts and commentators as 'nuclear apartheid' (Biswas 2001) because of how international agreements such as the Non-Proliferation Treaty and the Limited Test Ban Treaty 'sought to preserve the superpowers' nuclear arsenals while constraining the ability of presumed outsiders to join the nuclear club ... allowing a select group of Western allied states to retain genocidal weapons in perpetuity, while others, many of them former colonies, renounced their intention to possess such weapons' (Maddock 2010, 6).

As Western states entrenched the racism and white supremacy of the global nuclear order throughout the Cold War, African Americans and people of colour played an important role in protesting against and challenging the harms of nuclear weapons (Intondi 2015). From the first use of nuclear weapons in 1945, African American activists pointed out that 'racism was the heart of Truman's decision to use nuclear weapons in Japan' and questioned why Truman didn't drop the bomb on Germany or Italy (Intondi 2015, 3). Subsequently, as Vincent Intondi has eloquently documented, the struggle for civil rights in the USA became inextricably linked with the campaign for nuclear abolition, as Black activists 'believed that equality, liberation, and a world free of nuclear weapons were and would remain, links in the same chain' (Intondi 2015, 5). In 1946, the African American anthropologist Zora Neale Hurston wrote that Truman 'is a monster. I can think of him as nothing else but the BUTCHER OF ASIA', and that same year the National Association for the Advancement of Colored People (NAACP) was already campaigning for nuclear disarmament at its annual conference (quoted in Intondi 2015, 15). Other African American activists such as Shirley Graham 'warned that children could only live in peace only in a world "without battleships, atom bombs and lynch ropes"' (quoted in Intondi 2015, 26).

Whilst Martin Luther King Jr is now celebrated for his campaign for civil rights, his championing of nuclear disarmament and abolition is often ignored. Ironically, the United States Strategic Command often commemorates Martin Luther King Day (United States Strategic Command 2022), despite King himself being overtly opposed to nuclear weapons, military institutions, and war. King's anti-nuclear advocacy is laid out in no uncertain terms in several speeches. In 1959, King said that 'every man, woman and child lives, not knowing if they shall see tomorrow's sunrise', and he asked, 'what will be the ultimate value of having established social justice in a context where all people, Negro and White, are merely free to face destruction by strontium 90 or atomic war?' (quoted in Intondi 2015, 64). In 1962, King challenged the notion of deterrence, and suggested that 'non-violence in the nuclear age was life's last chance' (quoted in Intondi 2015, 66). In 1964, when receiving the Nobel Peace Prize, King stated that 'equality with whites will hardly solve the problems of either whites or Negroes if it means equality in a society under the spell of terror and a world doomed to extinction' (quoted in Intondi 2015, 67). One month before his death, King pointed out that 'it is a wonderful thing to integrate lunch counters, public accommodations, and schools. But it would be rather absurd to work to get schools and lunch counters integrated and not be concerned with the survival of a world in which to integrate' (quoted in Intondi 2015, 80).

Malcolm X and the Black Panther Party also sought to highlight and challenge the interconnections of racism and nuclear weapons. The Black Panther Party's executive mandate number 1 stated that 'the dropping of atomic bombs on Hiroshima and Nagasaki' stood alongside 'the enslavement of black people at the very founding of this country, the genocide practiced on the American Indians and the confinement of the survivors on reservations, the savage lynching of thousands of Black men and women ... and now the cowardly massacre in Vietnam' as testimony 'to the fact that toward people of color the racist structure of America has but one policy: repression, genocide, terror, and the big stick' (quoted in Intondi 2015, 83).

After the Vietnam War ended, many African American activists pointed out that poverty in Black communities throughout the USA 'was linked to the government's nuclear policies' and many began to question 'why their children suffered from malnutrition as the administration continued to spend money on nuclear weapons' (Intondi 2015, 87). As people took to the streets of New York in 1982 in the largest protest against nuclear weapons in history, African American leaders argued that 'nuclear militarism and nuclear technology are clear expressions of racism ... there is no issue more overwhelming and all embracing than nuclear technology, militarism and power' (quoted in Intondi 2015, 105). Through decades of anti-nuclear advocacy African American activists had a direct impact on the arms control and disarmament policies of Ronald Reagan, who admitted that he took these steps because, 'from a propaganda point of view, we were on the defensive' (quoted in Intondi 2015, 107). Alongside their campaigns for civil rights and social justice, African American activists have long been united by a belief that 'successful antinuclear politics must comprehend the divisiveness of thinking in terms of racial difference, and that campaigns against racism should be linked to calls for disarmament if they are to be meaningful movements for equality and human rights' (Williams 2011, 168).

With this historical overview of how race, racism, and nuclear weapons are interconnected, I now trace how these issues have gained a new importance – one that has been largely overlooked – in much of the mainstream scholarship on the Third Nuclear Age.

Racism and the Third Nuclear Age

The brutal police murder of George Floyd which took place in broad daylight, in front of a crowd who filmed his murder, shook the world. It starkly demonstrated how those institutions that are supposed to maintain security can actually endanger people, threaten them, kill them, and make them less secure – especially if they are Black, or from an ethnic minority. Around the same time that the police murdered George Floyd, they were also involved in killing other Black Americans. In June, officers from the Atlanta Police Department shot and killed Rayshard Brooks who had fallen asleep in his car outside a fast-food restaurant. Earlier that year, in March, plain-clothes officers from the Louisville Metro Police Department in Kentucky forcibly entered the apartment of Breonna Taylor and proceeded to fire thirty-two bullets into her home after being confronted by Taylor's boyfriend who thought her flat was being broken into. Taylor was hit by five or six bullets and died at the scene. These incidents, as well as the February 2020 murder of Ahmaud Arbery who was shot dead by three white men who chased him around the streets whilst he was out jogging, provoked global Black Lives Matter protests and a widespread reckoning with institutional racism, police violence, white supremacy, and the threat that these issues pose to Black people, other minorities, and the societies in which they live.

The growth of the Black Lives Matter movement and the public outcry that followed the murder of George Floyd caused many institutions within the nuclear community – including universities, thank tanks, civil society organisations, and individuals – to acknowledge and decry systemic racism. However, as Kaitlyn M. Turner and colleagues pointed out in the *Bulletin of the Atomic Scientists* in August 2020, the nuclear community needs to do much more than acknowledge that racism exists if it is to 'dismantle long-standing structural inequalities' (Turner *et al.* 2020). According to Turner *et al.*, the 'fundamental problem hiding in plain sight' for those working on nuclear policy is that 'its history, logics, and culture "produce or sustain racial hierarchy," which, by scholar Ibram X. Kendi's definition, means it is racist' (Turner *et al.* 2020).

Turner *et al.* identify two ways in which the field of nuclear weapons, policy, and strategy is racist; first, it is epistemically racist in that nuclear weapons were developed in ways that served to normalise 'colonialist dehumanization, erasure, and exploitation of people of color' (Turner *et al.* 2020). Second, the field is institutionally racist because it continues to create and sustain 'barriers precluding Black and non-Black professionals of color from full participation, inclusion, and professional advancement' (Turner *et al.* 2020). In their analysis Turner and colleagues explore these two issues in detail, noting that the history of nuclear weapons development is one of minority and indigenous communities being displaced and poisoned for the building of nuclear facilities, the testing of nuclear weapons, and the disposal of nuclear waste. They also recognise that the enshrining in the NPT by nuclear weapons states of their right to have nuclear weapons 'indefinitely preserves an inequitable and unjust world order' (Turner *et al.* 2020) where the concerns of people in the Global South, and their wishes, hopes, and dreams – for example, for a world without nuclear weapons and for compensation from the nuclear weapons states for the poisoning of their homelands through nuclear tests – are ignored.

In addition to this, Turner *et al.* highlight how policy and analysis of nuclear weapons is institutionally racist due to how knowledge about nuclear weapons 'is produced in predominantly white spaces, where professionals of color must confront racial biases and structural racism daily' (Turner *et al.* 2020). For example, in 2016, Black students only accounted for 0.6 per cent of all the doctorates awarded for nuclear engineering in the USA, and, since 1970, 'only five women of color (out of 36 total women) have held leadership positions in the nuclear security policy field within the US government' (Turner *et al.* 2020). As Turner et al. powerfully put it:

> Mutually reinforcing, the mechanisms of epistemic and institutional racism in the nuclear field work in concert to erase the scholarship, history, and perspectives of people of color. Consciously or unconsciously, leaders in the nuclear field perpetuate epistemic racism through these institutionally racist practices, reinforcing the field's narrow logics and paradigms. (Turner *et al.* 2020)

Two years on, in 2022, institutional racism still hinders the participation of people of colour from the Global South in nuclear politics (Samuel 2022). As Olamide Samuel, a Nigerian expert on nuclear weapons, points out, 'nuclear politics affect all people, yet not all voices are given equitable access to the spaces where crucial deliberations and decisions are made'. After being prevented from attending the NPT Review Conference in the summer of 2022 due to difficulties in getting a visa, Samuel pointed out that he was not the only person to face these structural barriers. He noted that, 'Despite the fact that much of the negative human and environmental impacts are borne by people of colour across the global south, the spaces where decisions are made remain exclusively in western capitals – and the conversations remain limited to a select few' (2022). This epistemic and institutional racism is apparent not just within the field of nuclear policy and strategy, but rather in the broader machinations of International Relations and security studies as a whole.

As an academic discipline, International Relations was born out of and in service of empire, and the field of security studies has often focused on maintaining the security of white, Western, 'civilised' states from non-white, non-Western, 'barbaric' others. However, the importance of race as 'a central organising feature of world politics' (Zvobgo and Loken 2020) is often ignored, and the colonial, racist history of the discipline is often overlooked or whitewashed (Henderson 2013; Vitalis 2015; Gani and Marshall 2022). The importance of race and empire to the historical study of global politics is evident in the fact that the foundational journal of the discipline – the first academic IR journal ever established, way back in 1910 – was originally called the *Journal of Race Development*, and set out to discuss 'the problems which relate to the progress of races and states generally considered backward in their standards of civilization' (Blakeslee 1910, 1). Since 1922, the journal has been known as *Foreign Affairs* and is now one of the most prominent and influential outlets for the study of international politics (Zvobgo and Loken 2020). Race and racism continue to shape the study and practice of world politics, yet the mainstream, traditional approaches to the study of International Relations do 'not take race or racism seriously' (Zvobgo and

Loken 2020). This is a problem because so many of the issues at the heart of world politics, 'such as war, migration, human rights, development, and climate change', and of course nuclear weapons, 'have a disproportionate impact on black people, indigenous people, and people of color' (Zvobgo and Loken 2020).

Nuclear testing has proven to have had a disproportionate impact on those indigenous communities who lived in places where nuclear weapon states chose to develop and test their nuclear weapons. However, despite the evidence of the harms of nuclear testing, and a global moratorium on nuclear testing that has existed since the development of the Comprehensive Test Ban Treaty (which although the USA signed but hasn't ratified, it has still adhered to), in May 2020 the *Washington Post* reported that the Trump administration was discussing the possibility of testing a new nuclear weapon. This further highlights how race is significant in the new nuclear age.

The United States has not tested a nuclear weapon since 1992, so why did the Trump administration want to do so in the summer of 2020? One of the main reasons was the administration's belief that testing a nuclear weapon would put pressure on China and Xi Jinping to start engaging with arms control negotiations; however, nuclear experts have noted that this was misguided. James Acton, the director of the nuclear policy programme at the Carnegie Endowment for International Peace, said that it was 'a hugely mistaken line of reasoning' that was 'more likely to fuel an arms race than to dampen it' (quoted in Ploughshares Fund 2020a). Tom Collina, another nuclear weapons expert, agreed, and suggested that this was not a serious move to propose a three-way arms control initiative, but simply a way for the Trump administration to undermine 'a tremendously important set of agreements' that are in place in order to 'reduce nuclear risks' (quoted in Ploughshares Fund 2020a).

Trump himself had spent the past few months talking about a 'super duper missile' that was in development, and in a meeting of national security officials the Trump administration discussed plans to test a nuclear weapon because they believed it could prove to be helpful in negotiating a trilateral arms control agreement between the USA, Russia, and China. However, the testing of a nuclear weapon is not needed to modernise the American nuclear arsenal, and it would not serve to help American interests because it would encourage Russia and China to also test nuclear weapons. If America were to test a nuclear weapon, it would, in the words of Daryl Kimball, the executive director of the Arms Control Association, 'be the starting gun to an unprecedented nuclear arms race' (quoted in Hudson and Sonne 2020). In addition to this, an American nuclear test could 'also disrupt the negotiations with North Korean leader Kim Jong-un, who may no longer feel compelled to honor his moratorium on nuclear testing' (Kimball quoted in Hudson and Sonne 2020), whilst also undermining any attempt to get Iran to return to the negotiating table so as to limit its nuclear weapons development programme.

The reporting of the Trump administration's desire to test a nuclear weapon coincided with the imminent 75th anniversary of the Trinity test and the 75th anniversary of the American atomic bombing of Hiroshima and Nagasaki. Whilst the United States did not eventually test a nuclear weapon in the summer of 2020, the President's announcement that they wanted to was enough to seem like, as Matt Korda from the Federation of American Scientists aptly put it, 'a giant middle finger not only to the Hibakusha – the survivors of those bombings – but also to the millions of Americans exposed to radioactive fallout during the cold war nuclear tests that still suffer from adverse health effects to this day' (quoted in Ploughshares Fund 2020b).

Race is a significant factor in these renewed discussions of nuclear testing because nuclear tests have disproportionate effects on people of colour, and the Trump administration's discussion of renewing testing was motivated by a fear of an ascendent China. Around the time of these discussions, Marshall Billingslea, Trump's special presidential envoy for arms control, stated that, 'Beijing is in the midst of a sizeable buildup' of its nuclear arsenal and that China 'is intent on building up its nuclear forces and using those forces to try to intimidate the United States and our friends and our allies' (2020). Even though in 2020 China had a stockpile of 350 nuclear warheads (of which 272 were operationally deployed), whereas the USA had a stockpile ten times the size of China's – with 3,800 nuclear warheads stockpiled and 1,750 deployed – Billingslea proclaimed that China posed a nuclear threat for several reasons. First, because China was no longer pursuing a minimal deterrent; second, because China's nuclear weapons policy was 'secretive and non-transparent'; and third, because it was moving towards 'a triad of delivery vehicles, a launch on warning posture, and exploration of low-yield nuclear weapons' whilst also refusing 'any opportunity to engage in good faith negotiation on these most important topics' (Billingslea 2020).

Billingslea's position reeks of hypocrisy because the United States itself does not maintain a minimum deterrent, has a secretive and non-transparent nuclear weapons policy, maintains a nuclear triad, with a launch-on-warning posture, and in its 2018 Nuclear Posture Review outlined how it wanted to develop a low-yield nuclear weapon – all whilst the Trump administration expressed a blatant disregard for good faith negotiations by withdrawing from the Iran deal, the INF Treaty, the Open Skies Treaty, and making no serious effort to renew New START. However, more than this, this hypocrisy is underpinned by a racist logic which views similar actions in drastically different ways. Whilst what China does is seen as 'irresponsible', 'dangerous', evil, and threatening, when the USA does the same thing it is seen and described as being 'responsible' and 'modernizing and sustaining what we have' so as to 'safeguard American national security and the protection of the American people' (Billingslea 2020). This othering of other states and peoples has been integral to US foreign policy since the inception of the American state (Campbell 1992), and US foreign policy towards China has been, and continues to be, underpinned by a racist, orientalist view. As the anthropologist Hugh Gusterson has argued, 'in Western discourse nuclear weapons are represented so that "theirs" are a problem whereas "ours" are not' (1999, 114). Recognising this fact is not to legitimate China's nuclear weapons, modernisation, and build-up, nor is it to support the oppressive authoritarianism of the Chinese state. Instead, it is to point out 'the dangers inherent in the continued maintenance of our own nuclear arsenals and the fact that our own actions are often a source of the instabilities we so fear in [other] nations' (Gusterson 1999, 133).

Alongside the looming spectre of a return to nuclear weapons tests that were underpinned by structural racism and an orientalist view of China, other events between May and July 2020 pointed to the important role that race and racism plays in the Third Nuclear Age. The date 8 May marked the two-year anniversary of the withdrawal of the Trump administration from the JCPOA, since which Iran had come closer to producing a nuclear weapon than ever before. Trump's approach to Iran was emblematic of his approach to states and people in the Middle East and the Global South. At home, Trump introduced a Muslim ban, incarcerated record numbers of refugees from South America, and, when speaking about migration from Africa, asked, 'Why are we having all these people from shithole countries come here?' (quoted in Kendi 2019). These words and policies create a racial hierarchy where whiteness is privileged over people of colour from different parts of the world, and this racism leads to individuals from state institutions murdering Black men and people of colour in the streets, whilst also shaping nuclear policies that are underpinned by the exploitation of the Global South, disproportionally affect indigenous people, and are reliant on racist conceptions of other people as threats.

Conclusion: why we need critical nuclear race theory

The brutal police murder of George Floyd provoked widespread outrage about how the very institutions that are supposed to keep us safe often fail to do so and are, for many minorities, a source of danger rather than safety.

George Floyd's murder followed a string of horrific racist acts of violence that led to the deaths of Rayshard Brooks, Breonna Taylor, and Elijah McClain, all of which occurred in the context of an American presidency that openly espoused racism, white supremacism, and courted violent extremists on the far right. In the summer of 2020, the spread of Black Lives Matter protests across the globe led to many institutions reflecting on their racist, colonial histories and how they continued to perpetuate racism in 2020.

In the field of nuclear policy, the summer of 2020 saw a broader reflection on how nuclear weapons were designed, developed, and deployed in ways that violently impacted people of colour in disproportionate ways. It is important to continue this reflection because, as Turner and colleagues explain, 'future scholars and professionals in the nuclear field may be unaware of how racism and colonialism intertwine with the technologies and policies that they work on' (2020). If we remain ignorant of the racialised dynamics of nuclear weapons then we may prevent and hinder a 'rectification of racial injustices' when we analyse and make policy on nuclear weapons (Turner *et al.* 2020). For Turner *et al.*, we need to acknowledge and address 'epistemic injustices and institutional racism… to create a truly antiracist future in the nuclear community' (2020).

Addressing the inherent racism of nuclear weapons, and the policies and strategies that sustain them, begins with acknowledgement, but it must also include accountability and action. This prerogative not only needs individuals to push for change and racial justice, but it also needs to involve organisations in the field prioritising racial inclusion. In addition, the study and policy of nuclear politics needs to go beyond the confines of traditional scholarship that entrenches biases, and open up to 'valuable insights on justice and equity' from other, multidisciplinary areas such as 'critical race theory, in science and technology studies, and in postcolonial and feminist studies' (Turner *et al.* 2020).

This call for intersectional insights into the field of nuclear weapons policy has been heeded by Gabriele Schwab, who advocates a critical nuclear race theory in our approach to the politics and culture of nuclear weapons. Fundamentally, this approach enhances critical nuclear studies by placing race at the forefront of our understanding of the Third Nuclear Age. Doing so shifts our attention from abstract notions of national security to how nuclear weapons – and the policies and strategies that sustain them – disproportionately impact people of colour and are bound up with colonialism, racism, and white supremacy. Critical nuclear race theory encourages us to trace and challenge how 'both everyday racism and the nuclear threat persist as slow and structural violence over and above their specific manifestations' (Schwab 2020, 94).

Critical nuclear race theory (Schwab 2020, 104) involves, first, a recognition and a grounding in the history of colonialism where nuclear weapons are inseparable from the histories of empire, racism, and war that created them. Second, it highlights how campaigns for social justice need to be anti-nuclear, and, third, how anti-nuclear movements need to be anti-racist, locally grounded but global in scope, with, fourth, an intersectional approach that is mindful of the environment, class, and gender. Fifth, critical nuclear race theory needs to mobilise against the ways in which the nuclear-military-industrial complex constructs an ecology of fear for others, a denial of the threat that nuclear weapons pose, and a moral inversion where our weapons are deemed to be safe whereas those of others are viewed as threats. Central to this endeavour is how we need to challenge what is considered as common-sense and normal in the realm of how we think about nuclear weapons – what Schwab calls 'a nuclear colonisation of the mind' (Schwab 2020, 104) – that permeates foreign policy, but is also evident in the political economy of the nuclear complex, popular culture concerning nuclear weapons, and the social relations that sustain all of these in our everyday lives.

Incorporating an intersectional approach to critical nuclear studies that accounts for race, racism, and colonialism enables us to see the links between the murder of George Floyd, the history the Manhattan Project, the bombing of Hiroshima and Nagasaki, the indigenous people who have been affected by nuclear testing, and contemporary American foreign policy towards China, Iran, and North Korea. Nuclear weapons perform

> the work of death at the global scale, either through hitherto unimaginable mass killings, if not a nuclear holocaust, or through the slow violence of radioactive contamination that poisons air, water, soil, and food. This slow violence encompasses the entire earth, including the very bodies of those who inhabit it, albeit disproportionately – at least for the time being. (Schwab 2020, 103)

Building from this, in the next chapter we turn to the events of August to October 2020 to explore the significance of other intersectional, global issues, such as how the political economy of the nuclear weapons complex further hinders how states can keep their populations secure when, in the middle of a global pandemic, 'money meant for face masks' was instead given to militaries and arms companies. In doing so we examine the significance of capitalism in the Third Nuclear Age, alongside the harm nuclear weapons and militaries cause (and can potentially cause) to the climate, how this exacerbates the climate crisis, and how this then, in a vicious cycle, exacerbates the interconnected crises of today.

7

'Money meant for face masks': August to October 2020

> Trump administration spent money meant for face masks and other PPE on jet engine parts.
>
> Aaron Gregg and Yeganeh Torbati, 22 September 2020

Every day, I walk my dog down by the River Clyde that runs through the heart of Glasgow. Just before we reach the river, we pass the high-rise flats of the Glasgow Harbour complex, where the modern towers that rise above us are currently covered in scaffolding and an array of external elevators used by workers to remove and replace the flammable cladding on the outside of the buildings. After the 2017 Grenfell Tower fire in London – where seventy-two people were killed by a fire that spread up unsafe, flammable cladding that had been attached to the building to make it look aesthetically pleasing – the cladding on the outside of Glasgow Harbour was found to be equally as dangerous and in need of replacement. Now, in early August three years later, as I passed under the shadow of the looming towers, I thought about how we expect the state to keep us safe in our own homes – yet as Grenfell, recent acts of police brutality, and the response to COVID-19 were making clear, the state very often fails to do so.

On reaching the water's edge I always take a moment to look out across the river. Directly across from the Glasgow Harbour flats lies the enormous BAE Govan shipyard where workers are busy building new type-26 class frigates for the Royal Navy which will primarily be used for 'anti-submarine' purposes. It's been fascinating to watch the ships come together over the years. From across the river you can see into the massive warehouses and watch parts of these great grey hulls being built; and then, one morning, you arrive and find the parts have been moved outside in front of the warehouse. There they sit, assembled into the final shape of the enormous ships that will soon be launched to sail in seas far from here.

The waterfront of the river Clyde at Glasgow Harbour has a peculiar meaning for me. It is a nice place to walk my dog, to stroll on an evening with Rhiannon, our baby, and friends, as we watch the sunset out west towards the Firth of Clyde. It is also a place where two competing visions of security stand in vivid contrast on each side of the river. At Glasgow Harbour, the cladding replacement symbolises the state's responsibility to keep us safe and secure from harm in our homes. Across the river in Govan, the BAE shipyard shows how the state deploys massive resources towards militaries and the contractors that provide their equipment to supposedly keep us safe from foreign harms, out there, over and beneath the tossing waves of who-knows-where.

Of course, just down the water from where I'm standing in Glasgow lies His Majesty's Naval Base Clyde, home to Britain's nuclear-armed submarines. And on this day – the 75th anniversary of the American atomic bombing of Hiroshima – I reflect on the horrors that were inflicted on unsuspecting people by a nuclear weapon with a yield of approximately 15 kilotons. I recoil when I realise that the nuclear submarines based so close to where I am carry an estimated forty nuclear warheads that each have a yield of 100 kilotons. Given that an estimated 140,000 people died in Hiroshima, the destructive power of just one of Britain's modern nuclear warheads is terrifying. As I look across the water, I think of how we seem to have learned nothing from the horrors of history.

This chapter builds upon earlier arguments about the need to reconceptualise how security is approached and practised by arguing that militarisation and the entrenchment of the nuclear-military-industrial complex across economics, politics, media, and society exists as a form of exterminism that presents more dangers than it prevents (Enloe 2000; Der Derian 2009; Jackson *et al.* 2020). I begin by exploring the issues of militarism, militarisation, and exterminism and how they came to be defining features of societies after the first use of nuclear weapons in 1945. In particular, I draw attention to how militarism has had negative impacts on people and the planet we live on. I then explore the political economy of the Third Nuclear Age where states spend billions of dollars on nuclear weapons every year, even in the midst of the COVID-19 pandemic and an ongoing climate crisis.

Militarism, militarisation, and exterminism

There is a lot of money being made in the defence industry. In 2020, BAE Systems – the company building warships on the banks of the river Clyde – made a profit of £1.9 billion on a revenue of £19.27 billion despite the COVID-19 pandemic (BAE Systems 2021). These figures made BAE Britain's biggest defence contractor, and the seventh biggest defence contractor in the world (Defense News 2021). Across the globe, defence spending reached $1,981 billion in 2020 (Silva, Tian, and Marksteiner 2021, 1). This was an increase of 2.6 per cent on the previous year, and it was 'the biggest year-on year rise' in defence spending since the 2008 global financial crisis (Silva, Tian, and Marksteiner 2021, 11). According to International Monetary Fund figures, the global economy shrank by 3 per cent in 2020, yet defence spending rose. As one defence industry report put it, '2020 was good for the industry despite the crippling coronavirus' (Gould 2021). Throughout 2020 the nine nuclear-armed states spent a total of £72.6 billion on nuclear weapons (ICAN 2021). To put this into perspective, in 2020, the entire budget of the UN was $3 billion, and the World Health Organisation's budget was $5.84 billion.

How and why did defence spending – and spending on nuclear weapons in particular – reach such dizzying heights? One of the main reasons is because of a political and social phenomenon called militarism and its associated processes of militarisation. Militarism refers to 'the tendency to regard military efficiency as the paramount interest of the state' (Bacevich 2013, 239), where states and other actors are disposed to understand military force as a normal, necessary, and positive component of global politics (Åhäll 2016; Jackson *et al.* 2020; Gani 2021). Militarisation refers to the processes by which states, societies, groups, and individuals come to 'imagine military needs and militaristic presumptions to be not only valuable but also normal' (Enloe 2000, 3). These processes are diverse and complex, involving

> an intensification of the labor and resources allocated to military purposes, including the shaping of other institutions in synchrony with military goals. Militarization is simultaneously a discursive process, involving a shift in general societal beliefs and values in ways necessary to legitimate the use of force, the organization of large standing armies and their leaders, and the higher taxes or tribute used to pay for them. Militarization is intimately connected not only to the obvious increase in the size of armies and resurgence of militant nationalisms and militant fundamentalisms but also to the less visible deformation of human potentials into the hierarchies of race, class, gender, and sexuality, and to the shaping of national histories in ways that glorify and legitimate military action. (Lutz 2002, 723)

Subsequently, the materiality of militarism – evidenced by incredible levels of defence spending – is made possible through 'a diverse range of media, communication, and everyday sites and practices' where war and political violence become normalised (Jackson *et al.* 2020, 1048).

One of the most prominent warnings of the dangers of militarism does not come from critical scholars; instead it can be found in the 1961 farewell address of the Republican US President and former Second World War army general Dwight D. Eisenhower. In this speech, Eisenhower worried about the corrupting influence of what he called 'the military-industrial complex', where he stated that, 'until the latest of our world conflicts, the United States had no armaments industry' but now there existed 'an immense military establishment and a large arms industry' that had acquired 'unwarranted influence'. For Eisenhower, the military-industrial complex had led to 'the potential for the disastrous rise of misplaced power' that could 'endanger our liberties or democratic processes' (1961).

Unfortunately, Eisenhower's warning was not heeded. The US economy became one of 'a permanent war economy' (Melman cited in Gusterson 2007, 163). Given the ascendancy of America as a global economic hegemon, this then structured the global economy and societies across the world in ways that favoured high military spending and privileged military force as a solution to political problems. Militarism took hold in the minds of elites, but also in popular discourse where, in 'equally damaging' ways, militarism has 'helped shape a degraded popular culture saturated with racial and nationalist stereotypes, aestheticized destruction, and images of violent hypermasculinity' (Gusterson 2007, 164).

Throughout the Cold War, E. P. Thompson argued that the growth of the military-industrial complex and the ways in which modern militarism had come to entrench the existence and proliferation of nuclear weapons had led to a new phenomenon of 'exterminism'. For Thompson, the arms races of the Cold War thrust civilisation 'in a direction whose outcome must be the extermination of multitudes' (Thompson 1982a, 20). This was because of how the arms races and the potential breakout of nuclear war risked the extermination of human life, but also in how nuclear weapons lent 'a terrible inertia to present political and economic structures' whilst also 'impeding free development of the broad social movements' that would be necessary to challenge the status quo 'on which the precarious and partial peace we still know appears to rest' (foreword to Thompson 1982a, vii). Not only did nuclear weapons threaten the extermination of life and civilisation, but in Thompson's view they already served to exterminate the possibilities for democratic political action across national borders. The impediments that nuclear weapons cause to democratic political action will be explored in the next chapter. However, here it is worth noting that since Thompson's writing, scientific research warns us of another serious facet of the exterminism of nuclear weapons: how they harm the environment, and how the use of even a small number of nuclear weapons in a localised region (such as between India and Pakistan) would cause catastrophic climate change that would affect all life on earth.

The harmful environmental effects of militaries – and especially those militaries in possession of nuclear weapons – has been well documented by scientists. Since ancient times, war has involved 'the degradation of land and ecosystems – including scorched earth practices, the diversion of rivers, the destruction of plants (through defoliation) and animals (such as bison on the Great Plains), the burning of oil wells, and the use of chemical and biological weapons' (Clark and Jorgenson 2012, 557). The development and testing of nuclear weapons has added to this toxic degradation and created radioactive fallout that has spread across the world; in doing so, it has given rise to 'a conception of global ecological crisis' (Clark and Jorgenson 2012, 557). Militaries deplete natural resources, cause damage to the physical environment, destroy ecosystems as well as the flora and fauna that sustain them, whilst leaving behind waste that can be toxic and radioactive – in essence, 'all aspects of military activity defile our environment in some way' (Singer and Keating 1999, 326). The negative impact of militaries on our climate is exacerbated by the fact that militaries, their operations, and the production facilities they use are exempt from environmental regulations and laws under the guise that their activities are essential for national security. Because of this unaccountable environmental damage, militarism has been referred to as 'the single most ecologically destructive human endeavour' (Gould 2007, 331).

Scientists refer to the harmful environmental impacts of militarism as the 'treadmill of destruction' (Hooks and Smith 2004; Clark and Jorgenson 2012). This idea builds upon the notion that our current economic system is a 'treadmill of production' where the nature of growth under capitalism increases demands on natural resources and leads to the environment being polluted (Gould, Pellow, and Schnaiberg 2004). However, due to the fact that militaries have their own 'expansionary dynamics' – including the requirement for vast quantities of capital, energy, and other raw materials – whilst also producing 'specific forms of environmental degradation' (Clark and Jorgenson 2012, 558), we need to pay particular attention to the environmental impacts of militarism because these cannot simply be reduced to being effects of capitalist production (Hooks and Smith 2004, 22). Because militaries produce 'a broad array of impacts that undermine environmental sustainability ... [they] must be considered a key driver of ecological degradation' (Clark and Jorgenson 2012, 566).

Nuclear weapons play a major role in this treadmill of destruction. Not only does their use threaten to make the environment they are used in uninhabitable, but every aspect of their production has a negative environmental impact and exacerbates economic and environmental inequality. For example, the extraction of uranium through mining is dangerous for the people who do it and damaging to the environment, and the places where nuclear weapons are produced and stored are 'among the most toxic places on earth' (Hooks and Smith 2004, 20), not to mention how the places where nuclear weapons have been tested are scarred for decades, if not centuries. Unfortunately, 'technologies to clean these places do not exist – and it may prove impossible to develop them' (Hooks and Smith 2004, 32), and whilst militaries may have shrunk in terms of personnel since the end of the Cold War, their continued reliance on nuclear weapons and the modernisation of these weapons ensures that their 'ability to kill people and poison the environment grows sharply' (Hooks and Smith 2004, 33).

One recent study of the energy consumption and carbon emissions of 136 countries found that 'nuclear weapon possession is consistently associated with higher total carbon emissions', and that it was 'the strongest of the key independent variables' in their analysis that studied the effects of other variables such as GDP per capita, military spending per soldier, total population, and urban population (Lengefeld and Smith 2013, 22). The existence of nuclear weapons already has a disastrous impact on the environment, yet the potential use of nuclear weapons poses exceptionally horrific environmental harm.

In 1982, the same year that Thompson's *Exterminism and Cold War* was published, the scientists Paul J. Crutzen and John W. Birks wrote about the atmospheric effects of nuclear war that would cause a 'twilight at noon' (1982), and a year later a collective of scientists (including the prominent astronomer Carl Sagan) wrote about how multiple nuclear explosions would cause a global 'nuclear winter' (Turco *et al.* 1983). According to these scientists, nuclear war would cause cities, croplands, and forests to burn, destroying fossil fuels and causing a thick layer of smoke to envelop parts of the planet. This smoke would prevent sunlight reaching the surface of the earth for several weeks or months, therefore 'rendering any agricultural activity in the Northern Hemisphere virtually impossible if the war takes place during the growing season' (Crutzen and Birks 1982, 125).

Inspired by the discovery that previous mass extinction events had been caused by particles clouding the atmosphere, scientists finally began to understand how nuclear weapons could cause another mass extinction event. By using the most advanced modelling techniques available at the start of the 1980s, scientists found that nuclear war would have a truly catastrophic impact on the environment that would be 'manifested by significant surface darkening over many weeks, subfreezing land temperatures persisting for up to several months, large perturbations in global circulation patterns, and dramatic changes in local weather and precipitation rates – a harsh "nuclear winter" in any season' (Turco *et al.* 1983, 1290). These effects would not only arise from a massive nuclear war but would likely happen from even a 'small' nuclear exchange that measured between 100 and 1,000 megatons if cities were targeted (due to the smoke and emissions caused by the burning of large amounts of combustible material in urban areas). In both a limited nuclear exchange and an all-out nuclear war, fallout would be intense and widespread in 'plumes of radioactive debris extending hundreds of kilometres downwind of targets' (Turco *et al.* 1983, 1290).

Despite the potential immensity of the environmental harms posed by the risk of nuclear war, scientists soon saw that they had underestimated these effects. By 1984, the eminent scientific journal *Nature* published research that demonstrated that 'the climatic effects of a nuclear war might persist longer than previously calculated' (Robock 1984, 670) and could last up to one year. This would be because of two factors; first, how smoke and dust from nuclear war in the northern hemisphere would travel to the southern hemisphere and cool tropical regions, and second, because of how snow and sea ice would create a feedback loop that would cause 'longer and larger' cooling effects (Robock 1984, 668).

Over the years, scientists have continued to improve their predictions of the climate effects of nuclear war by using more up-to-date knowledge about climate change as well as accounting for changes in the global security environment. In 2007, Robock and colleagues found that the effects of nuclear war would persist not just for a few weeks, months, or years but for over a decade. By using the latest available data and NASA modelling, they found that the smoke cloud caused by nuclear war would cause a global average surface cooling of -8 degrees Celsius for several years, and that after a decade there would still be a cooling of -4 degrees (Robock, Oman, and Stenchikov 2007, 6). In comparison, during the last ice age 18,000 years ago global average cooling was -5 degrees Celsius, so the use of nuclear weapons would result in 'climate change unprecedented in speed and amplitude in the history of the human race' (Robock, Oman, and Stenchikov 2007, 6). Consequently, nuclear war 'would so disrupt the food supply that it would be suicide for the attacking country' and would affect the entire planet (Robock, Oman, and Stenchikov 2007, 12).

More recent research adds to this grim picture. In 2019, Toon *et al*. modelled what would happen if Pakistan and India attacked each other with nuclear weapons. These countries are understood to be two of the most likely nations to use nuclear weapons given how they are engaged in a territorial dispute in the Kashmir region and how relations between the two became increasingly tense under the leadership of India's Hindu authoritarian populist prime minister Narendra Modi and his Islamic authoritarian populist Pakistani counterpart Imran Khan (Pulla 2019). If the two countries were to use only a quarter of their nuclear weapons, not only would there be between 50 and 125 million fatalities, but smoke from burning cities would cause 'widespread starvation and ecosystem disruption far outside of the war zone itself' (Toon *et al*. 2019, 1) as the productivity of major crop-growing regions and fishing areas would decline by between a quarter and a half for at least three years (Toon *et al*. 2019, 9).

Another study focused on the specific impact of nuclear war between India and Pakistan on the global food system. In this study, the soot caused by fires burning after a nuclear attack would cause global caloric production of major crops such as maize, wheat, and rice to fall by 12 per cent. This would be a loss four times bigger than any previous historical decrease caused by drought or volcanic eruptions (Jägermeyr *et al.* 2020, 7071). For a decade after the initial explosions, nuclear weapons would 'be more harmful to global agriculture than the same amount of warming associated with anthropogenic climate change' (Jägermeyr *et al.* 2020, 7075). These findings are based on less than 1 per cent of the worldwide nuclear arsenal being detonated, yet the impact would be global, severely affecting the food supply for 3.7 billion people (Jägermeyr *et al.* 2020, 7077). In addition, nuclear war would also likely cause a 'nuclear Niño' that would affect sea temperatures and lead to a 'sustained decrease in regional maritime productivity, in turn reducing fish catch' (Coupe *et al.* 2021, 8), thereby further hindering the ability of nuclear war survivors to sustain themselves. In the event of even a 'small' nuclear war, there would be no crops, no meat, no fish – no food – for vast numbers of survivors (Xia *et al.* 2022).

Nuclear weapons have a tremendously negative impact on the environment, and if they were ever to be used again in war the results would be truly catastrophic. Arising in its modern form after the end of the Second World War, militarism has led to incredible amounts of money being spent on militaries and the nuclear weapons that they possess. This nuclear militarism not only depletes state finances, it also depletes natural resources and harms the environment. The 'extermination of multitudes' that Thompson worried nuclear weapons would bring about is in fact actually already happening due to the 'treadmill of destruction' where militaries in nuclear weapons states are a key factor in driving the contemporary climate crisis. If nuclear weapons were to be used once again, that would in turn cause a climate crisis worse than that unfolding around us now, and severe impacts to the ecosystem would lead to survivors likely starving.

So far in this chapter we've explored the historical development of militarism, the exterminist impact of nuclear weapons on the environment, as well as the potential extermination of people and entire ecosystems that would arise from a small number of nuclear weapons being used. In what follows, I draw upon the events of August to October 2020 to argue that these issues are of profound importance in the new nuclear age.

The treadmill of destruction in the Third Nuclear Age

Despite the onslaught of the COVID-19 pandemic, state spending on militaries and nuclear weapons increased in 2020. This is despite the fact that by

August 2020 COVID-19 had caused hundreds of thousands of deaths, placed unparalleled strains on public health services, and demonstrated how woefully underprepared states were to keep their citizens and key workers safe from harm. The nine nuclear-armed states spent a total of $72.6 billion on nuclear weapons in 2020 (ICAN 2021). The USA was the biggest spender, spending a total of $37.4 billion on nuclear weapons in 2020 – three times the amount of China, which spent $10.1 billion. Russia spent $8 billion, followed by the UK with $6.2 billion, and France with $5.7 billion. India spent $2.48 billion, whilst Israel and Pakistan spent approximately $1 billion, and North Korea spent $667 million (ICAN 2021).

In 2020 President Trump requested, and Congress approved, a total defence budget of $740.5 billion for the 2021 fiscal year. This incredible sum of money was over 30 per cent larger than the combined national defence budgets of every other nuclear weapons state (see Figure 1). It was ninety times the size of the budget for the Centers for Disease Control and Prevention (CDC) that year, and an increase of $100 billion from when Donald Trump first became president. As the 2020 defence budget was passing through Congress, Senator Bernie Sanders tabled an amendment to cut the money allocated to the military by 10 per cent – $74 billion – and to spend that money instead on domestic healthcare, childcare, housing, and education in the most impoverished parts of America. Polling released by the think tank Data for Progress in the summer of 2020 showed that 56 per cent of respondents supported reducing defence spending by 10 per cent in order to address domestic issues like fighting COVID-19 and providing healthcare (Pocan 2020). Only 25 per cent of respondents opposed the defence spending cuts, and, in response to the polling, the progressive Democrat congressman Mark Pocan said, 'the American people know that new nukes, cruise missiles, or F-35s won't help them get their next unemployment check, or pay next month's rent, or put food on their family's table, or pay for the costs of healthcare in a global pandemic' (quoted in Gould 2020). Despite public support for reductions in defence spending, Congress passed the highest peacetime defence budget in the history of the world.

The sheer volume of money spent on defence spending by the US government is symptomatic of rampant militarism. Between August and October 2020 this militarism was further evidenced by two other defence spending controversies. In September 2020, journalists at the *Washington Post* reported that $1 billion in emergency funding that had been given to the Pentagon to 'prevent, prepare for, and respond to coronavirus' had 'instead been mostly funnelled to defense contractors and used to make things such as jet engine parts, body armor and dress uniforms' (Gregg and Torbati 2020).

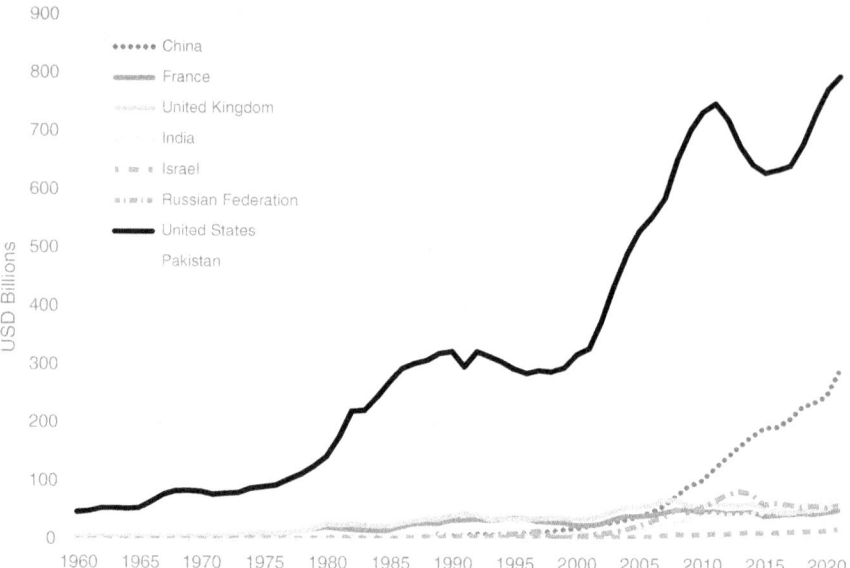

Figure 1 Military expenditure of nuclear weapons states 1960–2021 (current USD). World Bank 2022: https://data.worldbank.org/indicator/MS.MIL.XPND.CD?locations=US-RU-CN-GB-FR-IL-PK-IN&most_recent_value_desc=true
Source: Stockholm International Peace Research Institute (SIPRI), Yearbook: Armaments, Disarmament and International Security.

This 'money meant for face masks' was given to defence contractors who spent it on 'projects that [had] little to do with the coronavirus response' and was justified by the Pentagon as being needed to support firms who were facing financial hardship due to COVID-19 (Gregg and Torbati 2020). However, hundreds of millions of this funding was channelled to subsidiaries of large corporations like General Electric and Rolls Royce who are two of the largest defence contractors in the world.

In a statement at the time, Ellen Lord, who was responsible for acquisitions at the Pentagon during the Trump administration, asserted that it was okay that money meant for face masks had been given to these contractors because 'we need to always remember that economic security and national security are very tightly interrelated and our industrial base is really the nexus of the two' (quoted in Gregg and Torbati 2020). Rather tellingly, this focus on economic and national security neglects the fact that during a global pandemic, human security should take precedent. You can't have an industrial base and economic security if your workers can't work because they are ill or dying from COVID-19. National security is meaningless if your population are dying because there are shortages of PPE and medical equipment. In the middle of a pandemic, the money meant for face masks and the billions spent on defence would be better spent on, well, face masks and public health measures.

One of the reasons military spending has reached such vertiginous heights is because of a revolving door between Pentagon officials and defence companies. Prior to joining the Pentagon, Ellen Lord had been the CEO of a defence contractor called Textron Systems, and after leaving her role in January 2021 she became a senior adviser for both the defence lobbying firm The Chertoff Group and Clarifai, a company that develops AI for the Department of Defence. Lord also took up positions on the board of the defence firms AAR Corp and Science Applications International Corporation – two companies who had together received billions in dollars under Lord's tenure in charge of procurement at the Pentagon. Even Trump himself had once said that, 'I think anybody that gives out these big contracts should never ever, during their lifetime, be allowed to work for a defense company, for a company that makes that product' (Reuters 2016), yet when in office he did not 'drain the swamp' by putting an end to the revolving door between defence contractors and the Pentagon.

Lord is just one of hundreds of people who make career moves from defence firms to government and then jump back again. One recent study found that 'there were 645 instances of the top 20 defense contractors in fiscal year 2016 hiring former senior government officials, military officers, Members of Congress, and senior legislative staff as lobbyists, board members, or senior executives in 2018' (Smithberger 2018, 9). You might think that the close ties between industry and government would at least make the defence industry more efficient, but you would, in fact, be wrong. In the summer of 2020, the Government Accountability Office found that between 2018 and 2019 major defence acquisition projects had grown beyond their budgets by a total of $628 billion and were 54 per cent more expensive than originally costed whilst also being delayed by an average of two years (United States Government Accountability Office 2020, 24). Evidently, this revolving door grants the defence industry such undue influence on government that defence budgets become ever more bloated, whilst the projects these budgets are spent on increase in cost and are not delivered on time. At the same time, a 'nonproliferation complex' (Craig and Ruzicka 2013, 329) of think tanks and non-governmental organisations receives funding from nuclear weapons manufacturers and governments that base their security on nuclear deterrence, and then produces research and policy positions that unsurprisingly support the continued maintenance and growth of nuclear arsenals (see Egeland and Pelopidas 2023).

Alongside the money-meant-for-face-masks scandal, in September 2020 the US Air Force announced that it was awarding a $13.3 billion contract to the defence firm Northrup Grumman to modernise the American intercontinental ballistic missile (ICBM) system. The contract to develop a new missile system for the US Air Force's Ground-Based Strategic Deterrent was awarded to Northrup Grumman without any competition. The Air Force originally estimated that the Ground-Based Strategic Deterrent programme would cost $62 billion, though this estimate has since increased to $95.8 billion and does not include the cost of the new W87-1 nuclear warheads which are expected to cost $12.4 billion (Reif 2020). The entire Ground-Based Strategic Deterrent programme is designed to replace America's Minuteman III missiles – a literal Cold War relic, conceived in the 1950s and originally launched in the 1960s – which are based across the American Midwest in Montana, North Dakota, and Wyoming. Colorado and Nebraska also host silo-based nuclear missiles, and collectively these states are known as America's 'nuclear sponge' as they are designed to draw a potential nuclear attack away from other cities like New York and Washington, DC. In 1978 the Air Force chief of staff said that missile silos in these states would act as 'a great sponge to absorb' (quoted in Wilson 1978) a Soviet nuclear attack, and that because so many missiles would be needed to destroy the silos an adversary would be deterred from attacking the USA.

The logic of the nuclear sponge persists to this day, and it is problematic to modernise it for several reasons. First, even if you support nuclear weapons and deterrence, then you must admit that land-based nuclear weapons are an easy target for adversaries. Unlike submarine-based weapons, adversaries can easily find out where your land-based weapons are, and they are therefore redundant and vulnerable to attack. No nuclear weapons state needs land-based weapons to deter others when they can deploy these weapons on submarines. Second, if you live in Montana, North Dakota, Wyoming, Colorado, and Nebraska or their neighbouring states, it is probably not much solace that in the event of nuclear war you would die so that the people of New York might live. Alongside this, land-based nukes have been prone to accidents and close calls. In 1980, whilst a nuclear missile was being repaired in a silo in Arkansas, a worker dropped a socket down the silo, which pierced the fuel tank, caused an explosion, and launched the nuclear warhead flying into the woods. Thankfully, it did not explode.

Since the 1980s there have been other close calls and unnecessary, ridiculous risks related to nuclear-armed ICBMs. Recently ICBM service personnel were found to have taken drugs and cheated on their regular proficiency exams. In 2021 Air Force staff were found to have shared secret information about nuclear weapons on online flashcards (Postma 2021). Someone who is high, cheating on exams designed to make sure they know how to operate complex systems, and willingly shares top secret information online is probably not someone who should be responsible for maintaining nuclear weapons. The widespread occurrence of these issues suggests that the problem is not of a singular bad apple but a rotten barrel. The Ground-Based Strategic Deterrent does not ensure the security of anyone; it is 'a nuke no-one needs' (William Hartung in Ploughshares Fund 2020b) that exists to serve the interests of the Air Force (in maintaining a role in nuclear deterrence), local politicians (who claim that the ICBMs bring jobs to their states), and defence contractors (who make billions from them). The only thing the people who actually live near these missile silos get is the opportunity to be sacrificed in a nuclear war.

Over the course of August–October 2020, as the American military spent taxpayers' money meant to fight COVID-19 on other things, and as the US Air Force gave one defence firm $13.3 billion to develop an obsolete, dangerous missile system, militaries across the globe continued to harm the environment on a day-to-day basis. Scientists estimate that in 2020, militaries were responsible for 6 per cent of the global total of carbon emissions: more than the combined emissions contributions of both the shipping and aviation sectors (Parkinson 2020). Globally, there are twice the number of military aircraft (53,563) than there are in the civilian fleet of planes and helicopters (23,715), and, because military planes fly higher in the atmosphere and burn more fuel than civilian ones, they can cause 'additional atmospheric heating effects' (Conflict and Environment Observatory 2021). The lack of transparency around military carbon emissions figures means that the real emissions could be much higher than expected (Spray 2021), yet it is undisputed that militaries are contributing to climate change in catastrophic ways. This is a vicious cycle, because, as the International Panel on Climate Change finds through a synthesis of research, 'changes in climate variability increase the risk of armed conflict' (Adger *et al.* 2014, 773) and 'climate change will be an increasingly important driver of human insecurity in the future' (Adger *et al.* 2014, 779). As militaries contribute to climate change by releasing emissions, climate change is likely to cause more conflicts (Mach *et al.* 2019), more conflicts cause militaries to release more emissions, and more emissions cause more climate change, which then causes more conflicts. Repeat ad infinitum until there is no one left to wage war, nor a planet left to wage it on.

Conclusion: why we need to halt the nuclear treadmill of destruction

There can be no security on a dead planet. The latest scientific modelling demonstrates that even a 'small' nuclear war would have long-term impacts on our environment that would make growing food or catching fish almost impossible in countries that are home to billions of people. Those lucky enough to survive the blasts would likely in time starve to death even if they lived thousands of miles away. In an instant, nuclear war would cause climate change at a level unforeseen since the last Ice Age. Yet, nuclear weapons already contribute to environmental harm. Militaries are some of the worst polluters in the world, having three times as much impact on carbon emissions as deforestation does. Militaries burn more fuel than civilian shipping and aviation, and produce toxic, radioactive waste at the same time. The scars of nuclear weapons development and testing are still felt, if not seen, in places where uranium was mined, nuclear weapons assembled, and nuclear bombs detonated. Worse still, those militaries responsible for such harms are not included in state agreements to reduce and limit emissions and environmental damage.

The Third Nuclear Age is unfolding at the same time as the climate crisis. Research suggests that every year ten million people die from the effects of air pollution, and every year the global economy loses $8.1 trillion because of pollution (Wallace-Wells 2021). If the United States were to decarbonise its economy, it 'could prevent 4.5 million premature deaths, 1.4 million hospitalisations, 1.7 million cases of dementia and 300 million lost work days' in the USA every year (Wallace-Wells 2021). This would not only benefit human lives but would also benefit the US economy to the tune of $700 billion a year, therefore the energy transition away from carbon 'would pay for itself through public health gains alone' (Wallace-Wells 2021). It is in the interest of all humans to reduce emissions and address the climate crisis. Militaries, especially those of nuclear weapons states, cause massive environmental harms yet they are largely left unaccountable in how states attempt to reduce emissions and prevent temperatures rising.

In the context of the climate crisis, we need to halt the military treadmill of destruction because it contributes to insecurity by causing environmental damage and diverting state resources away from actions that would actually improve the security of people and planet. Alongside this, climate change that is in part caused by the treadmill of destruction exacerbates the conditions that lead to conflict. The ever-increasing level and frequency of climate change poses a danger as it contributes to increasing probabilities of conflict in the Third Nuclear Age.

The summer of 2020 was the hottest summer ever recorded in the northern hemisphere. Wildfires in California spread over 1.6 million hectares, which broke the record for 'most hectares burned in a single year', and by October, Arctic sea ice was at its lowest levels since records began for that month. In August, record levels of rainfall fell in China and Pakistan. In September, record flooding in the Sahel region of Africa was displacing people from their homes at the same time as record fires blazed across wetland areas of South America. In October, the UK had its wettest day on record. The year 2020 was not only the joint hottest year since records began, but it also set a record for levels of CO_2 (carbon dioxide) in the atmosphere (Carrington 2021). In 2020, CO_2 levels were 62 per cent higher than they were in 1990 (World Meteorological Organization 2020, 2). The head of the World Meteorological Organization – a specialised agency of the UN responsible for providing the framework for international collaboration on climate change – reported that 2020 was evidence of 'relentless, continuing climate change, an increasing occurrence and intensification of extreme events, and severe losses and damage, affecting people, societies and economies' (World Meteorological Organization 2021). The UN Secretary-General António Guterres also pointed out that, 'unless there are immediate, rapid and large-scale reductions in greenhouse gas emissions, limiting warming to 1.5 °C will be impossible, with catastrophic consequences for people and the planet on which we depend' (Reuters 2021). In the Third Nuclear Age, the climate crisis presents new challenges to society.

Human activity is changing the climate and this climate change in turn has a devastating impact on human life whilst also making conflict more likely. Climate change therefore causes a threat to stability and security in the Third Nuclear Age. The climate crisis can only be seriously addressed if we begin to recognise the role that militaries play in exacerbating it, and then work to change that. States continue to spend billions on their militaries and defence contractors who take incredible sums of taxpayers' money. This is driven by militarism and the undue influence of defence contractors in government spending. What seems like blatant corruption and cronyism, evidenced by the revolving door between government officials and defence contractors, serves to make a handful of people very rich whilst money is wasted on redundant nuclear weapons technologies like ICBMs that function as a 'nuclear sponge' in case nuclear war breaks out. If it did, people living in the 'nuclear sponge' states would be incinerated in an instant and the planet would be harmed for decades.

The treadmill of destruction already causes environmental harm and it races forward in one direction – towards an 'exterminism of multitudes' (Thompson 1982a, 20): of states, nations, people, and life itself. In the next chapter, we turn to how the exterminism of the Third Nuclear Age is also present in the political systems that govern nuclear weapons states. In turning to the events of November 2020 to January 2021, I explore the implications of the 2020 US presidential election and the subsequent storming of the Capitol on 6 January 2021 for the Third Nuclear Age. I place these events in the context of the global rise of populist authoritarianism as a mode of government that is increasingly evident in nuclear weapons states, from Trump's America to Putin's Russia, via Modi's India, Netanyahu's Israel, and Xi's China. I also explore the devastating potential of sole authority over nuclear weapons, and together examine how these issues create, as the poet Amanda Gorman eloquently put it in her poem for the inauguration of President Biden, 'a force that would shatter our nation rather than share it'.

8

'A force that would shatter our nation rather than share it': November 2020 to January 2021

> We've seen a force that would shatter our nation, rather than share it.
> Amanda Gorman, 20 January 2021

Watching American presidential elections from afar can be a stressful affair. You have to stay up all night to watch the results roll in as the announcers erratically jump from state to state and district to district. You must also try to make sense of the electoral college system which doesn't quite map on to the popular vote and is a relic of a time long ago. In 2020, you also had to worry about whether the election would be won by a man who had spent the past four years as president setting the Third Nuclear Age in motion by withdrawing from arms control treaties, threatening nuclear war with North Korea, and proposing bright ideas like nuking hurricanes. On election night in November 2020, I had bought popcorn, chocolate, and bags of sweets to keep Rhiannon and myself awake as the results came in, but the election was too close to call for another few days. Eventually, we breathed a sigh of relief as Joe Biden was declared president-elect. After the seemingly apocalyptic events of 2020, a glimmer of hope for the future had finally arrived.

This sense of hope was shattered two months later, when, on 6 January, we were once again glued to our television screen. This time, the bright lights of the studio were replaced by overcast skies and violent scenes as a mass of flag-waving insurrectionists scaled the walls of the US Capitol building and broke inside. Watching this unfold seemed urgently menacing and dreadful. What was this mob going to do inside the Capitol? Where were the police? Was this a coordinated assault on American democracy? Was this the start of a civil war? We checked our phones as images of insurrection from inside the Capitol began circulating on social media. Crowds of people in Trump memorabilia were storming through the building. People were looting items and sitting at the desks of politicians. Was that a gallows you could see on the lawn? Did those guys have zip ties to handcuff and kidnap Congress members? Wait, was that guy dressed like a Viking?

Yes, he was. Sort of. He was dressed as the 'QAnon Shaman': topless, tattooed, his face daubed in red, white and blue face paint, with a horned fur hat on his head. He was also carrying a spear. The QAnon Shaman – a thirty-three-year-old man from Arizona called Jake Angeli – was a grimly comic figure on a dark day for democracy. Angeli was a believer in the QAnon conspiracy theory. This conspiracy theory originated on the Internet forum 4chan in October 2017 when a user under the name Q – a supposed allusion to the fact that they had top secret, Q security clearance from the US Department of Energy and access to information about nuclear weapons and materials – posted that a storm was coming. According to Q, Hillary Clinton and other liberal figures like George Soros would soon be arrested for being part of a global paedophile ring. After the prominent far-right conspiracy theorist Alex Jones talked about QAnon on his *Infowars* show, the movement grew, and in July 2018 QAnon believers took part en masse in a Trump rally prior to the 2018 midterms (Campbell 2018). From then on, QAnon became a highly visible part of Donald Trump's supporter base in the United States. Members of the group believed that Trump himself was waging a war against the 'deep state' – a secret cabal of Satan-worshipping, paedophile government officials, bankers, and celebrities. Described as 'every conspiracy, all at once, an orchestra tune-up of theories' (Campbell 2018), QAnon eventually fed into the widespread conspiracy amongst Trump supporters that the 2020 election was rigged and that the presidency was stolen from Donald Trump.

The events of 6 January marked the culmination of Trump's 'Stop the Steal' campaign, by which, since losing to Joe Biden in November 2020, Trump refused to cede the presidency. The day began with a Trump rally on the Ellipse park outside the White House where Trump spoke to his supporters, told them the election was stolen, and said that those assembled needed to 'fight. We fight like hell. And if you don't fight like hell, you're not going to have a country anymore. Our exciting adventures and boldest endeavours have not yet begun … the best is yet to come. So we're going to, we're going to walk down Pennsylvania avenue … we're going to the Capitol' (quoted in Naylor 2021). By the end of the day five people would be dead, and the world would be shocked by a violent riot at the democratic heart of America.

As the Capitol was stormed, Vice President Mike Pence was in the building accompanied by military aides who carried with them the nuclear 'football' – a device that enables the Vice President to order a nuclear attack if the President is incapacitated. As insurrectionists stormed the Capitol and chanted 'hang Mike Pence', they came within 30 metres of Pence and his nuclear football before he was evacuated off site. Even if they could never have used the football to launch nuclear weapons, the insurrectionists could have paraded the football around and 'caused widespread panic and chaos' (Collina quoted in Borger 2021) as well as revealing nuclear launch codes and the list of American nuclear attack options available to the Vice President. The 6 January incident narrowly avoided being an overt nuclear crisis, yet it revealed a deeper issue at the heart of global nuclear politics: that the most sophisticated nuclear arsenal in the world was in the hands of a man who refused to accept that he had lost the presidency. As Julian Borger, a journalist with *The Guardian*, noted at the time, 'perhaps the only thing scarier than the football being surrounded by a mob is the thought of Trump being alone with it' (2021).

Indeed, after the events of 6 January, General Mark Milley, Donald Trump's Chairman of the Joint Chiefs of Staff – the highest ranked military officer in the United States – had to reassure other politicians that 'the nuclear triggers are secure ... and we're not going to allow anything crazy, illegal, immoral or unethical to happen ... I have no direct authority ... but I have a lot of ability to prevent bad things from happening' (quoted in Woodward and Costa 2021, xx). He simultaneously summoned a meeting of officers responsible for dealing with the launch of nuclear weapons and told them that 'if you get calls ... no matter who they're from, there's a process here, there's a procedure. No matter what you're told you do the procedure. You do the process. And I'm part of this procedure' (quoted in Woodward and Costa 2021, xxvii). As the head of the US military, Milley was concerned that in the dying days of his presidency Trump would initiate military action or even launch nuclear weapons at an adversary. The events of 6 January and the fallout of the November US elections therefore stand as a vital moment that reveals another important aspect of the Third Nuclear Age: how nuclear weapons are inherently anti-democratic, and how the rise of nationalist, authoritarian populist leaders increases the risks of nuclear conflict and unparalleled catastrophe.

This chapter therefore examines how nuclear weapons erode democracy and how authoritarian conspiracy theories that influence populist movements of the modern era pose a serious threat to the planet, especially in states that have leaders with the sole authority to use nuclear weapons (Meier and Vieluf 2021). As the storming of the US Capitol made clear, democratic states such as the USA are not immune to instability and violence striking at the heart of state institutions, and the Third Nuclear Age is wrought with exterminist dangers that threaten the social and political fabric of democratic states. As the poet Amanda Gorman eloquently put it in her poem written for the inauguration of President Biden, populism is 'a force that would shatter our nation rather than share it' – and so too are nuclear weapons.

The nuclear democratic deficit

There is a democratic deficit at the heart of global nuclear politics. Writing in 1985, the political theorist Robert Dahl noted that 'no decisions can be more fateful for Americans, and for the world, than decisions about nuclear weapons. Yet these decisions have largely escaped the control of democratic process' (1985, 3). Dahl continued to point out how the world had 'turned over to a small group of people decisions of incalculable importance to ourselves and mankind, and it is very far from clear how, if at all, we could recapture a control that in fact we never had' (1985, 6–7). In subsequent decades, and despite the end of the Cold War, the situation has not improved (Hanson 2022, 22–9). Political scientists have noted that states, international institutions, and the current structure of international politics are suffering from a 'democratic deficit' (Moravcsik 2004; Follesdal and Hix 2006). This democratic deficit is caused by the fact that many state policies, and policies by international institutions such as the European Union, as well as the broader structuring of the international system do not reflect what most people want or need, and that there are insufficient checks and balances on decision makers, alongside a distinct lack of democratic input or control over national and international politics (Moravcsik 2004, 336–7). In this chapter, we explore the contours of what I call the nuclear democratic deficit, where nuclear weapons policies lack much, if any, democratic input, control, or accountability, even in the nuclear weapons states that are democratic.

The nuclear democratic deficit manifests in several ways. First, decisions about the development, testing, possession, targeting, and potential use of nuclear weapons have been and continue to be shaped by a small number of military and political elites. Second, the authority to launch nuclear weapons often lies with one individual, even in democratic states that possess nuclear weapons such as the USA, France, and the UK, where the president and the prime minister have sole authority to order a nuclear attack. In other nuclear democracies such as India and Pakistan, other military and political figures will supposedly be involved in decisions to launch nuclear weapons; however, what this would look like in practice is unclear, due to how, for example, any state leader would be confronted with very tight time constraints if they were faced with the decision to retaliate to an incoming nuclear attack. Third, there is a lack of transparency and accountability in the realm of nuclear doctrine, developments, and decision making. Finally, the continued existence of nuclear weapons is driven by nine states that possess nuclear weapons, and such a situation is evidence of a global nuclear order that constitutes both a 'nuclear apartheid' (Biswas 2001) between the nuclear weapons haves and have-nots, and 'thermonuclear subjugation' (Scarry 2014, 22) of citizens across the globe.

How decisions about nuclear weapons have been, and continue to be, made by a small number of elites is the first major way in which nuclear weapons undermine democracy. In states that possess nuclear weapons, 'only a minute proportion of the population' (Hanson 2022, 23) formulates and has any impact on nuclear policy and decisions that potentially affect the entire planet. This issue stems from the earliest days of the First Nuclear Age, when the development of the first nuclear weapons and the war plans that informed how they would be used were shaped by the 'wizards of Armageddon' (Kaplan 1991) – a small group of white, American, male policy makers, scientists, and military personnel who operated in top secret. In addition, the narrow way that nuclear expertise has been, and still is, defined by these elites – viewing nuclear weapons and deterrence as essential to global security – leads to the legitimisation of past and present nuclear weapons policies, and the continued existence of nuclear weapons and doctrines of deterrence, whilst also limiting the possibilities for innovation and other ways of thinking about nuclear weapons and security that may lead to disarmament and abolition (Pelopidas 2011, 2016). These elites have been 'arguably afforded more secrecy than any other decision making branch of government' (Hanson 2022, 25) under the guise that nuclear weapons and national security are too dangerous and serious to allow the public to know too much about them, let alone have any input into important decisions in this area. What we subsequently see in the realm of nuclear policy is the undue influence of elites who have a narrow view of national security as military security, of nuclear weapons as necessary to ensure that security through deterrence, and of nuclear disarmament as an impossibility.

Whilst few people are involved in decisions about the development of nuclear weapons and plans about how they will potentially be used, there are an even smaller number of people who have their finger on the nuclear trigger. In the United Kingdom, the decision to use nuclear weapons lies solely with the prime minister, who, like the American president, has sole authority over when to launch nuclear weapons. The decision of the United States to develop the atomic bomb and then to drop it on Hiroshima and Nagasaki was made by Presidents Roosevelt and Truman respectively, with no input from other democratically elected politicians. The decision of the United Kingdom to develop nuclear weapons was also not democratically driven by widespread public support for the bomb, but instead was influenced by a small group of politicians. In 1946, Ernest Bevin, the Labour politician who was then foreign secretary, remarked in a cabinet meeting that 'we've got to have this thing over here whatever it costs ... we've got to have the bloody Union Jack on top of it' (quoted in Hogg and Laucht 2012, 482), and there has only ever been limited public and parliamentary debate about

Britain's nuclear weapons (Hanson 2022, 27). So, too, in France does the authority to launch nuclear weapons lie solely with the French president.

The nuclear launch policies in democratic states are the same as those in authoritarian nuclear weapons states such as China, Russia, and North Korea where the power to use nuclear weapons lies in the hands of Xi Jinping, Vladimir Putin, and Kim Jong-un respectively. In India and Pakistan, the decision to use nuclear weapons lies with each country's Nuclear Command Authority which consists of political and military officials; however, the final say on dropping the bomb still lies with the prime minister of both states. Israel, meanwhile, has never confirmed nor denied the existence of its nuclear weapons, so little is known about their launch authority, though it is likely to rest with the prime minister. The sole authority over nuclear weapons in most nuclear weapons states can be understood as 'nuclear despotism' (Deudney 2010, 255) because of how such important decision-making power is concentrated 'into the hands of one individual', whereby 'whatever their formal constitutional principles, all nuclear-armed states have become "monarchical" because decision making about nuclear use has devolved into the hands of one individual' (Deudney 2010, 255). Due to this concentration of nuclear decision-making power, every nuclear power is now a 'nuclear monarchy' (Deudney 2010, 255) that operates under the 'nuclear totalitarianism' (Deudney 2010, 256) of strict hierarchies where state leaders have sole authority over their nuclear arsenals.

The nuclear democratic deficit is further exacerbated by the secrecy that surrounds nuclear weapons and the distinct lack of transparency and accountability concerning them. Nuclear weapons policy suffers from a distinct lack of external scrutiny, and demands for transparency and accountability in this area 'have invariably been discounted or suppressed' (Hanson 2022, 26). Nuclear weapons 'undermine democracy as a result of the extreme secrecy nuclear policies are thought to demand' (Booth 1999, 21), and this regime of official secrecy 'suppresses and distorts nuclear information' whilst also cultivating 'a climate of permanent emergency that promotes public inertia and acquiescence to authoritarian rule' (Taylor 2007, 671). At the same time, the undue influence of the military and defence contractors in nuclear policy subverts democratic norms when defence budgets soar but funding for other public goods such as education, health, housing, and critical infrastructure is decimated. Not only do politicians defer to, and benefit from, the interests of military and defence contractors, but 'a timid and amnesiac news media' fails to sufficiently interrogate nuclear policies or hold elites to account, whilst anti-nuclear views that support disarmament and the abolition of nuclear weapons are demonised 'as extreme, irrelevant, and unpatriotic' (Taylor 2007, 672). This leaves the general public 'fragmented, alienated, uninformed, and unable to participate in deliberation with forceful and reasoned discourse' as citizens struggle to 'acquire, deliberate, and act on information concerning nuclear policy' (Taylor 2007, 671). Recent studies have affirmed that 'procedures to ensure transparency and accountability are impossible in nuclear weapons policymaking ... [and] A potential consequence of this is that it could lead to a more general acceptance of political deception and a greater degree of cynicism and suspicion' (Cooke and Futter 2018, 511–12) as the public are alienated from nuclear policy.

The Glasgow trade unionist Jimmy Reid once claimed that the alienation of the public from political and economic decisions is one of the central causes of harm in modern societies: alienation from the decisions that shape their lives leads to a 'feeling of despair and hopelessness that pervades people who feel with justification that they have no real say in shaping or determining their own destinies' (1972, 5). Citizens are utterly alienated from nuclear weapons policy, and, 'once citizens no longer feel qualified to participate in decisions about their very survival, the connection between the governing and the governed is severed' (Benedict 2012). This nuclear alienation is accompanied by what Ken Booth calls 'nuclear amnesia' (1999, 12), since people have largely forgotten the effects that nuclear weapons had on people in Hiroshima and Nagasaki, as well as forgetting the subsequent decades of fears, crises, near-misses, accidents, and worries of nuclear conflict throughout the Cold War. The alienation of the public from nuclear policy, and their forgetting of the horrors of nuclear weapons, and the crises of the Cold War 'has greatly suited the policy elite, because it has allowed them to carry out their nuclear policies in ways and at the pace they have preferred' (Booth 1999, 13). With the end of the Cold War, reductions in nuclear arsenals rather than complete disarmament and abolition were 'a result of nuclear complacency' where the opportunity for a truly meaningful change to international security 'went begging' (Booth 1999, 13; Egeland 2020b).

Beyond these factors, nuclear weapons serve to undermine democracy in two other fundamental ways. First, they constitute a 'nuclear apartheid' (Biswas 2001) between states that have nuclear weapons and those that do not, and second, they lead to an international system where citizens live under 'thermonuclear subjugation' (Scarry 2014, 22). The contemporary global nuclear order is enshrined in the Non-Proliferation Treaty that gives the P5 nuclear weapons states the right to maintain nuclear weapons and is intended to stop other states from developing them. As such, the NPT engages 'states in a collaborative exercise within which some states will always remain marginal' (Biswas 2014, 73) and upholds a 'global unequal order that sustains the desire for and production of nuclear weapons' (Biswas 2014, 74). Not only is there a lack of democracy *between* the nuclear weapons states and those that do not possess them, but the existence of nuclear weapons erodes the democratic rights of citizens in *all* states on earth. This is because the lives of billions of people are at risk if nuclear weapons are used, and this means that those who are at risk of nuclear annihilation have 'lost the capacity for self-preservation' and 'have ceased to be, with respect to their own survival, rights-bearing persons' (Scarry 2014, 6). The looming spectre of unparalleled catastrophe leaves people across the planet 'disempowered, disabled ... frozen in structures of thermonuclear subjugation' (Scarry 2014, 22) because decisions about the fate of the earth now lie 'wholly outside the social contract' (Scarry 2014, 24).

The nuclear democratic deficit has been a feature of global politics since the advent of the atomic bomb. Nuclear weapons policies have always been decided upon by a small number of people, with little regard for what the public think or want. Even in democratic nuclear weapons states, the decision to use nuclear weapons lies with one individual state leader, and nuclear weapons policies lack transparency and escape full public debate or oversight. The nuclear desires of only nine states that possess nuclear weapons shape global politics and reify an undemocratic nuclear order, whilst also eroding core democratic rights such as the right of people to live their lives free from threats of death and violence. In the next section of this chapter I explore how these issues are significant in the Third Nuclear Age. I draw particular attention to how the two factors of authoritarian populism and declining democracy further increase the risk of unparalleled catastrophe, whilst also demonstrating how the development of the TPNW (Treaty on the Prohibition of Nuclear Weapons) marks an important step in the democratisation of nuclear politics.

Nuclear populism and democracy in 'this winter of peril and possibility'

In his inauguration speech on 20 January 2021, President Biden warned that 'we have much to do in this winter of peril and possibility' (2021). For Biden, this 'winter of peril' was caused by the threat to democracy posed by the conflagration of COVID-19, racial injustice, the climate crisis, and the rise of 'political extremism, white supremacy, domestic terrorism' that were evident on 6 January. In the United States, the rise of nationalist authoritarianism that culminated in Trump's efforts to steal an election is evidence of two issues that are important in the Third Nuclear Age. The first of these issues is the global rise of populist authoritarianism that is prevalent in nuclear weapons states. The second issue is a global democratic backsliding, where progress towards a more democratic world is halting and backsliding, as democratic standards are being eroded in states that possess nuclear weapons such as the USA, UK, and India.

The election of Donald Trump has been described as the 'most dramatic case' (Norris and Inglehart 2019, 4) of populism in contemporary democracies. Trump, a figure who was politically inexperienced and better known for his appearances on reality TV shows and wrestling matches, came to lead the largest military power on earth and used 'populist rhetoric to legitimize his style of governance, while promoting authoritarian values that threaten the liberal norms underpinning American democracy' (Norris and Inglehart 2019, 4). On 6 January, Trump's populist, nationalist rhetoric was evident in the speech that he gave to his supporters prior to them storming the Capitol, where he made anti-elite claims to speak for 'the American people' against other politicians, the media, and corporations where he proclaimed, 'Together, we will drain the Washington swamp and we will clean up the corruption in our nation's capital' (quoted in Naylor 2021). Trump's authoritarian values were laid bare in his fantastical claims that the election was stolen from him and that in response his supporters needed to 'fight like hell' (quoted in Naylor 2021). The effects of this populist authoritarianism were then rendered visible in the violence of the Capitol insurrection. However, populist authoritarianism also has an impact on the broader politics of the Third Nuclear Age beyond the halls of power in Washington, DC.

Populism is 'a style of rhetoric' that challenges the authority of elites and claims that 'the people' are the only source of political authority, rather than elected officials or other establishment figures such as the media, judges, scientists, or international organisations (Brubaker 2017; Chatterje-Doody and Crilley 2019; Norris and Inglehart 2019, 4–6). Populism is often authoritarian as it has the 'rhetorical veneer of "people power"', but populist leaders like Trump are concerned with ensuring security against outsiders through illiberal means, conformity with traditions, and maintenance of obedient loyalty to a strong leader (Norris and Inglehart 2019, 7).

The recent global rise of 'nationalist, anti-elitist, illiberal, and anti-pluralist set of ideas and politics conducted in the supposed interests of "the people" … has begun to influence the effectiveness of time-honored institutions of the nuclear order' (Meier and Vieluf 2021, 2). In their landmark study of the effects of populism on nuclear politics, Oliver Meier and Maren Vieluf identify three ways in which populism increases nuclear dangers. First, populist leaders talk about nuclear weapons differently than other leaders. They 'often speak loosely about nuclear weapons' (Meier and Vieluf 2021, 11), brag about them as a symbol of strength, and proclaim that they are ready to use them. Populists trivialise the risks of nuclear war or accident, and exaggerate the benefits of having nuclear arsenals (Meier and Vieluf 2021, 13). This rhetoric idealises nuclear weapons, incentivises others to pursue developing them, and 'make it more difficult for third parties to judge the intentions behind strong statements' about nuclear weapons (Meier and Vieluf 2021, 13). Second, whilst there is a democratic deficit in nuclear policy making in nuclear weapons states, there are at least small groups of experts involved in planning decisions; yet populist leaders' desire to depart from routine policy can 'empower officials with radical views' (Meier and Vieluf 2021, 13) and make nuclear policy more unpredictable. On a day-to-day basis the emboldened hawkish nuclear policies of populists can be dangerous. During a crisis they could be deadly because populists tend to be risk takers and value strong displays of military power over diplomacy and cooperation. Furthermore, the authoritarian proclivities of populist leaders also lead to a stranglehold over security policy. Third, populist leaders undermine the institutions and mechanisms that maintain some semblance of order in nuclear politics. By viewing 'global institutions and international arrangements as disadvantageous for their own countries' (Meier and Vieluf 2021, 17), populist leaders have withdrawn from international treaties, ended international dialogues, and denounced international alliances. The fact that the United States had a populist leader in Donald Trump, the United Kingdom had Boris Johnson as prime minister, and France nearly saw Marine Le Pen elected as president suggests that in the Third Nuclear Age the distinction between 'responsible' nuclear weapons states and 'irresponsible' ones has been shattered, as populist leaders undermine the notion that nuclear powers show restraint (Meier and Vieluf 2021, 2).

In addition to these issues, the rise of populist authoritarianism also configures the Third Nuclear Age in two other ways. First, authoritarian populism that feeds upon economic insecurity and authoritarian attitudes gives rise to polarisation within democratic societies (Jennings and Stoker 2018, 159), and this polarisation serves to make the governance of states, including nuclear weapons states, more difficult as citizens disagree on core national issues and crises become normalised – Brexit and the election of Trump being two cases in point. Second, populism gives rise to the spread of disinformation and post-truth politics, where people no longer know what to believe and thus feel apathy towards the political process and political institutions (Crilley 2018; Crilley and Chatterje-Doody 2019). Together, the loose talk and nuclear threats of populist leaders, their valuing of national strength over international dialogue, their undermining of international institutions and cooperation, as well as the polarisation of societies and the proliferation of political apathy, make it harder for the world to deal with nuclear dangers; arms control and disarmament become more difficult, and the nuclear taboo is eroded.

The rise of populist authoritarianism across the planet has been accompanied by a global democratic backsliding to levels not seen since 1989.

One recent study has found that the three decades of democratic developments that followed the end of the Cold War have now unravelled as 'dictatorships are on the rise and harbor 70% of the world population – 5.4 billion people' (Boese *et al.* 2022, 6). The Economist Democratic Index ranks countries according to their electoral processes, the functioning of their governments, the political participation and culture, and the civil liberties of their citizens. Of the nuclear weapons states, only the UK is classed as a 'full democracy', ranking 18th on the global democratic index. France, Israel, the USA, and India are ranked as 22nd, 23rd, 26th, and 46th respectively and are classed as 'flawed democracies' because, whilst citizens may enjoy civil liberties and elections may be free and fair, there are serious problems of governance or weak democratic institutions. Pakistan places 104th and is classed as a 'hybrid regime' because of democratic irregularities, widespread corruption, and weak rule of law. On the most recent democratic index, Russia is ranked 124th, China is 148th, and North Korea is 165th. All of these states are classed as 'authoritarian' because their regimes lack any substantial democratic participation and citizens essentially have no political freedoms or democratic rights (Economist Intelligence Unit 2021).

The majority of nuclear weapons states are categorised as undemocratic, and those states that have nuclear weapons but are also classed as democracies are mainly flawed and at risk of democratic backsliding. Research suggests that the number of democracies peaked in 2006 (Walter 2022, 26) and that a record number of countries are 'autocratizing' and moving away from democracy (Boese *et al.* 2022). India, for example was downgraded from a democracy to an electoral autocracy in 2020 because of how the anti-pluralist political BJP party led by Narendra Modi is driving a turn to autocracy. This is happening elsewhere across the globe, and there are few signs of pro-democratic mobilisation in the face of widespread assaults on freedom of expression, repression of civil society, the undermining of electoral management bodies, and diminishing opposition parties and movements (Boese *et al.* 2022, 18–20). The backsliding of democracy is evident in increasing polarisation to toxic levels within countries, increasing government misinformation, an increasing number of coups, and the fact that we are now living in 'a new peak' of civil wars across the globe (Walter 2022, 11).

The increase in civil wars has been driven by declining democratic standards as shifting demographics within states, the growth of inequality, and the weakening of institutions to serve elite interests has coincided with the rise of factionalism and populist demagogues who have used new media technologies to exacerbate tensions and mobilise their supporters (Walter 2022, xvii). These factors are not only apparent in states already consumed by civil wars, but also in many democracies such as the United States which is 'quickly approaching the open insurgency stage, which means we are closer to civil war than any of us would like to believe' (Walter 2022, 159). It is not insignificant that the events of 6 January were understood by many of the insurrectionists themselves to be the 'spark that started a new civil war' (Tatenhove quoted in Pengelly 2022a) as they wore T-shirts emblazoned, in the style of Marvel's *Captain America: Civil War* movie logo, with 'MAGA CIVIL WAR January 6 2021'.

The Third Nuclear Age is marked not only by an increasing risk of conflict between nuclear weapons states but also by an increasing risk of conflict *within* nuclear weapons states themselves. Civil war poses severe dangers to the stability of states that possess nuclear weapons and to the security of such incredibly dangerous weapons. Far-right extremists in America today hold 'an apocalyptic belief that modern society is irredeemable and that its end must be hastened, so that a new order can be brought into being' (Walter 2022, 175). Experts view this as an ideology that will lead to ethnic cleansing and genocide, and what better way to bring about these horrific acts than through the detonation of nuclear weapons? It is perhaps no coincidence that one of the most prominent far-right accelerationist groups in the USA today – the Nationalist Socialist Order which was originally named the Atomwaffen Division (AWD) – was named after the German word for nuclear weapons (Walter 2022, 176–7). The far-right insurgency and domestic terrorism that experts believe could soon break out into a Second American Civil War would no doubt target military sites and installations. Given that the security of American nuclear bases has been lax, alongside the fact that ex-military or still-serving personnel are increasingly involved in far-right domestic terrorist attacks (Jones *et al.* 2021; see also Kennard 2012), it is not beyond the bounds of possibility that far-right extremists will have American nuclear weapons in their sights. Throughout the Second Nuclear Age a large concern was that Islamist extremists such as al-Qaeda would obtain a nuclear weapon; however, now, in the Third Nuclear Age, it is domestic, white, far-right terrorists who pose a serious risk of obtaining a nuclear weapon or attacking a nuclear installation inside the USA.

Conclusion: why we need to democratise nuclear politics

The nuclear democratic deficit has been present since the advent of the First Nuclear Age. Now, in the Third Nuclear Age, this nuclear democratic deficit is worsening as populist authoritarianism is on the rise and democracy is in decline. Such a situation exacerbates the risk of nuclear danger through nuclear weapons states becoming governed by populist, authoritarian leaders who make nuclear threats, value nuclear weapons and the threat of their use as a symbol of strength, and view cooperation and dialogue as something that weakens their own standing. Meanwhile, declining democratic standards remove oversight over governments, reduce their accountability, and lead to citizens having less say in their countries' national security policies. Democratic backsliding shifts states towards autocracy, and it is in this shift away from democracy towards a zone of 'anocracy' (somewhere between democracy and authoritarianism) that states are at most risk of civil war. As the 6 January storming of the US Capitol illustrates, the United States is not immune to organised violence inside of its borders, and as a civil war inside the United States seems like an ugly possibility, the risk of domestic nuclear terrorism inside the USA is an increasing, unprecedented risk.

Nine nuclear weapons states hold the potential to annihilate most of life on earth. In these nuclear weapons states, small numbers of people have influence on their nuclear policies, and these policies do not reflect the will of the people. Research suggests that the majority of people support nuclear abolition (Rosendorf, Smetana, and Vranka 2021, 189). Subsequently, we need to democratise nuclear politics. But how? One of the most promising steps towards the democratisation of nuclear politics and the disarmament of nuclear weapons came in January 2021 when the Treaty on the Prohibition of Nuclear Weapons (TPNW) entered into force after obtaining fifty ratifications. The TPNW provides a legal mechanism for non-nuclear weapons states to reject nuclear weapons from their territories and it signifies a shift in, or a rejection of, the global nuclear order whilst also supporting the victims of nuclear weapons use and testing as well as environmental remediation for areas affected by nuclear weapons. The TPNW is a cause for optimism in the Third Nuclear Age. It offers a glimmer of hope that nuclear abolition has popular support across the globe and is within our reach. In the concluding chapter I will draw together the key themes of this book and provide an overview of events from the end of January 2021 up until the time of going to print in early 2023, and highlight how the problems of the Third Nuclear Age will not be solved simply by the nuclear weapons states saying that 'a nuclear war cannot be won and must never be fought'.

Conclusion: it's not enough to say 'a nuclear war cannot be won and must never be fought': February 2021 to the present

> A nuclear war cannot be won and must never be fought.
> Joint Statement of the Leaders of the Five Nuclear-Weapon States,
> 3 January 2022

> Russia remains one of the most powerful nuclear states ... there should be no doubt for anyone that any potential aggressor will face defeat and ominous consequences should it directly attack our country.
> Vladimir Putin, 24 February 2022

The plane that dropped the first nuclear bomb on Hiroshima sits in the National Air and Space Museum just outside of Washington, DC, across the Potomac River, in the state of Virginia. The museum houses a host of important civilian and military aircraft in two huge aircraft hangars. There's a space shuttle, a Concorde, an F-14 Tomcat (like the one Tom Cruise flies in *Top Gun*), a Lockheed SR-71 Blackbird (the fastest jet-propelled aircraft in the world, apparently), a General Atomics Predator Drone (equipped with two Hellfire missiles) – and the *Enola Gay*, the Boeing B-29 Superfortress that dropped the atomic bomb that annihilated the city of Hiroshima in 1945. Dropping that bomb killed 140,000 people, but the information plaque next to the *Enola Gay* doesn't tell you that. Instead, it states that the B-29 Superfortress 'was the most sophisticated propeller-driven bomber of World War II' and that it 'found its niche on the other side of the globe'. The plaque states that this plane 'dropped the first atomic weapon used in combat on Hiroshima, Japan' but contains no reference to the lives it took or the devastation it caused. As I'm looking at the shining chrome fuselage of the plane, contemplating everything it set in motion, two Americans stand next to me. One of them turns to the other and says 'kaboom!'. The other one laughs as they walk away.

I was in Washington, DC to attend the Arms Control Association's Annual Meeting in June 2022, where various policy makers and nuclear experts were gathered to discuss the challenges facing the future of nuclear arms control and disarmament. At the time, Russia was four months into its brutal invasion of Ukraine, Vladimir Putin had recently made threats to use nuclear weapons, and a few days before I landed in Washington, Joe Biden had outlined 'What America Will and Will Not Do in Ukraine' in the pages of the *New York Times* (2022). Biden wrote about the need to stand 'by Ukraine in its hour of need' for fear that if the world did not oppose Russian aggression there would be 'catastrophic consequences the world over' (2022). Biden recognised that 'many people around the world are concerned about the use of nuclear weapons' and said that 'Russia's occasional rhetoric to rattle the nuclear saber is itself dangerous and extremely irresponsible … Any use of nuclear weapons in this conflict on any scale would be completely unacceptable to us as well as the rest of the world and would entail severe consequences' (2022). As Putin's nuclear threats of 'ominous consequences' provoked Biden's threats of 'severe consequences' – the essence, you see, of deterrence – and as the risk of nuclear war felt closer than it had since the height of the Cold War, the Third Nuclear Age was well underway.

This book has been an attempt to document the dawn of the Third Nuclear Age, where I focused on the eighteen-month period from the collapse of the INF Treaty in August 2020 up until the renewal of New START and the entry into force of the Treaty on the Prohibition of Nuclear Weapons in January 2021, and this conclusion serves to draw out the key themes of the book. In what follows, I reflect on the core issues of the Third Nuclear Age as they arose in the time period covered herein, and I highlight how the Third Nuclear Age lives on by examining how the issues covered have been further entrenched by the events that followed, between the end of January 2021 until the time of going to print in early 2023. Then, in order to end on a note of optimism, I outline what can be done to bring about the death of the Third Nuclear Age and take us beyond to a more peaceful, secure era, where 'nuclear ages' themselves are a thing of the past.

The Third Nuclear Age lives

My trip to Washington, DC turned out to be a microcosm of the issues explored in this book. I saw the humanitarian impact of nuclear weapons silenced at the *Enola Gay* exhibit in a museum sponsored by the three largest arms companies in the world (Lockheed Martin, Boeing, and Raytheon). I saw policy makers from the State Department express support for arms control initiatives but express faith in 'a safe, secure, and effective nuclear deterrent' (Stewart 2022) even as Russia was busy bombing Ukraine and using nuclear deterrence as a cover to do so. I saw other State Department representatives warn of the dangers of China developing more nuclear weapons without saying anything about the modernisation of America's own nuclear arsenal. I saw diplomats from non-nuclear weapons states express anger and disappointment that the nuclear powers had done so little to work towards disarmament in recent years. I saw Americans joke about dropping nuclear weapons. I saw 'RIP George Floyd' graffitied on a wall. I saw security barriers outside the Capitol building. I saw kids in 'Trump Save America' hats on the steps of the Lincoln Memorial. I caught COVID-19 on the flight home.

From the issue of arms control treaties collapsing, through to the global health crisis and narrow conceptualisation of security as military security, via the everyday politics of jokes about nuclear weapons as well as hats declaring support for a populist president, the Third Nuclear Age lives on. It began with the collapse of the INF Treaty in August 2019 as the USA and Russia stepped back from an arms control treaty that had eradicated an entire class of nuclear weapons since before the end of the Cold War. The end of the INF Treaty coincided with a further erosion of the nuclear taboo that had been evident in Donald Trump's threats of 'fire and fury' against North Korea and was then moronically manifest in Trump's bright idea to nuke hurricanes.

These trends towards the collapse of arms control and the hollowing out of the nuclear taboo then came to be further solidified in the immediate testing of hypersonic missiles by Russia and the USA. Whilst the development of these technologies and the deployment of new 'low yield' nuclear weapons are now important issues in the Third Nuclear Age, so too are popular culture and media that inform how many people come to know about nuclear weapons – whether that be critical songs that imagine the end of the world brought about by nuclear war, or through the vitriolic desire of politicians to show how strong they are by nonchalantly saying they would launch nuclear weapons.

As 2020 began, COVID-19 locked down the world and starkly revealed how the prioritisation of military security left states lacking what would ensure the human security of their citizens. The world struggled with the pandemic as health services were inundated and lacked the appropriate number of beds, ventilators, PPE, staff, and other equipment to prevent millions of deaths. The fact that British prime minister Boris Johnson and US president Donald Trump were also hospitalised after falling seriously ill with COVID-19 also revealed the dangers of nuclear sole authority when a state leader is ill, on experimental drugs, or otherwise incapacitated. The Third Nuclear Age is therefore one of misplaced security priorities, where a lack of preparedness for other security threats, such as pandemics and climate change, leaves populations at risk of disaster.

The shocking police murder of George Floyd in May 2020 revealed the extent to which racism, white supremacy, and colonialism shape state institutions. In a summer during which racial injustice was at the forefront of public discourse, the 75th anniversary of the American atomic bombing of Hiroshima and Nagasaki made clear the long lineage of racism in nuclear policy. The racism that led to the exploitation of indigenous communities in mining uranium, developing nuclear weapons and testing them on indigenous land, then dropping them on Japan in 1945, now manifests as a racism towards the likes of Iran and China, and the continued exploitation of indigenous communities in the Third Nuclear Age.

Nuclear weapons spending, and military spending in general, has now reached record heights during the Third Nuclear Age. This spending coincides with the challenges of the climate crisis, a crisis which is in turn exacerbated by militaries and the development and deployment of nuclear weapons. If nuclear weapons were ever to be used, the results would be catastrophic for life on earth and the planet itself. Yet states continue to invest billions in nuclear weapons because of the entrenchment of militarism and the stranglehold that defence companies exert on public spending through a revolving door of industry, lobbying, and military and government personnel.

All of these issues are then exacerbated by a nuclear democratic deficit and the rise of authoritarian populism in nuclear weapons states. Nuclear policy making and important decisions have always been left to a small number of individuals. The sole authority of state leaders to decide when to use nuclear weapons, and to potentially cause billions of deaths, is illustrative of how undemocratic our nuclear world is. In the Third Nuclear Age, the spread of authoritarian populism and the backsliding of democratic standards across the globe bring new challenges as populist leaders make loose nuclear threats whilst also hollowing out international institutions and cooperation – all whilst the risk of civil war within nuclear weapons states increases as those that were previously stable democracies shift towards autocracy.

The time frame covered in this book ended with Joe Biden becoming president and on his first day in office immediately extending New START for another five years with Vladimir Putin. That same month – January 2021 – the Treaty on the Prohibition of Nuclear Weapons entered into force as fifty states ratified it. The renewal of New START seemed to signal that nuclear arms control was back on the agenda of the nuclear weapons states, and the TPNW demonstrated that non-nuclear weapons states were taking nuclear disarmament into their own hands after years of inaction from nuclear weapons states. Although support for the TPNW has gone from strength to strength and provides a note of optimism at the outset of the Third Nuclear Age, the actions of the nuclear weapons states since January 2021 suggest that the challenges of the Third Nuclear Age are here to stay. My brief nuclear diary of these events and developments reveals how this is so:

February 2021

The UK's £31 billion programme to replace the current Trident nuclear submarines with a Dreadnought class of submarines is further delayed, with the first submarines now expected to enter into service in the early 2030s. The first Dreadnought was originally scheduled to be delivered in 2024.

Satellite images reveal that Israel has expanded its Dimona nuclear facility used to make the fissile material for their nuclear weapons.

The USA agrees to return to multilateral talks with Iran with the hope of negotiating the return of the JCPOA.

The British Labour Party announces that its 'support for the UK's nuclear deterrent is non-negotiable'.

March 2021

Researchers and investigative journalists release the Moruroa Files – a set of declassified documents that have been used to re-evaluate the impact of French nuclear testing in the Pacific. The files show that French nuclear testing in the 1960s affected 110,000 people with radiation doses way beyond safe limits and caused cancers amongst those affected in French Polynesia (Philippe and Statius 2021).

The Federation of American Scientists finds that the development of the USA's new $100 billion Ground-Based Strategic Deterrent is driven by industry lobbyists and politicians in states which will benefit economically rather than by a proper assessment of the USA's nuclear deterrent needs (Korda 2021, 64).

The UK lifts its cap on the number of nuclear warheads it can maintain in its stockpile by more than 40 per cent. The limit was previously 180 warheads but can now be up to 260. The UK simultaneously announces that it will 'no longer give public figures for our operational stockpile, deployed warhead or deployed missile numbers' (HM Government 2022, 77).

For the first time in a year, North Korea test fires two ICBMs that land in the sea off the coast of Japan.

April 2021

Israel attacks the Natanz nuclear facility in Iran with a cyber attack that causes a power cut. In response, Iran declares it will now enrich uranium to 60 per cent, which is just below the level needed for nuclear weapons-grade fissile material.

May 2021

The former head of the British Foreign Office tells the House of Lords that the UK's increase of its nuclear warhead stockpile cap 'does not increase deterrence. It is expensive and incompatible with our obligations under the nuclear non-proliferation treaty' (quoted in Wintour 2021).

Henry Kissinger says that deteriorating relations between the United States and China are 'the biggest problem for the world. Because if we can't solve that, then the risk is that all over the world a kind of cold war will develop between China and the United States'. He goes on to state that, 'For the first time in human history, humanity has the capacity to extinguish itself in a finite period of time' (quoted in Ni 2021).

June 2021

The International Atomic Energy Agency announces to the UN that it hasn't been able to access information for monitoring Iran's nuclear development since February when international inspectors were restricted from entering Iranian facilities.

Iran elects a new president – Ebrahim Raisi – who is viewed as Iran's 'own hard-line populist' (Erdbrink 2017).

July 2021

Satellite images reveal that China is building over 100 new missile silos in the desert of the landlocked province of Gansu in the north of the country.

Conservative councillors in the British county of Essex force an artist to remove a small garden of flowers and benches dedicated to the memory of Britain's first atomic test. A plaque on one of the benches describes how British nuclear testing contaminated indigenous land and that the garden 'reflects Britain's historical and ongoing identity as a colonial nuclear state'. One Conservative councillor describes the garden as 'offensive' and 'attacking our country' (Ferguson 2021).

August 2021

The 76th anniversary of the American atomic bombing of Hiroshima and Nagasaki.

The 40th anniversary of the Greenham Common march where women walked from Wales to RAF Greenham Common and chained themselves to the fence around the base, forming the Greenham Common Women's Peace Camp – one of the longest and most prominent protests against nuclear weapons in history.

After twenty years of being present in Afghanistan, NATO forces withdraw from the country and the Taliban soon take over as Kabul falls much sooner than expected. In their desperation to flee, several Afghans cling to the outside of American military planes as they take off from Kabul airport only to fall to their deaths.

The International Atomic Energy Agency announces it is 'deeply troubled' by evidence that North Korea has restarted a reactor to produce plutonium for nuclear weapons.

September 2021

North Korea fires a ballistic missile from a train.

Iran agrees to begin negotiations with the International Atomic Energy Agency to once again monitor their nuclear sites.

The USA, UK, and Australia announce a trilateral security partnership called 'Aukus' in order to deter Chinese expansion in the Indo-Pacific. Under this arrangement the USA and UK will supply Australia with nuclear-powered submarines; it replaces a previous $90 billion agreement Australia had with France to supply submarines. The French describe the deal as 'a stab in the back' (quoted in Chrisafis and Boffey 2021). The Chinese say that it expresses a 'Cold War zero-sum mentality', a 'malicious exploitation of loopholes in the Nuclear non-proliferation treaty and the International Atomic Energy Agency safeguards mechanism', and something that 'has seriously undermined regional peace and stability, intensified the arms race and undermined international non-proliferation efforts' (quoted in Chrisafis and Boffey 2021).

The BBC releases the TV thriller *Vigil* – a story of murder and Russian spies set on a British Trident submarine.

Leonor Tomero – one of President Biden's appointees to write his own administration's Nuclear Posture Review – is forced out of her job after her position is removed in a Pentagon 'reorganization effort' (Seligman, Ward, and McLeary 2021). Tomero was previously critical of the Pentagon's large and expanding nuclear budget, and her departure is largely believed to have been caused by congressional Republicans who pressured Pentagon officials to remove her from the NPR.

October 2021

Pakistan's 'father of the bomb' Abdul Qadeer Khan dies. Pakistan's prime minister Imran Khan tweets that he is 'deeply saddened' by his passing and remembers him for 'his critical contribution in making us a nuclear weapon state'.

China confirms that it successfully tested a hypersonic missile that can carry nuclear warheads earlier in the year. The test surprises many commentators, who didn't think China could launch hypersonic missiles.

North Korea launches a new submarine-based ballistic missile.

December 2021

Negotiations begin with Iran, the P5 nuclear powers, Germany, and the EU in Vienna in an attempt to salvage the 2015 JCPOA.

January 2022

North Korea test launches seven ballistic missiles in a month, including a hypersonic missile and its longest-range missile since 2017.

The Doomsday Clock is set once again at 100 seconds to midnight.

The P5 nuclear weapons states – the USA, Russia, China, the UK, and France – release a rare joint statement that repeats the Reagan–Gorbachev pledge that 'a nuclear war cannot be won and must never be fought' (White House 2022). The statement also notes how these states 'reaffirm the importance of addressing nuclear threats and emphasize the importance of preserving and complying with our bilateral and multilateral non-proliferation, disarmament, and arms control agreements and commitments'. In addition, the P5 point out that they are committed to the NPT Article VI obligation to pursue negotiation to end nuclear arms races and to pursue nuclear disarmament. The joint statement concludes by underlining 'our desire to work with all states to create a security environment more conducive to progress on disarmament with the ultimate goal of a world without nuclear weapons with undiminished security for all' (White House 2022).

February 2022

On the orders of Vladimir Putin, the Russian military invades Ukraine.

Putin announces that he is placing Russia's nuclear forces on high alert.

Putin states that anyone who opposes his invasion of Ukraine 'will face defeat and ominous consequences should it directly attack our country'. In another speech, Putin makes an overt nuclear threat when he warns that anyone who intervenes in his war 'must know that Russia will respond immediately, and the consequences will be such as you have never seen in your entire history'.

March 2022

The UN Secretary General António Guterres says that 'The prospect of nuclear conflict, once unthinkable, is now back within the realm of possibility.'

Former US president Donald Trump suggests that President Biden should threaten Putin with nuclear attack and 'wipe out Russia' (quoted in Pengelly 2022b). Trump also suggests that Biden should 'bomb the shit out of Russia' by disguising American aircraft with Chinese flags. 'And then,' Trump adds, 'we say, China did it, we didn't do it, China did it, and then they start fighting with each other and we sit back and watch' (quoted in Place 2022).

The day after these comments, an average of American favourability polls gives Trump a 42.4 per cent favourability rating (Five Thirty Eight 2022a). This is 0.3 per cent higher than Joe Biden's favourability rating on the same day (Five Thirty Eight 2022b).

Former Russian president Dmitry Medvedev says that Russian nuclear doctrine clearly states that Russia will use nuclear weapons if it is existentially threatened by opponents who use conventional weapons.

April 2022

The CIA director William Burns says that, 'given the potential desperation of President Putin and the Russian leadership, given the setbacks that they've faced so far militarily, none of us can take lightly the threat posed by a potential resort to tactical nuclear weapons or low-yield nuclear weapons' (quoted in D'Agostino and Diaz-Maurin 2022).

Ukrainian President Volodymyr Zelensky warns that Ukraine needs to prepare for Russian nuclear attack. 'We shouldn't wait for the moment when Russia decides to use nuclear weapons… We must prepare for that', Zelensky says, as he suggests his country needs anti-radiation medication and nuclear-proof air raid shelters (quoted in D'Agostino and Diaz-Maurin 2022).

Russia launches a Sarmat ICBM that can carry ten or more nuclear warheads. In a television statement Putin says, 'This truly unique weapon will strengthen the combat potential of our armed forces, reliably ensure Russia's security from external threats and provide food for thought for those who, in the heat of frenzied aggressive rhetoric, try to threaten our country' (quoted in D'Agostino and Diaz-Maurin 2022).

Russia properly notifies the United States of the test as part of their New START obligations and the Pentagon describes the test as 'routine', 'not a surprise', and not a threat to the USA or its allies (DW 2022).

The Biden administration's 2023 budget request indicates that military facilities in the UK will be upgraded in order to once again store American nuclear weapons after they were previously removed from British soil in 2008. Other bases in Belgium, Germany, the Netherlands, and Turkey that already host American nuclear weapons are also due to be upgraded.

May 2022

North Korea test launches an ICBM after Kim Jong-un announces that his country will use nuclear weapons 'at any time' if North Korea is threatened.

The long-awaited sequel to the Cold War action film *Top Gun* is released in cinemas with a barely aged Tom Cruise reviving his role as a fighter pilot who must now destroy a well-protected uranium enrichment plant in *Top Gun: Maverick*.

June 2022

North Korea takes the presidency of the Conference on Disarmament – a multilateral forum supposedly focused on arms control and disarmament that meets at United Nations headquarters in Geneva.

The Stockholm International Peace Research Institute releases its annual report into global nuclear forces and states that the 'post-cold war decline in nuclear arsenals is ending' (SIPRI 2022), because of the fact that 'All of the nuclear-armed states are increasing or upgrading their arsenals and most are sharpening nuclear rhetoric and the role nuclear weapons play in their military strategies' (SIPRI 2022). SIPRI predicts that nuclear arsenals will increase in the coming decade and that 'there are clear indications that the reductions that have characterized global nuclear arsenals since the end of the cold war have ended' (SIPRI 2022).

The first meeting of states party to the Treaty on the Prohibition of Nuclear Weapons meets in Vienna, Austria. The meeting ends with sixty-five states party to the treaty and eighty-six other state signatories condemning 'unequivocally any and all nuclear threats, whether they be explicit or implicit and irrespective of the circumstances' (TPNW 1MSP 2022b, 2) whilst also adopting an action plan for the future. The action plan focuses on universalising the TPNW, implementing timelines for eliminating nuclear weapons, as well as providing victim assistance and environmental remediation for those affected by nuclear weapons (TPNW 1MSP 2022a).

August 2022

At the opening of the NPT Review Conference in New York, the UN Secretary-General António Guterres says that the conference is meeting 'at a time of nuclear danger not seen since the height of the Cold War', and that 'today, humanity is just one misunderstanding, one miscalculation away from nuclear annihilation'.

Russia temporarily suspends the arrangement of the New START treaty provision that allows US inspectors into Russian nuclear weapon facilities.

The tenth NPT Review Conference ends on 26 August with no agreement on the final outcome as Russia objects to the final document that expressed concern about military activity around the Russian-held Zaporizhzhia nuclear plant in Ukraine.

Mar-a-Lago, the summer residence of Donald Trump, is raided by FBI agents who find that Trump is illegally storing classified documents – some that potentially contain top secret nuclear information – on his resort.

Mikhail Gorbachev, former leader of the Soviet Union and one of the architects of the INF Treaty, dies in Moscow. The 1998 Pizza Hut TV advertisement featuring Gorbachev soon goes viral. 'Because of him we have many things … like Pizza Hut!' is certainly one way to be remembered, even though the company that owns Pizza Hut withdrew from Russia in July 2022 following Putin's invasion of Ukraine.

Jacinda Ardern, the prime minister of New Zealand, writes in an op-ed that 'nuclear catastrophe is not an abstract threat but a real world risk' and calls on 'the nuclear weapons states – the US, Russia, China, France and the UK – to step back from the nuclear abyss, and provide that leadership by committing to negotiate a new multilateral nuclear disarmament framework'.

In a Conservative Party leadership hustings, Liz Truss (who would eventually win the contest only to be ousted as prime minister forty-five days later) is asked how she would feel if she launched nuclear weapons knowing that 'it would mean global annihilation'. She replies that she thinks it's an 'important duty' and she is 'ready to do that'. The audience of Conservative Party members breaks out in applause.

September 2022

Liz Truss becomes prime minister.

Vladimir Putin warns that Russia is willing to use 'all the tools at its disposal' to defend itself if needed, stating that 'This is not a bluff. And those who try to blackmail us with nuclear weapons should know that the weathervane can turn and point towards them.'

October 2022

President Biden warns that the Russian use of tactical nuclear weapons in Ukraine would cause 'Armageddon'.

North Korea tests ballistic missiles, fires one over Japan, and says that they simulated launching tactical nuclear weapons against South Korea.

It is sixty years since the Cuban missile crisis.

Russia makes false allegations that Ukraine is preparing to use a dirty bomb – a conventional explosive laced with radioactive material.

The Biden administration cancels the development of a submarine-based nuclear missile programme began under Donald Trump, but the administration continues the development of Trump's 'low-yield' W76-2 warhead.

Australia ends its opposition to the TPNW at the UN.

Liz Truss resigns as prime minister after just forty-five days in office.

November 2022

Joe Biden and Xi Jinping meet in person for the first time and agree that a nuclear war 'should never be fought'.

December 2022

The trailer for Christopher Nolan's new film *Oppenheimer* – a biopic of Robert J. Oppenheimer and the development of nuclear weapons – is released online.

January 2023

On New Year's Day Kim Jong-un announces an 'exponential increase' in North Korea's nuclear arsenal.

In a leaked memo, a four-star US general states that 'my gut tells me that we will fight [China] in 2025' (Minihan quoted in Kube and Gains 2023).

The Doomsday Clock is set at 90 seconds to midnight – the closest it has ever been – because of Russia's nuclear threats after the invasion of Ukraine.

February 2023

Just prior to the one-year anniversary of Russia's invasion of Ukraine, Russia suspends its participation in New START, and Putin states that 'in the current situation, Russia's ministry of defence and Rosatom must ensure that Russia is ready to test its nuclear weapons', before adding, 'of course, we will not do it first. But if the US conducts the tests, we will do it as well' (quoted in Roth and Borger 2023).

Media reports circulate about a recently published study which found that the best place to survive a nuclear winter brought about by nuclear war would be island nations in the Southern Hemisphere such as Australia and New Zealand, though the authors point out that, 'at present, there is no widely understood planning for nuclear winter' and that the collapse of society 'is possible even in locations considered likely to survive' (Boyd and Wilson 2022, 16).

The above nuclear diary draws attention to a chaotic series of events that constitute the continued challenges and threats of the Third Nuclear Age. Russia's brutal invasion of Ukraine and Putin's nuclear threats have brought the realities of an eroding nuclear taboo and potential nuclear confrontation to the fore of global politics. China's testing of hypersonic missiles mirrors Russia's and the USA's own developments, and their building of more missile silos further reinforces the modern challenges of multipolar nuclear powers and new nuclear technologies. The end of strategic dialogue between Russia and the United States, alongside the suspension of parts of New START and no attempts to initiate further nuclear negotiations suggests arms control is waning. As nuclear weapons states continue to modernise or increase their arsenals, nuclear policies across the globe are changing as a result of nuclear weapons becoming ever more entrenched in state security policies. Gendered and racialised ways of thinking influence these decisions, because the bomb, and a willingness to use it, is seen as a necessity for masculine virile leaders threatened by distant foreign others. Military and nuclear weapon budgets reach record highs. Popular culture and the media once again tackle the topic of nuclear weapons on prime-time television as people feel a sense of heightened atomic anxiety. Populist authoritarian leaders continue to be a feature of nuclear weapon states – Liz Truss for Leader! Trump 2024! – all of this occurring at a time when the crises of COVID-19 and climate change lay bare the risks to the planet of conceptualising security so narrowly in military terms. What then, can be done? How can the risks and challenges of the Third Nuclear Age be addressed? How can we bring about the end of the Third Nuclear Age?

The death of the Third Nuclear Age

The challenges of the Third Nuclear Age have few easy solutions, yet there are things that state leaders, civil society organisations, activists, scholars, students, and ordinary people can do to avert unparalleled catastrophe. First, the state leaders of nuclear weapons states need to not only make a renewed commitment to nuclear arms control and nuclear disarmament, but also take substantive steps towards them. It is not enough to say that 'a nuclear war cannot be won and must never be fought' when you are modernising and expanding your nuclear arsenals as if you are preparing to fight and win a nuclear war. Signatories of the NPT are obliged to work towards nuclear disarmament, and it is imperative that they do so. Stalling on this obligation is not only infuriating for everyone else but also dangerous for the entire planet. If disarmament requires a more stable and better security environment, then work to make that happen – global security is what states make of it. If nuclear abolition can't be achieved overnight, then arms control measures and agreements can be developed to work towards this goal and to reduce nuclear risks in the immediate future. Bring back the INF Treaty, end Russia's invasion of Ukraine, implement multilateral dialogues over hypersonic and dual-use technologies, don't try and match the nuclear capabilities of adversaries in a like-for-like way. Research has shown that with the technology available today it would take less than ten years to dismantle and destroy all nuclear weapons on the planet (Kütt and Mian 2019, 2). We know how to dismantle and destroy nuclear weapons, and we need leaders who have the courage to do so.

Second, the nuclear taboo needs to be strengthened. State leaders can no longer claim to be responsible nuclear powers when nuclear threats are made so often and accompanied by the continued development and deployment of nuclear weapons. Strengthening norms around the nuclear taboo and non-use of nuclear weapons is something that needs leadership from those in the halls of power but it also requires a demand from the people below. Perhaps the only silver lining of the renewed spectre of nuclear war in modern global politics is that it will spur further demand for nuclear non-use and abolition.

Third, we need to rethink what matters in nuclear politics. Russia's invasion of Ukraine has revealed once again how nuclear deterrence can shield a horrific conventional war of territorial expansion by preventing others from intervening. Nuclear deterrence may have worked in Ukraine as there has been no nuclear war. But at what cost? Thousands of dead Ukrainian civilians. Tens of thousands of dead Ukrainian and Russian military personnel. Millions of Ukrainians displaced from their homes. The crippling of the Ukrainian and Russian economies. A global energy, food, and cost-of-living crisis. All this deterrence yet the bodies keep piling up. Are the concepts and practices at the heart of contemporary nuclear politics effective in ensuring security? Or do they make us less safe? How can we resist the dominant orthodoxy of theory and practice when it comes to nuclear weapons? Here, we need to reconsider what might constitute knowledge in nuclear politics, the sites we see as important, and what counts as effective resistance to the status quo.

Intimately tied to this point is the fourth need: to rethink security to keep the planet and the people on it safe. When state leaders prioritise maintaining nuclear arsenals and increasing military spending whilst a pandemic runs rampant and kills millions, and as we also stare into the eye of an oncoming storm of catastrophic climate change, it is clear that our security priorities are misplaced. An 'exterminism of multitudes' (Thompson 1982a, 20) faces us if we carry on this way. Pandemic preparedness, adequate global public health, and preventing climate change are just some of the real security issues that could be funded if we were to step out of an outdated national, military security mindset of the Cold War caveman – me man, me strong, me have nuclear bomb. The challenges that face the world today are too serious, too global, and too imminent for the follies of the nuclear national security state to continue. Nuclear weapons already cause global health and climate problems, and their potential use threatens global health and the climate on a scale previously unimaginable. Coronavirus can't stop America's nukes, but America's nukes can't stop coronavirus. Neither can Russia's, nor China's, nor anyone else's. No one's nukes can stop the next pandemic. And just as you can't nuke a hurricane to stop it reaching land, you can't nuke your way out of climate change.

Our endeavour to rethink security needs to be intersectional. This is the fifth need, if we are to end the Third Nuclear Age and replace it with something better. Critical nuclear race theory can help to draw attention to the imbalanced impact of nuclear weapons policy on indigenous people, people of colour, and those in the Global South who continue to be affected by the development, testing, use, and deployment of nuclear weapons. Nuclear policies are racialised, shaped by colonial legacies and an everyday racism where foreign others are viewed as dehumanised threats.

Sixth, the nuclear treadmill of destruction needs to be stopped. Higher and higher military spending harms the planet as militaries are exempt from climate change accords, and nuclear weapons possession harms the environment. We are trapped in a vicious circle of militaries contributing to climate change and climate change then making conflict more likely. We need to break this by reducing military and nuclear weapons spending, contesting militarism as a social and political force by, for example, ending the revolving door between arms companies, lobbyists, the military, and government, and rejecting the notion that nuclear weapons are necessary for international security.

Finally, we need to democratise nuclear politics. The fate of the earth is in the hands of a few elite figures unfit to govern. Donald Trump: impeached twice for abusing power and inciting insurrection. Vladimir Putin: invaded Ukraine. Xi Jinping: oppressed human rights in China to the worst level since the Tiananmen Square massacre. Kim Jong-un: ordered the execution of his own uncle and half-brother. Narendra Modi: causing democracy to backslide by attacking opposition to his rule whilst also overseeing border skirmishes with Pakistan and China. Benjamin Netanyahu: indicted for corruption. Imran Khan: charged under anti-terror laws for attacking the judiciary in his own country. Boris Johnson: forced from office after lying to members of his own cabinet. Liz Truss: forced out of office for being so incompetent that her policies tanked the British economy. All recently had, or still have, control of vast nuclear arsenals. Whilst Joe Biden and Emmanuel Macron may look like saints in comparison to their brethren leaders, both nearly lost elections to populist authoritarian figures. The world's nuclear weapons are not in safe, responsible hands, yet they threaten the safety of all of us – the majority of whom oppose their use and existence. Ending sole authority, entrenching democracy, and ensuring that the voices of those who oppose nuclear weapons are heard in the halls of power is essential for ending the Third Nuclear Age.

The road to a more peaceful world beyond the Third Nuclear Age may seem fanciful, but there is cause to be optimistic and hopeful for the Third Nuclear Age's demise. The ascendancy of the humanitarian initiative to a formalised Treaty on the Prohibition of Nuclear Weapons shows that activists, civil society organisations, and non-nuclear weapons states can come together and change the discourse around nuclear weapons whilst also having an impact on international law (Acheson 2021; Hanson 2022). Even if no nuclear state will join the TPNW anytime soon, it sends a signal that the rest of the world opposes the nuclear status quo, and it is the kind of political pressure needed to bring about change. Putin's invasion of Ukraine and his nuclear threats have brought about an erosion of the nuclear taboo, but they have also eroded the collective nuclear amnesia that has fallen upon the world since the end of the Cold War. As the threat of nuclear war, accident, and unparalleled catastrophe seem closer than they have in decades, popular and political attention to preventing them is once again mounting. Whether this will build up enough political will to implement serious global nuclear arms control and disarmament measures (like we saw in the 1980s) remains to be seen, but it is a possibility, and one that we should work towards to make more likely.

The opportunity to imagine and make a better future for our planet lies in our hands, and it is urgent now that the ugly face and harmful effects of the Third Nuclear Age are so apparent. We need critical nuclear studies to make sense of, and work to change, our current moment. But we also need state leaders to lead the world to a better place. For that, we need to demand nuclear arms control. Demand disarmament. Demand that new technologies are limited. Demand that states invest in public health and stopping climate change rather than militaries. Demand an end to the racial injustice of nuclear weapons. Demand an end to the insanity of military spending. Demand an end to the revolving door of government, the military, and defence contractors. Demand that Russia leaves Ukraine. Demand diplomacy. Demand an approach to security that keeps you and your environment safe. Demand democracy.

The status quo of our global nuclear order will lead to nothing but exterminism, yet this status quo is not natural, nor is it impossible to change. We can avoid the fire and fury. We can avoid the consequences like never before seen in history. This book has chronicled the development of the Third Nuclear Age, but these developments are not set in stone. The world is one of our making. We can, and we must, make sure this era ends not with a bang, but with a change to our modes of thinking, and an avoidance of unparalleled catastrophe.

References

Abbasi, Kamran. 2020. Covid-19: politicisation, 'corruption', and suppression of science. *BMJ* m4425. doi: 10.1136/bmj.m4425

Abbasi, Kamran. 2021. Covid-19: Social murder, they wrote – elected, unaccountable, and unrepentant. *BMJ* 372:n314. doi: 10.1136/bmj.n314

Abraham, Itty. 2006. The ambivalence of nuclear histories. *Osiris* 21 (1): 49–65.

Acheson, Ray. 2019. The nuclear ban and the patriarchy: a feminist analysis of opposition to prohibiting nuclear weapons. *Critical Studies on Security* 7 (1): 78–82.

Acheson, Ray. 2021. *Banning the Bomb, Smashing the Patriarchy*. Lanham, MD: Rowman & Littlefield.

Acheson, Ray. 2022. Abolition, not arms control: against reinforcing nuclear weapons through 'reform'. *Zeitschrift für Friedens-und Konfliktforschung* 1–9. doi: 10.1007/s42597-022-00080-w

Acton, James M. 2018. Escalation through entanglement: how the vulnerability of command-and-control systems raises the risks of an inadvertent nuclear war. *International Security* 43 (1): 56–99. doi: 10.1162/isec_a_00320

Adger, W. Neil, Juan M. Pulhin, Jon Barnett, Geoffrey D. Dabelko, Grete K. Hovelsrud, Marc Levy, Ursula Oswald Spring, and Coleen H. Vogel. 2014. Human security. In *Climate Change 2014: Impacts, Adaptation, and Vulnerability. Part A: Global and Sectoral Aspects. Contribution of Working Group II to the Fifth Assessment Report of the Intergovernmental Panel on Climate Change*, edited by Christopher B. Field *et al.*, pp. 755–91. Cambridge: Cambridge University Press.

Åhäll, Linda. 2016. The dance of militarisation: a feminist security studies take on 'the political'. *Critical Studies on Security* 4 (2): 154–68.

Ahmed, Sara. 2004. Affective economies. *Social Text* 22 (2): 117–39.

Alexievich, Svetlana. 2005. *Voices from Chernobyl*, trans. Keith Gessen. London: Dalkey Archive Press.

Alexis-Martin, Becky. 2019a. *Disarming Doomsday*. London: Pluto Press.

Alexis-Martin, Becky. 2019b. The nuclear imperialism-necropolitics nexus: contextualizing Chinese-Uyghur oppression in our nuclear age. *Eurasian Geography and Economics* 60 (2): 152–76.

Ali, Idrees. 2019. U.S. Defense Secretary says he favors placing missiles in Asia. *Reuters*. www.reuters.com/article/us-usa-asia-inf-idUSKCN1UT098 (accessed 14 February 2023).

Assistant Secretary of Defense. 1978. History of the custody and deployment of nuclear weapons, July 1945 through September 1977. https://nsarchive2.gwu.edu/news/19991020/history-of-custody.pdf (accessed 14 February 2023).

Atherton, Kelsey D. 2020. Trump inherited the drone war but ditched accountability. *Foreign Policy*, 22 May. https://foreignpolicy.com/2020/05/22/obama-drones-trump-killings-count/ (accessed 14 February 2023).

Bacevich, Andrew J. 2013. *The New American Militarism: How Americans Are Seduced by War*. Oxford: Oxford University Press.

BAE Systems. 2021. *2020 Full-Year Results*. 25 February. www.baesystems.com/en-uk/article/2020-full-year-results (accessed 14 February 2023).

Baker, John Carl. 2017. Notes on late exterminism, the Trump stage of civilization. Blog, 16 June. https://www.versobooks.com/blogs/3277-notes-on-late-exterminism-the-trump-stage-of-civilization (accessed 14 February 2023).

Baron, Jonathon, Rebecca Davis Gibbons, and Stephen Herzog. 2020. Japanese public opinion, political persuasion, and the Treaty on the Prohibition of Nuclear Weapons. *Journal for Peace and Nuclear Disarmament* 3 (2): 299–309.

BBC News. 2014. US nuclear force cheating scandal widens. *BBC News*, 30 January. www.bbc.co.uk/news/world-us-canada-25967081 (accessed 14 February 2023).

BBC News. 2019. INF nuclear treaty: US pulls out of Cold War-era pact with Russia. *BBC News*, 2 August. www.bbc.co.uk/news/world-us-canada-49198565 (accessed 14 February 2023).

Belcher, Emma. 2020. Transforming our nuclear future with ridiculous ideas. *Bulletin of the Atomic Scientists* 76 (6): 325–30. doi: 10.1080/00963402.2020.1846420

Bell, Duncan. 2022. *Dreamworlds of Race: Empire and the Utopian Destiny of Anglo-America*. Princeton, NJ: Princeton University Press.

Bendix, Aria. 2019. A real-life character in HBO's 'Chernobyl' says reporters have accused her of killing her baby. Here's her side of the story. *Insider*, 23 December. https://www.businessinsider.com/chernobyl-hbo-character-lyudmilla-ignatenko-bbc-interview-baby-2019-12 (accessed 14 February 2023).

Benedict, Kennette. 2012. Democracy and the bomb. *Bulletin of the Atomic Scientists*, 15 November. https://thebulletin.org/2012/11/democracy-and-the-bomb/ (accessed 14 February 2023).

Bernstein, Barton J. 1995. The atomic bombings reconsidered. *Foreign Affairs* 74 (1): 135–152. doi: 10.2307/20047025.

Biden, Joe. 2021. Inaugural Address by President Joseph R. Biden, Jr, 20 January. www.whitehouse.gov/briefing-room/speeches-remarks/2021/01/20/inaugural-address-by-president-joseph-r-biden-jr/ (accessed 15 February 2023).

Biden, Joe. 2022. What America will and will not do in Ukraine. *New York Times*, 31 May. www.nytimes.com/2022/05/31/opinion/biden-ukraine-strategy.html (accessed 15 February 2023).

Billingslea, Marshall. 2020. Transcript: Special Presidential Envoy Marshall Billingslea on the future of nuclear arms control. Hudson Institute, 22 May. www.hudson.org/research/16062-transcript-special-presidential-envoy-marshall-billingslea-on-the-future-of-nuclear-arms-control (accessed 15 February 2023).

Biswas, Shampa. 2001. 'Nuclear apartheid' as political position: race as a postcolonial resource? *Alternatives* 26 (4): 485–522.

Biswas, Shampa. 2014. *Nuclear Desire: Power and the Postcolonial Nuclear Order*. Minneapolis: University of Minnesota Press.

Blakeslee, George H. 1910. Introduction. *Journal of Race Development* 1 (1): 1–4.

Bleiker, Roland. 2001. The aesthetic turn in international political theory. *Millennium* 30 (3): 509–33.

Blitzer, Wolf. 2003. Search for the 'smoking gun'. *CNN*, 10 January. https://edition.cnn.com/2003/US/01/10/wbr.smoking.gun/ (accessed 15 February 2023).

Blume, Lesley. 2020. *Fallout: The Hiroshima Cover-up and the Reporter Who Revealed It to the World*. London: Scribe.

Boese, Vanessa A., Nazifa Alizada, Martin Lundstedt, Kelly Morrison, Natalia Natsika, Yuko Sato, Hugo Tai, and Staffan I. Lindberg. 2022. *Democracy Report 2022: Autocratization Changing Nature?* V-Dem Institute. https://v-dem.net/media/publications/dr_2022.pdf (accessed 15 February 2023).

Booth, Ken. 1999. Nuclearism, human rights and constructions of security (part 1). *International Journal of Human Rights* 3 (2): 124.

Booth, Ken. 2005. *Critical Security Studies and World Politics*. Boulder, CO: Lynne Rienner.

Borger, Julian. 2021. Mike Pence's 'nuclear football' was potentially at risk during Capitol riot. *The Guardian*, 12 February. www.theguardian.com/us-news/2021/feb/12/mike-pence-nuclear-football-capitol-riot (accessed 15 February 2023).

Boyd, Matt, and Nick Wilson. 2022. Island refuges for surviving nuclear winter and other abruptsunlight-reducing catastrophes. *Risk Analysis*. Early View: 1–19. https://doi.org/10.1111/risa.14072 (accessed 9 March 2023)

Bracken, Paul. 2003. The structure of the Second Nuclear Age. *Orbis* 47 (3): 399–413.

Braithwaite, Rodric. 2019. *Armageddon and Paranoia: The Nuclear Confrontation since 1945*. London: Profile Books.

Braut-Hegghammer, Målfrid. 2019. Proliferating bias? American political science, nuclear weapons, and global security. *Journal of Global Security Studies* 4 (3): 384–92. doi: 10.1093/jogss/ogz025

Braut-Hegghammer, Målfrid. 2020. 2020 is the year to worry about nuclear weapon. *Washington Post*, 6 January. www.washingtonpost.com/politics/2020/01/06/is-year-worry-about-nuclear-weapons/ (accessed 15 February 2023).

Brians, Paul. 1987. *Nuclear Holocausts: Atomic War in Fiction, 1895–1984*. Kent, OH: Kent State University Press.

Brigg, Morgan, and Roland Bleiker. 2010. Autoethnographic international relations: exploring the self as a source of knowledge. *Review of International Studies* 36 (3): 779–98.

Bright, Sam, Hardeep Matharu, Katie Tarrant, Max Colbert, Daisy Bata, and Iain Overton. 2021. Mapping the pandemic: £1 billion in contracts awarded to conservative donors. *Byline Times*, 29 March. https://bylinetimes.com/2021/03/29/mapping-the-pandemic-1-billion-in-contracts-awarded-to-conservative-donors/ (accessed 15 February 2023).

Brodie, Bernard, ed. 1946. *The Absolute Weapon: Atomic Power and World Order*. New York: Harcourt, Brace.

Broinowski, Adam. 2015. Nuclear imperialism. In *The Palgrave Encyclopedia of Imperialism and Anti-Imperialism*, ed. Z. Cope and I. Ness, pp. 1–10. London: Palgrave Macmillan.

Brown, Seyom. 2018. The Trump administration's Nuclear Posture Review (NPR) in historical perspective. *Journal for Peace and Nuclear Disarmament* 1 (2): 268–80.

Brubaker, Rogers. 2017. Why populism? *Theory and society* 46 (5): 357–85.

Bull, Hedley. 1965. *The Control of the Arms Race*, 2nd edn. Praeger for the Institute for Strategic Studies.

Bulletin of the Atomic Scientists. 2020. Press Release – it is now 100 seconds to midnight. Bulletin of the Atomic Scientists, 23 January. https://thebulletin.org/2020/01/press-release-it-is-now-100-seconds-to-midnight/ (accessed 15 February 2023).

Bulletin of the Atomic Scientists. 2021. At doom's doorstep: It is 100 seconds to midnight. https://thebulletin.org/wp-content/uploads/2022/01/2022-doomsday-clock-statement.pdf (accessed 15 February 2023).

Burke, Anthony. 2009. Nuclear reason: at the limits of strategy. *International Relations* 23 (4): 506–59.

Burke, Anthony. 2016. Nuclear politics: beyond positivism. *Critical Studies on Security* 4 (1): 1–5.

Burke, Anthony, Stefanie Fishel, Audra Mitchell, Simon Dalby, and Daniel J. Levine. 2016. Planet politics: a manifesto from the end of IR. *Millennium* 44 (3): 499–523.

Bush, G. W. 2002. President Bush outlines Iraqi threat. The White House, 7 October. https://georgewbush-whitehouse.archives.gov/news/releases/2002/10/20021007-8.html (accessed 15 February 2023).

Byline Times and the Citizens. 2021. £121.7 million increase in profits for COVID contract winners with Conservative links. *Byline Times*, 12 October. https://bylinetimes.com/2021/10/12/121-7-million-increase-in-profits-for-covid-contract-winners-with-tory-links/ (accessed 15 February 2023).

Callamard, Agnès. 2020. *Use of Armed Drones for Targeted Killings: Report of the Special Rapporteur on Extrajudicial, Summary or Arbitrary Executions*. United Nations.

Calvert, Jonathan, and George Arbuthnott. 2021. *Failures of State: The Inside Story of Britain's Battle with Coronavirus*. London: Mudlark.

Calvert, Jonathan, George Abuthnott, and Joanthan Leake, *Sunday Times*, 19 April 2020.

Campbell, Andrew. 2018. The QAnon conspiracy has stumbled into real life, and it's not going to end well. *Huffington Post*, 24 July. www.huffingtonpost.com/entry/qanon-conspiracy-real-life_us_5b54bbafe4b0b15aba8fe484 (accessed 15 February 2023).

Campbell, David. 1992. *Writing Security: United States Foreign Policy and the Politics of Identity*. Minneapolis: University of Minnesota Press.

Carrington, Damian. 2021. Climate crisis: 2020 was joint hottest year ever recorded. *The Guardian* 8 January. www.theguardian.com/environment/2021/jan/08/climate-crisis-experts-2020-joint-hottest-year-ever-recorded (accessed 15 February 2023).

Center for Defense Information. 1981. U.S. nuclear weapons accidents: danger in our midst. *The Defense Monitor* 10 (5). https://fas.org/nuke/norris/nuc_81010001a_n22.pdf (accessed 15 February 2023).

Chaloupka, William. 1992. *Knowing Nukes: The Politics and Culture of the Atom*. Minneapolis: University of Minnesota Press.
Channel 4 News. 2020. Revealed: PPE stockpile was out-of-date when coronavirus hit UK. *Channel 4 News*, 7 May. www.channel4.com/news/revealed-ppe-stockpile-was-out-of-date-when-coronavirus-hit-uk (accessed 15 February 2023).
Chatterje-Doody, Precious N., and Rhys Crilley. 2019. Populism and contemporary global media: populist communication logics and the co-construction of transnational identities. In *Populism and World Politics*, ed. Frank A. Stengel, David B. MacDonald, and Dirk Nabers, pp. 73–99. Springer.
Chernobrov, Dmitry. 2022. Strategic humour: public diplomacy and comic framing of foreign policy issues. *British Journal of Politics and International Relations* 24 (2): 277–96.
Choi, Shine, and Catherine Eschle. 2022. Rethinking global nuclear politics, rethinking feminism. *International Affairs* 98 (4): 1129–47.
Chrisafis, Angelique, and Daniel Boffey. 2021. 'Stab in the back': French fury as Australia scraps submarine deal. *The Guardian*, 16 September. www.theguardian.com/world/2021/sep/16/stab-in-the-back-french-fury-australia-scraps-submarine-deal (accessed 15 February 2023).
Churchill, Winston. 1953. Statement to House of Commons. Hansard.
Churchill, Winston. 1955. Statement to House of Commons. Hansard.
Cirincione, Joseph. 2018. A no-cost, no-brainer of a nuclear deal. *Defense One*, 10 July. www.defenseone.com/ideas/2018/07/no-cost-no-brainer-nuclear-deal/149603/ (accessed 15 February 2023).
Cirincione, Joseph. 2020. Urgent action is needed to put the lid on a new and costly global arms race. American Foreign Service Association. www.afsa.org/restoring-nuclear-diplomacy (accessed 15 February 2023).
Clark, Brett, and Andrew K. Jorgenson. 2012. The treadmill of destruction and the environmental impacts of militaries 1. *Sociology Compass* 6 (7): 557–69.
Clements, Ben, and Catarina P. Thomson. 2021. The 'ultimate insurance' or an 'irrelevance' for national security needs? Partisanship, foreign policy attitudes, and the gender gap in British public opinion towards nuclear weapons. *European Journal of International Security*, 8 July: 1–22. doi: 10.1017/eis.2021.17. https://dx.doi.org/10.1017/eis.2021.17
Clinton, Bill. 1996. Address by President Bill Clinton to the UN General Assembly, 24 September. https://2009-2017.state.gov/p/io/potusunga/207410.htm (accessed 15 February 2023).
CNN. 2016. Full rush transcript: Donald Trump, CNN Milwaukee Republican Presidential Town Hall, 29 March. *CNN*. https://cnnpressroom.blogs.cnn.com/2016/03/29/full-rush-transcript-donald-trump-cnn-milwaukee-republican-presidential-town-hall/ (accessed 15 February 2023).
Cohn, Carol. 1987. Sex and death in the rational world of defense intellectuals. *Signs: Journal of Women in Culture and Society* 12 (4): 687–718.
Cohn, Carol. 2018. The perils of mixing masculinity and missiles. *New York Times*, 5 January. www.nytimes.com/2018/01/05/opinion/security-masculinity-nuclear-weapons.html (accessed 15 February 2023).

Conflict and Environment Observatory. 2021. The military's contribution to climate change. Conflict and Environment Observatory, 16 June. https://ceobs.org/the-militarys-contribution-to-climate-change/ (accessed 15 February 2023).

Considine, Laura. 2017. The 'standardization of catastrophe': nuclear disarmament, the Humanitarian Initiative and the politics of the unthinkable. *European Journal of International Relations* 23 (3): 681–702.

Cooke, Steve, and Andrew Futter. 2018. Democracy versus deterrence: nuclear weapons and political integrity. *Politics* 38 (4): 500–13.

Cooper, Ken. 1995. The whiteness of the bomb. *Postmodern Apocalypse: Theory and Cultural Practice at the End*, ed. Richard Dellamora, pp. 79–106. Philadelphia: University of Pennsylvania Press.

Cooper, Neil, and David Mutimer. 2011. Arms control for the 21st century: controlling the means of violence. *Contemporary Security Policy* 32 (1): 3–19.

Cordle, Daniel. 2017. *Late Cold War Literature and Culture: The Nuclear 1980s*. London: Springer.

Coupe, Joshua, Samantha Stevenson, Nicole S. Lovenduski, Tyler Rohr, Cheryl S. Harrison, Alan Robock, Holly Olivarez, Charles G. Bardeen, and Owen B. Toon. 2021. Nuclear Niño response observed in simulations of nuclear war scenarios. *Communications Earth & Environment* 2 (1): 1–11.

Cox, Robert W. 1981. Social forces, states and world orders: beyond international relations theory. *Millennium* 10 (2): 126–55.

Craig, Campbell, and S. M. Amadae. 2021. The myth of the nuclear revolution: power politics in the atomic age. *Journal of Strategic Studies* 1: 1–9.

Craig, Campbell, and Jan Ruzicka. 2013. The nonproliferation complex."*Ethics & International Affairs* 27 (3): 329–48.

Crawford, Neta C. 2020. Afghanistan's rising civilian death toll due to airstrikes, 2017–2020. Costs of War Project at the Watson Institute for International and Public Affairs. https://watson.brown.edu/costsofwar/files/cow/imce/papers/2020/Rising%20Civilian%20Death%20Toll%20in%20Afghanistan_Costs%20of%20War_Dec%207%202020.pdf (accessed 15 February 2023).

Crenshaw, Kimberlé. 1990. Mapping the margins: intersectionality, identity politics, and violence against women of color. *Stanford Law Review* 43: 1241.

Crenshaw, Kimberlé. 1989. Demarginalizing the intersection of race and sex: a black feminist critique of antidiscrimination doctrine, feminist theory and antiracist politics. *University of Chicago Legal Forum*: 139.

Crilley, Rhys. 2018. International relations in the age of 'post-truth' politics. *International Affairs* 94 (2): 417–25.

Crilley, Rhys. 2021. Where we at? New directions for research on popular culture and world politics. *International Studies Review* 23 (1): 164–80. doi: 10.1093/isr/viaa027

Crilley, Rhys, and Precious Chatterje-Doody. 2019. Security studies in the age of 'post-truth' politics: in defence of poststructuralism. *Critical Studies on Security* 7 (2): 166–70.

Crilley, Rhys, and Precious N. Chatterje-Doody. 2021. From Russia with lols: humour, RT, and the legitimation of Russian foreign policy. *Global Society* 35 (2): 269–88.

Crilley, Rhys, and Louise Pears. 2021. 'No, we don't know where Tupac is': critical intelligence studies and the CIA on social media. *Intelligence and National Security* 36 (4): 599–614.

Croft, Stuart. 1996. *Strategies of Arms Control: A History and Typology*. Manchester: Manchester University Press.

Crutzen, Paul, and John Birks. 1982. The atmosphere after a nuclear war: twilight at noon. *Ambio* 11 (2/3): 114–25.

D'Agostino, Susan, and François Diaz-Maurin. 2022. Will Putin go nuclear? An updated timeline of expert comments. *Bulletin of the Atomic Scientists*, 6 June.

Dahl, Robert. 1985. *Controlling Nuclear Weapons: Democracy Versus Guardianship*. Syracuse, NY: Syracuse University Press.

Daniel, J. Furman, and Paul Musgrave. 2017. Synthetic experiences: how popular culture matters for images of International Relations. *International Studies Quarterly* 61 (3): 503–16. doi: 10.1093/isq/sqx053

Davies, Harry, David Pegg, and Felicity Lawrence. 2020. Revealed: value of UK pandemic stockpile fell by 40% in six years. *The Guardian*, 12 April. www.theguardian.com/world/2020/apr/12/revealed-value-of-uk-pandemic-stockpile-fell-by-40-in-six-years (accessed 15 February 2023).

Davis Gibbons, Rebecca, and Keir Lieber. 2019. How durable is the nuclear weapons taboo? *Journal of Strategic Studies* 42 (1): 29–54.

Debs, Alexandre, and Nuno P. Monteiro. 2017. *Nuclear Politics*, vol. 142. Cambridge: Cambridge University Press.

Defense News. 2021. Top 100 for 2021. *Defense News*.

Delbert, Caroline. 2020. Elon Musk needs 10,000+ missiles to nuke Mars. 'no problem,' he says. *Popular Mechanics*, 19 May. www.popularmechanics.com/science/a32588385/elon-musk-terraform-mars-nuclear-missiles/ (accessed 15 February 2023).

Department of Defense. 2010. Nuclear Posture Review. https://dod.defense.gov/Portals/1/features/defenseReviews/NPR/2010_Nuclear_Posture_Review_Report.pdf (accessed 15 February 2023).

Department of Defense. 2018. Nuclear Posture Review. https://media.defense.gov/2018/Feb/02/2001872886/-1/-1/1/2018-NUCLEAR-POSTURE-REVIEW-FINAL-REPORT.PDF (accessed 15 February 2023).

Department of Defense. 2019. DOD conducts ground launch cruise missile test. Department of Defense, 19 August. https://www.defense.gov/News/Releases/Release/Article/1937624/dod-conducts-ground-launch-cruise-missile-test/ (accessed 15 February 2023).

Department of Defense. 2020. Statement by the Department of Defense. 2 January. www.defense.gov/News/Releases/release/article/2049534/statement-by-the-department-of-defense/ (accessed 15 February 2023).

Der Derian, James. 2009. *Virtuous War: Mapping the Military-Industrial-Media-Entertainment-Network*. London: Routledge.

Derrida, Jacques. 1984. No apocalypse, not now (full speed ahead, seven missiles, seven missives). *diacritics* 14 (2): 20–31.

Deudney, Daniel. 1995. Nuclear weapons and the waning of the real-state. *Daedalus* 124 (2): 209–31.

Deudney, Daniel H. 2010. Bounding power. In Daniel Deudney, *Bounding Power*. Princeton, NJ: Princeton University Press.

Deudney, Daniel. 2020. *Dark Skies: Space Expansionism, Planetary Geopolitics, and the Ends of Humanity*. New York: Oxford University Press.

Doty, Roxanne Lynn. 1996. *Imperial Encounters: The Politics of Representation in North–South Relations*. Vol. 5. Minneapolis: University of Minnesota Press.

Dowd, Maureen. 2016. Donald the dove, Hillary the hawk. *New York Times*, 30 April.

Driver, Christopher. 1964. *The Disarmers: A Study in Protest*. London: Hodder & Stoughton.

DW. 2022. Russian ICBM test 'not deemed to be a threat' – Pentagon. DW.com, 21 April. www.dw.com/en/russian-icbm-test-not-deemed-to-be-a-threat-pentagon/a-61529853 (accessed 15 February 2023).

Economist Intelligence Unit. 2021. *Democracy Index 2021: The China Challenge*. Economist Intelligence Unit. www.eiu.com/n/campaigns/democracy-index-2021/ (accessed 15 February 2023).

Egel, Naomi, and R. Lincoln Hines. 2021. Chinese views on nuclear weapons: evidence from an online survey. *Research & Politics* 8 (3): 205316802110328. doi: 10.1177/20531680211032840

Egeland, Kjølv. 2020a. Spreading the burden: how NATO became a 'nuclear' alliance. *Diplomacy & Statecraft* 31 (1): 143–67.

Egeland, Kjølv. 2020b. Who stole disarmament? History and nostalgia in nuclear abolition discourse. *International Affairs* 96 (5): 1387–403.

Egeland, Kjølv. 2021. The ideology of nuclear order. *New Political Science* 43: 208–30. doi: 10.1080/07393148.2021.1886772

Egeland, Kjølv, and Benoît Pelopidas. 2023. No such thing as a free donation? Research funding and conflicts of interest in nuclear weapons policy analysis. *International Relations*, OnlineFirst.

Einstein, Albert, and Leo Szilard. 1939. Letter to President Roosevelt. Atomic Archive. www.atomicarchive.com/resources/documents/beginnings/einstein.html (accessed 15 February 2023).

Eisenhower, Dwight D. 1961. Farewell address. National Archives. https://www.archives.gov/milestone-documents/president-dwight-d-eisenhowers-farewell-address (accessed 15 February 2023).

Engel, E. L. 2019. Letter to Robert C. O'Brien. www.ft.com/content/f49dffe2-fb3f-11e9-a354-36acbbb0d9b6 (accessed 9 March 2023).

Enloe, Cynthia. 2000. *Maneuvers*. Berkeley: University of California Press.

Enloe, Cynthia. 2014. *Bananas, Beaches and Bases: Making Feminist Sense of International Politics*. Berkeley: University of California Press.

Erdbrink, Thomas. 2017. Iran has its own hard-line populist, and he's on the rise. *New York Times*, 18 May. www.nytimes.com/2017/05/18/world/middleeast/iran-ebrahim-raisi-president-election.html (accessed 15 February 2023).

Eschle, Catherine. 2018. Nuclear (in) security in the everyday: peace campers as everyday security practitioners. *Security Dialogue* 49 (4): 289–305.

Ewbank, Leo, James Thompson, Helen McKenna, Siva Anandaciva, and Deborah Ward. 2021. NHS hospital bed numbers: past, present, future. The King's Fund.

www.kingsfund.org.uk/publications/nhs-hospital-bed-numbers (accessed 15 February 2023).

Facini, Andrew. 2020. The low-yield nuclear warhead: a dangerous weapon based on bad strategic thinking. *Bulletin of the Atomic Scientists*, 28 January. https://thebulletin.org/2020/01/the-low-yield-nuclear-warhead-a-dangerous-weapon-based-on-bad-strategic-thinking/ (accessed 15 February 2023).

Fehér, Ferenc, and Heller Agnes. 1986. Doomsday or deterrence? On the antinuclear issue. *International Journal of Politics* 16 (1/2): 1–153.

Ferguson, Donna. 2021. 'Not in this town': artwork about Britain's 'nuclear colonialism' removed. *The Observer*, 17 July. www.theguardian.com/artanddesign/2021/jul/17/not-in-this-town-artwork-about-britains-nuclear-colonialism-removed (accessed 15 February 2023).

Fey, Marco, Annika E. Poppe, and Carsten Rauch. 2016. The nuclear taboo, Battlestar Galactica, and the real world: illustrations from a science-fiction universe. *Security Dialogue* 47 (4): 348–65.

Fihn, Beatrice, and Alicia Sanders-Zakre. 2020. You can't save a COVID-19 patient with nuclear arms. *Medicine, Conflict and Survival* 36 (2): 126–8. doi: 10.1080/13623699.2020.1761059

Fishel, Stefanie. 2015. Remembering nukes: collective memories and countering state history. *Critical Military Studies* 1 (2): 131–44.

Five Thirty Eight. 2022a. Do Americans have a favorable or unfavorable opinion of Donald Trump? An updating average, accounting for each poll's quality, recency, sample size and partisan lean. https://projects.fivethirtyeight.com/polls/favorability/donald-trump/ (accessed 15 April 2022).

Five Thirty Eight. 2022b. How popular is Joe Biden? An updating calculation of the president's approval rating, accounting for each poll's quality, recency, sample size and partisan lean. https://projects.fivethirtyeight.com/biden-approval-rating/ (accessed 15 April 2022).

Follesdal, Andreas, and Simon Hix. 2006. Why there is a democratic deficit in the EU? A response to Majone and Moravcsik. *JCMS: Journal of Common Market Studies* 44 (3): 533–62.

Freedman, Lawrence. 1987. *Why is Arms Control So Boring?* London: Council for Arms Control.

Freedman, Lawrence. 2013. Disarmament and other nuclear norms. *Washington Quarterly* 36 (2): 93–108. doi: 10.1080/0163660x.2013.791085

Freedman, Lawrence, and Jeffrey Michaels. 2019. *The Evolution of Nuclear Strategy: New, Updated and Completely Revised*. London: Springer.

Frisch, Otto, and Rudolf Peierls. 1940a. On the construction of a 'super-bomb' based on a nuclear chain reaction in uranium. Atomic Archive. www.atomicarchive.com/resources/documents/beginnings/frisch-peierls-2.html (accessed 15 February 2023).

Frisch, Otto, and Rudolf Peierls. 1940b. Properties of a radioactive 'super-bomb'. Atomic Archive. www.atomicarchive.com/resources/documents/beginnings/frisch-peierls-2.html (accessed 15 February 2023).

Futter, Andrew. 2018. *Hacking the Bomb: Cyber Threats and Nuclear Weapons*. Washington, DC: Georgetown University Press.

Futter, Andrew. 2021. *The Politics of Nuclear Weapons: New, Updated and Completely Revised*. London: Springer Nature.

Futter, Andrew, Samuel I. Watson, Peter J. Chilton, and Richard J. Lilford. 2020. Nuclear war, public health, the COVID-19 epidemic: lessons for prevention, preparation, mitigation, and education. *Bulletin of the Atomic Scientists* 76 (5): 271–6. https://doi.org/10.1080/00963402.2020.1806592.

Futter, Andrew, and Benjamin Zala. 2021. Strategic non-nuclear weapons and the onset of a Third Nuclear Age. *European Journal of International Security* 6 (3): 1–21. doi: 10.1017/eis.2021.2

Gamson, William A., and Andre Modigliani. 1989. Media discourse and public opinion on nuclear power: a constructionist approach. *American Journal of Sociology* 95 (1): 1–37.

Gani, Jasmine K. 2021. Racial militarism and civilizational anxiety at the imperial encounter: from metropole to the postcolonial state. *Security Dialogue* 52 (6): 546–66.

Gani, Jasmine K., and Jenna Marshall. 2022. The impact of colonialism on policy and knowledge production in International Relations. *International Affairs* 98 (1): 5–22.

Garrett, Bradley. 2020. *Bunker: Building for the End Times*. London: Simon & Schuster.

Gerstein, Daniel M. 2020. *The Strategic National Stockpile and COVID-19: Rethinking the Stockpile*. RAND.

Gorbachev, Mikhail S. 1991. Resignation speech, 26 December. World History Commons. https://worldhistorycommons.org/mikhail-gorbachevs-resignation-speech (accessed 15 February 2023).

Gorman, Amanda. 2021. The hill we climb. An inaugural poem for the country. www.cnbc.com/2021/01/20/amanda-gormans-inaugural-poem-the-hill-we-climb-full-text.html (accessed 9 March 2023).

Gottemoeller, Rose. 2011. New START Treaty – another success story. *Security Index: A Russian Journal on International Security* 17 (3): 7–8. doi: 10.1080/19934270.2011.587975

Gould, Joe. 2020. Defund Pentagon effort holds message for Biden. *Defense News*, 20 July. www.defensenews.com/congress/2020/07/20/defund-pentagon-effort-holds-message-for-biden/ (accessed 15 February 2023).

Gould, Joe. 2021. Riding the wave: defense revenues rise despite a dark 2020. *Defense News*, 12 July. www.defensenews.com/top-100/2021/07/12/riding-the-wave-defense-revenues-rise-despite-a-dark-2020/ (accessed 15 February 2023).

Gould, Kenneth A. 2007. The ecological costs of militarization. *Peace Review* 19 (3): 331–4.

Gould, Kenneth A., David N. Pellow, and Allan Schnaiberg. 2004. Interrogating the treadmill of production: everything you wanted to know about the treadmill but were afraid to ask. *Organization & Environment* 17 (3): 296–316.

Gray, Colin S. 1999. *The Second Nuclear Age*. London: Lynne Rienner.

Grayson, Kyle, Matt Davies, and Simon Philpott. 2009. Pop goes IR? Researching the popular culture–world politics continuum. *Politics* 29 (3): 155–63. doi: 10.1111/j.1467-9256.2009.01351.x

Green, Brendan Rittenhouse. 2020. *The Revolution That Failed: Nuclear Competition, Arms Control, and the Cold War*. Cambridge: Cambridge University Press.

Gregg, Aaron, and Yeganeh Torbati. 2020. Pentagon used taxpayer money meant for masks and swabs to make jet engine parts and body armor. *Washington Post*, 22 September. www.washingtonpost.com/business/2020/09/22/covid-funds-pentagon/ (accessed 15 February 2023).

Grove, Jairus Victor. 2019. *Savage Ecology: War and Geopolitics at the End of the World*. Durham, NC: Duke University Press.

Gusterson, Hugh. 1999. Nuclear weapons and the other in the Western imagination. *Cultural Anthropology* 14 (1): 111–43.

Gusterson, Hugh. 2007. Anthropology and militarism." *Annual Review of Anthropology* 36: 155.

Guterres, António. 2022. *Secretary-General's remarks to the Tenth Review Conference of the Parties to the Treaty on the Non-Proliferation of Nuclear Weapons*. www.un.org/sg/en/content/sg/statement/2022-08-01/secretary-generals-remarks-the-tenth-review-conference-of-the-parties-the-treaty-the-non-proliferation-of-nuclear-weapons-bilingual-delivered-follows-scroll-down-for (accessed 15 February 2023).

Hall, Stuart. 1997. Subjects in history: making diasporic identities. In *The House That Race Built*, ed. Wahneema Lubiano, pp. 289–99. New York: Pantheon.

Halliday, Fred. 1987. Vigilantism in International Relations: Kubálková, Cruickshank and Marxist theory. *Review of International Studies* 13 (3): 163. doi: 10.1017/s0260210500113580

Hansard. 2020. Wuhan coronavirus – debated on Monday 3 February 2020.

Hansen, Lene. 2013. *Security as Practice: Discourse Analysis and the Bosnian War*. London: Routledge.

Hanson, Marianne. 2022. *Challenging Nuclearism: A Humanitarian Approach to Reshape the Global Nuclear Order*. Manchester: Manchester University Press.

Harkinson, Josh. 2014. Hanging out with the disgruntled guys who babysit America's aging nuclear missiles. *Mother Jones*. www.motherjones.com/politics/2014/11/air-force-missile-wing-minuteman-iii-nuclear-weapons-burnout-1/ (accessed 15 February 2023).

Hecht, Gabrielle. 2002. Rupture-talk in the nuclear age: conjugating colonial power in Africa. *Social Studies of Science* 32 (5–6): 691–727. doi: 10.1177/030631270203200504

Hecht, Gabrielle. 2014. *Being Nuclear: Africans and the Global Uranium Trade*. Cambridge, MA: MIT Press.

Henderson, Errol A. 2013. Hidden in plain sight: racism in international relations theory. *Cambridge Review of International Affairs* 26 (1): 71–92.

Henry, Marsha. 2017. Problematizing military masculinity, intersectionality and male vulnerability in feminist critical military studies. *Critical Military Studies* 3 (2): 182–99.

Herbert, Jon, Trevor McCrisken, and Andrew Wroe. 2019. *The Ordinary Presidency of Donald J. Trump*. New York: Springer.

Hershey, John. 1946. *Hiroshima*. New York: Alfred A. Knopf.

Hersman, Rebecca. 2020. Wormhole escalation in the new nuclear age. *Texas National Security Review* 3 (3): 90–109. doi: 10.26153/tsw/10220

Heuser, Beatrice. 1995. The development of NATO's nuclear strategy. *Contemporary European History* 4 (1): 37–66.

Higuchi, Toshihiro. 2020. *Political Fallout: Nuclear Weapons Testing and the Making of a Global Environmental Crisis*. Stanford, CA: Stanford University Press.

HM Government. 2022. Global Britain in a competitive age: the integrated review of security, defence, development and foreign policy. www.gov.uk/government/publications/global-britain-in-a-competitive-age-the-integrated-review-of-security-defence-development-and-foreign-policy (accessed 15 February 2023).

Hoffman, David. 2009. *The Dead Hand: The Untold Story of the Cold War Arms Race and Its Dangerous Legacy*. London: Anchor.

Hogg, Jonathan. 2016. *British Nuclear Culture: Official and Unofficial Narratives in the Long 20th Century*. London: Bloomsbury.

Hogg, Jonathan, and Christoph Laucht. 2012. Introduction: British nuclear culture. *British Journal for the History of Science* 45 (4): 479–93. doi: 10.1017/s0007087412001008

Hohmann, James, and Mariana Alfaro. 2020. U.S. came 'much closer' to war with North Korea in 2017 than the public knew, Trump told Woodward. *Washington Post*, 16 September. www.washingtonpost.com/politics/2020/09/16/daily-202-us-came-much-closer-war-with-north-korea-2017-than-public-knew-trump-told-woodward/ (accessed 15 February 2023).

Hooks, Gregory, and Chad L. Smith. 2004. The treadmill of destruction: national sacrifice areas and Native Americans. *American Sociological Review* 69 (4): 558–75.

Hopkins, Nick. 2020. Leaked Cabinet Office briefing on UK pandemic threat – the key points. *The Guardian*, 24 April. www.theguardian.com/world/2020/apr/24/leaked-cabinet-office-briefing-on-uk-pandemic-threat-the-key-points (accessed 15 February 2023).

Horton, Richard. 2020. Just for the record: the UK government is deliberately rewriting history in its ongoing COVID-19 disinformation campaign. Twitter, 20 April. https://twitter.com/richardhorton1/status/1252183975893884933?ref_src=twsrc%5Etfw (accessed 15 February 2023).

Hoskins, Andrew. 2018. The forgetting conundrum. SoundCloud, 24 August. https://soundcloud.com/user-254586148/the-forgetting-conundrum (accessed 15 February 2023).

House of Commons Committee of Public Accounts. 2021. Improving the performance of major defence equipment contracts. https://publications.parliament.uk/pa/cm5802/cmselect/cmpubacc/185/report.html (accessed 9 March 2023).

Hudson, John, and Paul Sonne. 2020. Trump administration discussed conducting first U.S. nuclear test in decades. *Washington Post*, 22 May. www.washingtonpost.com/national-security/trump-administration-discussed-conducting-first-us-nuclear-test-in-decades/2020/05/22/a805c904-9c5b-11ea-b60c-3be060a4f8e1_story.html (accessed 15 February 2023).

ICAN. 2021. *Complicit: 2020 Global Nuclear Weapons Spending*. ICAN. https://d3n8a8pro7vhmx.cloudfront.net/ican/pages/2161/attachments/original/1622825593/Spending_Report_Web.pdf?1622825593 (accessed 15 February 2023).

Intondi, Vincent J. 2015. *African Americans Against the Bomb: Nuclear Weapons, Colonialism, and the Black Freedom Movement*. Stanford, CA: Stanford University Press.
Jackson, Susan T., Rhys Crilley, Ilan Manor, Catherine Baker, Modupe Oshikoya, Jutta Joachim, Nick Robinson, Andrea Schneiker, Nicole Sunday Grove, and Cynthia Enloe. 2020. Militarization 2.0: communication and the normalization of political violence in the digital age. *International Studies Review*. https://eprints.whiterose.ac.uk/163128/1/ISR%20forum%20%282020%29%20Militarization%202.0-%20Communication%20and%20the%20Normalization%20of%20Political%20Violence%20in%20the%20Digital%20Age.pdf (accessed 15 February 2023).
Jackson, Van. 2018. *On the Brink: Trump, Kim, and the Threat of Nuclear War*. Cambridge: Cambridge University Press.
Jacobs, Robert. 2010. *Filling the Hole in the Nuclear Future: Art and Popular Culture Respond to the Bomb*. Lexington, KY: Lexington Books.
Jacobs, Robert. 2013. Nuclear conquistadors: military colonialism in nuclear test site selection during the cold war. *Asian Journal of Peacebuilding* 1.
Jacobs, Robert A. 2022. *Nuclear Bodies: The Global Hibakusha*. New Haven, CT: Yale University Press.
Jägermeyr, Jonas, Alan Robock, Joshua Elliott, Christoph Müller, Lili Xia, Nikolay Khabarov, Christian Folberth, Erwin Schmid, Wenfeng Liu, and Florian Zabel. 2020. A regional nuclear conflict would compromise global food security. *Proceedings of the National Academy of Sciences* 117 (13): 7071–81.
Jamestown Foundation. 1999. Yeltsin really seeking ratification of CTBT? *Monitor* 5 (219).
Jantz, Eric. 2018. Environmental racism with a faint green glow. *Natural Resources Journal* 58 (2): 247.
Jennings, Will, and Gerty Stoker. 2018. The divergent dynamics of cities and towns: geographical polarisation after Brexit. *The Political Quarterly*, 27 November.
Jervis, Robert. 1990. Models and cases in the study of international conflict. *Journal of International Affairs* 44 (1): 81–101.
Johnson, Boris. 2020. PM speech in Greenwich, 3 February. https://www.gov.uk/government/speeches/pm-speech-in-greenwich-3-february-2020 (accessed 15 February 2023).
Jones, Seth G., Catrina Doxsee, Grace Hwang, and Jared Thompson. 2021. *The Military, Police, and the Rise of Terrorism in the United States*. Centre for Strategic and International Studies. www.jstor.org/stable/pdf/resrep31136.pdf?acceptTC=true&coverpage=false&addFooter=false (accessed 15 February 2023).
Jordan, Jerily. 2018. The fun and fractured world of Phoebe Bridgers. *Detroit Metro Times*, 18 February.
Kahn, Herman. 2017. *On Thermonuclear War*. London: Routledge.
Kaplan, Fred. 1991. *The Wizards of Armageddon*. Stanford, CA: Stanford University Press.
Kaplan, Fred. 2020. *The Bomb: Presidents, Generals, and the Secret History of Nuclear War*. New York: Simon & Schuster.

Kassenova, Togzhan. 2022. *Atomic Steppe: How Kazakhstan Gave Up the Bomb*. Stanford, CA: Stanford University Press.

Kaste, J. M., P. Volante, and A. J. Elmore. 2021. Bomb 137Cs in modern honey reveals a regional soil control on pollutant cycling by plants. *Nature Communications* 12 (1). doi: 10.1038/s41467-021-22081-8

Kendi, Ibram X. 2019. The day 'shithole' entered the presidential lexicon. *The Atlantic*, 14 January. www.theatlantic.com/politics/archive/2019/01/shithole-countries/580054/ (accessed 15 February 2023).

Kennard, Matt. 2012. *Irregular Army: How the US Military Recruited Neo-Nazis, Gang Members, and Criminals to Fight the War on Terror*. London: Verso.

Kennedy, John F. 1961. Address before the General Assembly of the United Nations, September 25. www.jfklibrary.org/archives/other-resources/john-f-kennedy-speeches/united-nations-19610925 (accessed 15 February 2023).

Kim, Michelle Hyun. 2020. Phoebe Bridgers is the spooky prophet of end times America. *Them Magazine*, 8 October.

Kissinger, Henry A. 2019. *Nuclear Weapons and Foreign Policy*. New York: Routledge.

Koch, Lisa Langdon, and Matthew Wells. 2021. Still taboo? Citizens' attitudes toward the use of nuclear weapons. *Journal of Global Security Studies* 6 (3). doi: 10.1093/jogss/ogaa024

Koch, Susan J. 2012. *The Presidential Nuclear Initiatives of 1991–1992*. https://ndupress.ndu.edu/portals/68/documents/casestudies/cswmd_casestudy-5.pdf (accessed 15 February 2023).

Korda, Matt. 21st March 2021. *Siloed Thinking: A Closer Look at the Ground-based Strategic Deterrent*. Federation of American Scientists. https://man.fas.org/eprint/siloed-thinking.pdf (accessed 15 February 2023).

Kristensen, Hans, M. 2020. World nuclear forces. In *SIPRI Yearbook 2020*, ed. Stockholm International Peace Research Institute, pp. 325–93. Oxford: Oxford University Press.

Kube, Courtney, and Mosheh Gains. 2023. Air Force general predicts war with China in 2025. *NBC News*. www.nbcnews.com/politics/national-security/us-air-force-general-predicts-war-china-2025-memo-rcna67967 (accessed 9 March 2023)

Kube, Courtney, Kristen Welker, Carol E. Lee, and Savannah Guthrie. 2017. Trump wanted tenfold increase in nuclear arsenal, surprising military. *NBC News*. www.nbcnews.com/politics/donald-trump/trump-wanted-dramatic-increase-nuclear-arsenal-meeting-military-leaders-n809701 (accessed 15 February 2023).

Kütt, Moritz, and Zia Mian. 2019. Setting the deadline for nuclear weapon destruction under the treaty on the prohibition of nuclear weapons. *Journal for Peace and Nuclear Disarmament* 2(2): 410–30.

Labour Party. 2019. *It's Time for Real Change: The Labour Party Manifesto 2019*. https://labour.org.uk/wp-content/uploads/2019/11/Real-Change-Labour-Manifesto-2019.pdf (accessed 15 February 2023).

Larsen, Jeffrey Arthur, and James M Smith. 2005. *Historical Dictionary of Arms Control and Disarmament*. London: Scarecrow Press.

Latham, Rob. 2016. Weaponizing the imagination. *Science Fiction Studies* 43 (2): 365. doi: 10.5621/sciefictstud.43.2.0365

Laware, Margaret L. 2004. Circling the missiles and staining them red: feminist rhetorical invention and strategies of resistance at the women's peace camp at Greenham Common. *Feminist Formations* 16 (3): 18–41.
LBC News. 2019. Jo Swinson responds to 'very fake news' story which said she fired stones at squirrels. *LBC News*, 19 November. https://www.lbc.co.uk/radio/presenters/iain-dale/jo-swinson-responds-to-viral-fake-story-squirrels/ (accessed 15 February 2023).
Legvold, Robert, and Christopher F. Chyba. 2020. Introduction: the search for strategic stability in a new nuclear era. *Daedalus* 149 (2): 6–16. doi: 10.1162/daed_e_01786
Lengefeld, Michael R., and Chad L. Smith. 2013. Nuclear shadows: weighing the environmental effects of militarism, capitalism, and modernization in a global context, 2001–2007. *Human Ecology Review* 20 (1): 11–25.
Levin, Bess. 2020. Report: Some people thinking a drug-addled maniac (Donald Trump) shouldn't be in charge of the nuclear codes. *Vanity Fair*, 12 October.
Lieber, Keir A., and Daryl G. Press. 2020. The myth of the nuclear revolution. In Keir A. Lieber and Daryl G. Press, *The Myth of the Nuclear Revolution*. Ithaca, NY: Cornell University Press.
Lipschutz, Ronnie D. 2001. *Cold War Fantasies: Film, Fiction, and Foreign Policy*. London: Rowman & Littlefield.
Lucas, Edward. 2014. *The New Cold War: Putin's Russia and the Threat to the West*. London: Palgrave Macmillan.
Luckham, Robin. 1984. Militarisation and the new international anarchy. *Third World Quarterly* 6 (2): 351–73.
Lutz, Catherine. 2002. Making war at home in the United States: militarization and the current crisis. *American Anthropologist* 104 (3): 723–35.
Mac, Annie. 2019. Sam Fender's Hypersonic Missiles named as Annie Mac's Hottest Record of the Year 2019. *Recordoftheday.com* (blog). www.recordoftheday.com/news-and-press/sam-fenders-hypersonic-missiles-named-as-annie-macs-hottest-record-of-the-year-2019 (accessed 15 February 2023).
Mach, Katharine J., Caroline M. Kraan, W. Neil Adger, Halvard Buhaug, Marshall Burke, James D. Fearon, Christopher B. Field, Cullen S. Hendrix, Jean-Francois Maystadt, and John O'Loughlin. 2019. Climate as a risk factor for armed conflict. *Nature* 571 (7764): 193–7.
MacKenzie, Donald. 1993. *Inventing Accuracy: A Historical Sociology of Nuclear Missile Guidance*. Cambridge, MA: MIT Press.
Macron, Emmanuel. 2020. Speech of the President of the Republic on the Defense and Deterrence Strategy. https://www.elysee.fr/en/emmanuel-macron/2020/02/07/speech-of-the-president-of-the-republic-on-the-defense-and-deterrence-strategy (accessed 15 February 2023).
Maddock, Shane J. 2010. *Nuclear Apartheid: The Quest for American Atomic Supremacy from World War II to the Present*. Chapel Hill: University of North Carolina Press.
Marani, Marco, Gabriel G. Katul, William K. Pan, and Anthony J. Parolari. 2021. Intensity and frequency of extreme novel epidemics. *Proceedings of the National Academy of Sciences* 118 (35): e2105482118.

Matharu, Hardeep. 2020. Britain's Chernobyl: COVID-19 and the cost of lies. *Byline Times*, 15 May. https://bylinetimes.com/2020/05/15/britains-chernobyl-covid-19-and-the-cost-of-lies/ (accessed 15 February 2023).

MAUD Committee. 1941. *Report by MAUD Committee on the Use of Uranium for a Bomb*. https://fissilematerials.org/library/maud.pdf (accessed 9 March 2023).

Maurer, Anaïs, and Rebecca H. Hogue. 2020. Introduction: transnational nuclear imperialisms. *Journal of Transnational American Studies* 11 (2).

McCarthy, Tom. 2014. Dozens of US nuclear missile officers caught up in drug and cheating scandals. *The Guardian*. www.theguardian.com/world/2014/jan/15/muclear-missile-officers-suspended-drug-cheating-scandals (accessed 15 February 2023).

McCrisken, Trevor, and Maxwell Downman. 2019. 'Peace through strength': Europe and NATO deterrence beyond the US Nuclear Posture Review. *International Affairs* 95 (2): 277–95.

McCurry, Justin. 2015. The man who survived Hiroshima: 'I had entered a living hell on earth'. *The Guardian*, 4 August. www.theguardian.com/world/2015/jul/31/japan-atomic-bomb-survivors-nuclear-weapons-hiroshima-70th-anniversary (accessed 15 February 2023).

Meier, Oliver, and Maren Vieluf. 2021. Upsetting the nuclear order: how the rise of nationalist populism increases nuclear dangers. *The Nonproliferation Review* 28: 1–23.

Meyer, David S. 1995. Framing national security: elite public discourse on nuclear weapons during the cold war. *Political Communication* 12 (2): 173–92. doi: 10.1080/10584609.1995.9963064

Meyn, Carina. 2018. Realism for nuclear-policy wonks. *The Nonproliferation Review* 25 (1–2): 111–28.

Michaels, Jeffrey, and Heather Williams. 2017. The nuclear education of Donald J. Trump. *Contemporary Security Policy* 38 (1): 54–77.

Miller, Nicholas L., and Narang, Vipin. 2019. Is a new nuclear age upon us? Why we may look back on 2019 as the point of no return. *Foreign Affairs*, 30 December. www.foreignaffairs.com/articles/2019-12-30/new-nuclear-age-upon-us (accessed 15 February 2023).

Milliken, Jennifer. 1999. The study of discourse in international relations: a critique of research and methods. *European Journal of International Relations* 5 (2): 225–54.

Ministry of Foreign Affairs of the People's Republic of China. 2019. Briefing by Mr. FU Cong, Director General of the Department of Arms Control and Disarmament of Ministry of Foreign Affairs. Department of Arms Control and Disarmament of Ministry of Foreign Affairs.

Ministry of Foreign Affairs of the Russian Federation. 2020. Foreign Ministry statement on the withdrawal of the United States from the INF Treaty and its termination. The Ministry of Foreign Affairs of the Russian Federation. https://russiaeu.ru/en/news/statement-russian-mfa-withdrawal-united-states-inf-treaty-and-its-termination (accessed 15 February 2023).

Minnion, John, and Philip Bolsover. 1983. *The CND Story: The First 25 Years of CND in the Words of the People Involved*. London: Allison & Busby.

Mitchinson, Rory. 2019. 'I want to sell out a show at St. James' Park before I die'. NUFC.com, 6 September. https://www.nufc.co.uk/news/features/i-want-to-sell-out-a-show-at-st-james-park-before-i-die/ (accessed 15 February 2023).
Moniz, Ernest J., and Sam Nunn. 2019. The return of Doomsday: the new nuclear arms race –and how Washington and Moscow can stop it. *Foreign Affairs* 98: 150.
Moore, Cerwyn, and Laura J. Shepherd. 2010. Aesthetics and International Relations: towards a global politics. *Global Society* 24 (3): 299–309. doi: 10.1080/13600826.2010.485564
Moravcsik, Andrew. 2004. Is there a 'democratic deficit' in world politics? A framework for analysis. *Government and Opposition* 39 (2): 336–63.
Morgenthau, Hans J. 1975. Some political aspects of disarmament. In *The Dynamics of the Arms Race*, ed. David Carlton and Carlo Schaerf, pp. 57–64. London: Croom Helm.
Moscow Times. 2019. Putin Says 'unparalleled' weapons tested at deadly nuclear accident site. *Moscow Times*, 22 November. www.themoscowtimes.com/2019/11/22/putin-says-unparalleled-weapons-tested-at-deadly-nuclear-accident-site-a68274 (accessed 15 February 2023).
Mutimer, David. 2000. *The Weapons State: Proliferation and the Framing of Security*. London: Lynne Rienner.
Mutimer, David. 2011. From arms control to denuclearization: governmentality and the abolitionist desire. *Contemporary Security Policy* 32 (1): 57–75.
Narang, Vipin. 2014. *Nuclear Strategy in the Modern Era: Regional Powers and International Conflict*. Oxford: Princeton University Press.
National Audit Office. 2020. Ministry of Defence: Managing infrastructure projects on nuclear-regulated sites. https://www.nao.org.uk/reports/management-of-nuclear-licensed-infrastructure-projects/ (accessed 15 February 2023).
NATO. 1949. The North Atlantic Treaty. North Atlantic Treaty Organization. https://www.nato.int/cps/en/natohq/official_texts_17120.htm (accessed 15 February 2023).
Naumes, Sarah. 2015. Is all 'I' IR? *Millennium* 43 (3): 820–32.
Naylor, Brian. 2021. Read Trump's Jan. 6 speech, a key part of impeachment trial. *NPR*, 10 February. www.npr.org/2021/02/10/966396848/read-trumps-jan-6-speech-a-key-part-of-impeachment-trial (accessed 15 February 2023).
New York Times. 1946. Atomic education urged by Einstein; scientist in plea for $200,000 to promote new type of essential thinking. *New York Times*, 25 May. www.nytimes.com/1946/05/25/archives/atomic-education-urged-by-einstein-scientist-in-plea-for-200000-to.html (accessed 15 February 2023).
Ni, Vincent. 2021. Failure to improve US–China relations 'risks cold war', warns Kissinger. *The Guardian*, 1 May. www.theguardian.com/us-news/2021/may/01/us-china-doomsday-threat-ramped-up-by-hi-tech-advances-says-kissinger (accessed 15 February 2023).
Norris, Pippa, and Ronald Inglehart. 2019. *Cultural Backlash: Trump, Brexit, and Authoritarian Populism*. Cambridge: Cambridge University Press.
Nye, Joseph S. 1991. Arms control and international politics. *Daedalus*: 145–65.
Obama, Barack. 2009. Remarks by President Barack Obama in Prague, April 5 2009. https://obamawhitehouse.archives.gov/video/The-President-in-Prague/#transcript (accessed 15 February 2023).

Obama, Barack. 2016. Statement by the President on North Korea's Nuclear Test. 9 September. https://obamawhitehouse.archives.gov/the-press-office/2016/09/09/statement-president-north-koreas-nuclear-test (accessed 15 February 2023).

O'Connor, Tom. 2018. Russia tests 'New Year's gift' weapon that could deliver nuclear strike 20 times speed of sound. *Newsweek*, 26 December. www.newsweek.com/russia-tests-new-years-weapon-nuclear-strike-1271822 (accessed 15 February 2023).

O'Neal, Adam. 2020. Coronavirus and the Chernobyl analogy. Wall Street Journal, 22 May. www.wsj.com/articles/coronavirus-and-the-chernobyl-analogy-11590167999 (accessed 15 February 2023).

Pappalardo, Joe. 2020. The coronavirus can't stop America's nukes. *Popular Mechanics*, 1 April.

Parkinson, Stuart. 2020. The carbon boot-print of the military. Responsible Science 2: 18–20. www.sgr.org.uk/sites/default/files/2020-08/SGR-RS02-Military-carbon-boot-print.pdf (accessed 15 February 2023).

Paul, Thazha V. 2009. *The Tradition of Non-Use of Nuclear Weapons*. Stanford, CA: Stanford University Press.

Paul, Thazha V. 2010. Taboo or tradition? The non-use of nuclear weapons in world politics. *Review of International Studies* 36 (4): 853–63.

Pauly, Reid B. C. 2018. Would US leaders push the button? Wargames and the sources of nuclear restraint. *International Security* 43 (2): 151–92.

Pearce, Fred. 2018. *Fallout: A Journey Through the Nuclear Age, from the Atom Bomb to Radioactive Waste*. London: Granta.

Pelopidas, Benoît. 2011. The oracles of proliferation: how experts maintain a biased historical reading that limits policy innovation. *Nonproliferation Review* 18 (1): 297–314.

Pelopidas, Benoît. 2016. Nuclear weapons scholarship as a case of self-censorship in security studies. *Journal of Global Security Studies* 1 (4): 326–36. doi: 10.1093/jogss/ogw017

Pelopidas, Benoît. 2017. The unbearable lightness of luck: three sources of overconfidence in the manageability of nuclear crises. *European Journal of International Security* 2 (2): 240–62. doi: 10.1017/eis.2017.6

Pelopidas, Benoît. 2020. Power, luck, and scholarly responsibility at the end of the world(s). *International Theory* 12 (3): 459–70. doi: 10.1017/s1752971920000299

Pelopidas, Benoît. 2021a. The birth of nuclear eternity. In *Futures*, ed. Sandra Kemp and Jenny Andersson. Oxford: Oxford University Press.

Pelopidas, Benoît. 2021b. Imaginer la possibilité de la guerre nucléaire pour y faire face. Le role de la culture populaire visuelle de 1950 à nos jours. *Cultures & Conflicts* 3–4: 123–24.

Pelopidas, Benoît, and Kjølv Egeland. 2020. What Europeans believe about Hiroshima and Nagasaki – and why it matters. *Bulletin of the Atomic Scientists*, 3 August. https://thebulletin.org/2020/08/what-europeans-believe-about-hiroshima-and-nagasaki-and-why-it-matters/ (accessed 15 February 2023).

Pelopidas, Benoît, and Zia Mian. 2023. Producing collapse. Nuclear weapons as preparations to end civilisation. In *How Worlds Collapse: What History, Systems,*

and Complexity Can Teach Us about Our Modern World and Fragile Future, ed. Miguel Centeno *et al*. London: Routledge.
Pengelly, Martin. 2022a. Trump sought to mount 'armed revolution', militia ex-spokesman says. *The Guardian*, 12 July. www.theguardian.com/us-news/2022/jul/12/jan-6-hearings-trump-capitol-attack-oath-keepers-ex-spokesperson-witness (accessed 15 February 2023).
Pengelly, Martin. 2022b. Trump: I would threaten Russia with nuclear submarines if still president. *The Guardian*, 23 March. www.theguardian.com/us-news/2022/mar/23/donald-trump-nuclear-weapons-russia (accessed 15 February 2023).
Peoples, Columba. 2010. *Justifying Ballistic Missile Defence: Technology, Security and Culture*. Vol. 112. Cambridge: Cambridge University Press.
Peoples, Columba, and Nick Vaughan-Williams. 2020. *Critical Security Studies: An Introduction*. London: Routledge.
Perry, William J., and Tom Z. Collina. 2020. *The Button: The New Nuclear Arms Race and Presidential Power from Truman to Trump*. Dallas, TX: BenBella Books.
Philippe, Sébastien, and Tomas Statius. 2021. *Toxique: enquête sur les essais nucléaires français en Polynésie*. Paris: Presses Universitaires de France.
Philippe, Sébastien, Sonya Schoenberger, and Nabil Ahmed. 2022. Radiation exposures and compensation of victims of French atmospheric nuclear tests in Polynesia. *Science & Global Security* 30 (2): 62–94.
Pifer, Steven. 2020. How COVID-19 might affect nuclear weapons and planning. *Brookings*, 18 May.
Pilkington, Ed, and Martin Pengelly. 2016. 'Let it be an arms race': Donald Trump appears to double down on nuclear expansion. *The Guardian*, 24 December. www.theguardian.com/us-news/2016/dec/23/donald-trump-nuclear-weapons-arms-race (accessed 15 February 2023).
Place, Nathan. 2022. Trump calls for US to put Chinese flags on fighter jets and 'bomb the s*** out of Russia. *The Independent*, 7 March. https://www.independent.co.uk/news/world/americas/us-politics/trump-china-flag-russia-ukraine-b2029695.html (accessed 15 February 2023).
Plokhy, Serhii. 2020. The world stopped another Chernobyl by working together. Coronavirus demands the same. *The Guardian*, 5 May. www.theguardian.com/commentisfree/2020/may/05/prevent-coronavirus-chernobyl-international-disaster (accessed 15 February 2023).
Ploughshares Fund. 2019. Press the Button. Podcast, 23 August.
Ploughshares Fund. 2020a. Press the Button. Podcast, 2 June.
Ploughshares Fund. 2020b. Press the Button. Podcast, 15 September.
Pocan, Mark. 2020. The American people agree: cut the Pentagon's budget. *Data for Progress*, 20 July. https://www.dataforprogress.org/blog/2020/7/20/cut-the-pentagons-budget (accessed 15 February 2023).
Pompeo, Michael R. 2020. U.S. withdrawal from the INF Treaty on August 2, 2019 – United States Department of State. US Department of State. https://2017-2021.state.gov/u-s-withdrawal-from-the-inf-treaty-on-august-2-2019/index.html (accessed 15 February 2023).

Postma, Foeke. 2021. US soldiers expose nuclear weapons secrets via flashcard apps. *Bellingcat*, 28 May. www.bellingcat.com/news/2021/05/28/us-soldiers-expose-nuclear-weapons-secrets-via-flashcard-apps/ (accessed 15 February 2023).

Press, Daryl G., Scott D. Sagan, and Benjamin A. Valentino. 2013. Atomic aversion: experimental evidence on taboos, traditions, and the non-use of nuclear weapons. *American Political Science Review* 107 (1):188–206.

Procter, James. 2004. *Stuart Hall*. London: Routledge.

Public Health England. 2017. *Exercise Cygnus Report*. London: Public Health England.

Pulla, Priyanka. 2019. India–Pakistan nuclear escalation: where could it lead? *Nature* 573 (7772): 16–18.

Putin, Vladimir. 2019. Statement by the President of Russia on the unilateral withdrawal of the United States from the Treaty on the Elimination of Intermediate-Range and Shorter-Range Missiles. http://en.kremlin.ru/events/president/news/61271 (accessed 15 February 2023).

Pym, Olivia. 2020. Phoebe Bridgers' music for the end of the world." *Esquire*, 15 June.

Rabinowitch, Eugene. 1953. The narrowing way. *Bulletin of the Atomic Scientists* 9 (8): 294–5.

Ray, Deepak K. 2022. Even a small nuclear war threatens food security. *Nature Food* 3: 1–2.

Reagan, Ronald. 1983. Address before the Japanese Diet in Tokyo. Ronald Reagan Presidential Library. https://www.reaganlibrary.gov/archives/speech/address-japanese-diet-tokyo (accessed 15 February 2023).

Reagan, Ronald. 1988. Transcript of President Reagan's press conference. *Washington Post*, 1988. www.washingtonpost.com/archive/politics/1988/12/09/transcript-of-president-reagans-press-conference/973fedd0-1de6-401d-a230-c99ee487175b/ (accessed 15 February 2023).

Reagan, Ronald, and M. Gorbachev. 1987. Remarks on signing the Intermediate-Range Nuclear Forces Treaty. Ronald Reagan Presidential Library. https://www.reaganlibrary.gov/archives/speech/remarks-signing-intermediate-range-nuclear-forces-treaty (accessed 15 February 2023).

Reid, James. 1972. *Alienation: Rectorial Address to the University of Glasgow*. Glasgow: University of Glasgow Publications.

Reif, Kingston. 2020. Air Force awards new ICBM contract. *Arms Control Today* 50 (8): 36–7.

Reilly, Katie. 2016. Read Hillary Clinton's speech on Donald Trump and national security. *TIME*. https://time.com/4355797/hillary-clinton-donald-trump-foreign-policy-speech-transcript/ (accessed 15 February 2023).

Reuters. 2016. Trump floats ban on defense firms hiring military procurement officials. *Yahoo Finance*, 9 December. https://finance.yahoo.com/news/trump-floats-ban-defense-firms-231624415.html (accessed 15 February 2023).

Reuters. 2019. U.N. chief says world will lose brake on nuclear war with end of INF treaty. Reuters, 1 August. www.reuters.com/article/us-russia-usa-missiles-un-idUSKCN1UR597 (accessed 15 February 2023).

Reuters. 2020a. Johnson – coronavirus will not stop me shaking hands. Reuters, 3 March. https://www.reuters.com/article/uk-health-coronavirus-britain-handshake-idUKKBN20Q1K2 (accessed 15 February 2023).

Reuters. 2020b. Who has the UK nuclear button while Johnson is ill? No comment. Reuters, 7 April. https://www.reuters.com/article/health-coronavirus-britain-nuclear-idUSL8N2BV1Z5 (accessed 15 February 2023).

Reuters. 2021. U.N. says world likely to miss climate targets despite COVID pause in emissions. Reuters, 16 September. www.reuters.com/business/environment/un-says-world-likely-miss-climate-targets-despite-covid-pause-emissions-2021-09-16/#:~:text=%22Unless%20there%20are%20immediate%2C%20rapid,we%20depend%2C%22%20Guterres%20said (accessed 15 February 2023).

Ritchie, Nick. 2013. "Valuing and devaluing nuclear weapons." *Contemporary Security Policy* 34 (1): 146-173.

Ritchie, Nick. 2019. A hegemonic nuclear order: understanding the Ban Treaty and the power politics of nuclear weapons. *Contemporary Security Policy* 40 (4): 409–34.

Robock, Alan. 1984. Snow and ice feedbacks prolong effects of nuclear winter. *Nature* 310 (5979): 667–70.

Robock, Alan, Luke Oman, and Georgiy L Stenchikov. 2007. Nuclear winter revisited with a modern climate model and current nuclear arsenals: still catastrophic consequences. *Journal of Geophysical Research: Atmospheres* 112 (D13).

Roosevelt, Franklin D. 1939. Letter to Albert Einstein. Atomic Archive. https://www.atomicarchive.com/resources/documents/beginnings/einstein.html (accessed 15 February 2023).

Rosendorf, Ondrej, Michal Smetana, and Marek Vranka. 2021. Disarming arguments: public opinion and nuclear abolition. *Survival* 63 (6): 183–200. doi: 10.1080/00396338.2021.2006454.

Roth, Andrew, and Julian Borger. 2023. Putin says Russia will halt participation in New Start nuclear arms treaty. *The Guardian*, 21 February. www.theguardian.com/world/2023/feb/21/putin-russia-halt-participation-new-start-nuclear-arms-treaty (accessed 9 March 2023)

Rothman, Lily. 2017. Survivors of the atomic bomb share their stories. *TIME*. https://time.com/after-the-bomb/ (accessed 15 February 2023).

Roy, Arundhati. 2016. *The End of Imagination*. London: Haymarket Books.

Royal Navy. 2019. Trafalgar Class Attack Submarine. www.royalnavy.mod.uk/the-equipment/submarines/attack-submarines/trafalgar-class (accessed 9 March 2023)

Rublee, Maria Rost, and Avner Cohen. 2018. Nuclear norms in global governance: a progressive research agenda. *Contemporary Security Policy* 39 (3): 317–40. doi: 10.1080/13523260.2018.1451428

Ruzicka, Jan. 2018. Behind the veil of good intentions: power analysis of the nuclear non-proliferation regime. *International Politics* 55 (3): 369–85.

Sabbagh, Dan. 2021. MoD wasting billions with 'broken' procurement system, MPs warn. *The Guardian*, 3 November. www.theguardian.com/uk-news/2021/nov/03/mod-wasting-billions-with-broken-procurement-system-mps-warn (accessed 15 February 2023).

Sagan, Carl. 1983a. Nuclear war and climatic catastrophe: some policy implications. *Foreign Affairs* 62 (2): 257–92.

Sagan, Carl. 1983b. The nuclear winter. *Parade Magazine*, 30 October.

Sagan, Scott D. 1993. *The Limits of Safety: Organizations, Accidents, and Nuclear Weapons*. Princeton, NJ: Princeton University Press.

Sagan, Scott D. 1996. Why do states build nuclear weapons? Three models in search of a bomb. *International Security* 21 (3): 54–86.

Sagan, Scott D., and Benjamin A. Valentino. 2017. Revisiting Hiroshima in Iran: what Americans really think about using nuclear weapons and killing noncombatants. *International Security* 42 (1): 41–79. doi: 10.1162/isec_a_00284

Said, Edward. 1978. *Orientalism: Western Concepts of the Orient*. New York: Pantheon.

Samuel, Olamide. 2022. Travelling while black: a first-hand account of the restrictive visa system impacting diversity at nuclear policy conferences. European Leadership Network, 8 August. https://www.europeanleadershipnetwork.org/commentary/travelling-while-black-a-first-hand-account-of-the-restrictive-visa-system-impacting-diversity-at-nuclear-policy-conferences/warn (accessed 15 February 2023).

Sanger, David E., and William J. Broad. 2020. Trump's virus treatment revives questions about unchecked nuclear authority. *New York Times*, 11 October.

Santese, Angela. 2017. Ronald Reagan, the nuclear weapons freeze campaign and the nuclear scare of the 1980s. *International History Review* 39 (3): 496–520. doi: 10.1080/07075332.2016.1220403

Sauer, Tom. 1998. *Nuclear Arms Control: Nuclear Deterrence in the Post-Cold War Period*. London: Macmillan.

Saunders, Robert A., Rhys Crilley, and Precious N. Chatterje-Doody. 2022. ICYMI: RT and youth-oriented international broadcasting as (geo) political culture jamming. *International Journal of Press/Politics* 27 (3): 696–717.

Scarry, Elaine. 2014. *Thermonuclear Monarchy: Choosing between Democracy and Doom*. New York: W. W. Norton.

Schelling, Thomas C. 2020. *Arms and Influence*. New Haven, CT: Yale University Press.

Schelling, Thomas C., and Morton H. Halperin. 1961. *Strategy and Arms Control*. New York: Twentieth Century Fund.

Schlosser, Eric. 2013. *Command and Control: Nuclear Weapons and the Illusion of Safety*. Harmondsworth: Penguin.

Schmemann, Serge. 2020. Trump's Chernobyl. *New York Times*, 14 March. www.nytimes.com/subscription/gateway/subcon/variants/variant-2.html (accessed 15 February 2023).

Schwab, Gabriele. 2020. *Radioactive Ghosts*. Minneapolis: Minnesota University Press.

Scott, Len, and R. Gerald Hughes. 2015. *The Cuban Missile Crisis: A Critical Reappraisal*. London: Routledge.

Seligman, Lara, Alexander Ward, and Paul McLeary. 2021. Pentagon's top nuclear policy official ousted in reorganization. *Politico*, 21 September. www.politico.com/news/2021/09/21/pentagon-top-nuclear-official-ousted-reorganization-513502 (accessed 15 February 2023).

Shepherd, Laura. 2013. *Critical Approaches to Security*. Abingdon: Routledge.

Silva, Diego Lopes da, Nan Tian, and Alexandra Marksteiner. 2021. Trends in world military expenditure, 2020. SIPRI Fact Sheet: 2. www.sipri.org/sites/default/files/2021-04/fs_2104_milex_0.pdf (accessed 15 February 2023).

Singer, J. David, and Jeffrey Keating. 1999. Military preparedness, weapon systems and the biosphere: a preliminary impact statement. *New Political Science* 21 (3): 325–43.

SIPRI (Stockholm International Peace Research Institute). 2022. Global nuclear arsenals are expected to grow as states continue to modernize – New SIPRI Yearbook out now. 13th June. https://sipri.org/media/press-release/2022/global-nuclear-arsenals-are-expected-grow-states-continue-modernize-new-sipri-yearbook-out-now (accessed 15 February 2023).

Smetana, Michal. 2018. A Nuclear Posture Review for the Third Nuclear Age. *Washington Quarterly* 41 (3): 137–57.

Smetana, Michal, and Michal Onderco. 2022. From Moscow with a mushroom cloud? Russian public attitudes to the use of nuclear weapons in a conflict with NATO. *Journal of Conflict Resolution* 67 (2–3): 183–209.

Smetana, Michal, and Carmen Wunderlich. 2021. Nonuse of nuclear weapons in world politics: toward the third generation of 'nuclear taboo' research. *International Studies Review* 23 (3): 1072–99.

Smith, Julia, Sara E. Davies, Huiyun Feng, Connie C. R. Gan, Karen A. Grépin, Sophie Harman, Asha Herten-Crabb, Rosemary Morgan, Nimisha Vandan, and Clare Wenham. 2021. More than a public health crisis: a feminist political economic analysis of COVID-19. *Global Public Health* 16 (8–9): 1–17. doi: 10.1080/17441692.2021.1896765

Smith, R. Jeffrey. 2019. Hypersonic missiles are unstoppable. And they're starting a new global arms race. *New York Times Magazine*, 19 June.

Smithberger, Mandy. 2018. *Brass Parachutes: The Problem of the Pentagon Revolving Door*. Project on Government Oversight. 5 November. www.pogo.org/report/2018/11/brass-parachutes (accessed 15 February 2023).

Smyth, Henry De Wolf. 1945. *Atomic Energy for Military Purposes*. York, PA: Maple Press.

Spray, Stuart. 2021. Global military carbon emissions 'significantly' under-reported. *The Ferret*, 9 November. https://theferret.scot/global-military-carbon-emissions-under-reported/ (accessed 15 February 2023).

Stavrianakis, Anna, and Jan Selby. 2012. *Militarism and International Relations: Political Economy, Security and Theory*. Abingdon: Routledge.

Steele, Brent J. 2013. Maintaining (US) collective memory: from Hiroshima to a critical study of security history. *Critical Studies on Security* 1 (1): 83–100.

Stein, Janice Gross. 2019. H-Diplo/ISSF Roundtable 11-4 on Trusting Enemies. *H-Diplo*, 25 October. https://networks.h-net.org/node/28443/discussions/5097205/h-diploissf-roundtable-11-4-trusting-enemies (accessed 15 February 2023).

Steinberg, Marc W. 1996. Culturally speaking: finding a commons between poststructuralism and the Thompsonian perspective. *Social History* 21 (2): 193–214.

Stewart, Mallory. 2022. Keynote Address for the Commemoration of the 50th Anniversary of the Arms Control Association. US Department of State, 2 June. www.state.gov/keynote-address-for-the-commemoration-of-the-50th-anniversary-of-the-arms-control-association/ (accessed 15 February 2023).

Strauss, Mark. 2016. Nuking hurricanes: the surprising history of a really bad idea. *National Geographic*, 30 November.

Sturgeon, Nicola. 2019. Why I'd never press the nuclear button. *The Guardian*, 24 November.
Sukin, Lauren, and Alexander Lanoszka. 2022. Poll: Russia's nuclear saber-rattling is rattling neighbors' nerves. *Bulletin of the Atomic Scientists*, 15 April. https://thebulletin.org/2022/04/poll-russias-nuclear-saber-rattling-is-rattling-neighbors-nerves/ (accessed 15 February 2023).
Swan, Jonathan, and Margaret Talev. 2019. Scoop: Trump suggested nuking hurricanes to stop them from hitting U.S. *Axios*, 25 August. www.axios.com/trump-nuclear-bombs-hurricanes-97231f38-2394-4120-a3fa-8c9cf0e3f51c.html (accessed 15 February 2023).
Tabatabai, Ariane, and Philip H. Gordon. 2020. The choice that's coming: an Iran with the bomb, or bombing Iran. *New York Times*, 7 January.
Taha, Hebatalla. 2022. Atomic aesthetics: gender, visualization and popular culture in Egypt. *International Affairs* 98 (4): 1169–87.
Tannenwald, Nina. 1999. The nuclear taboo: the United States and the normative basis of nuclear non-use. *International Organization* 53 (3): 433–68.
Tannenwald, Nina. 2007. *The Nuclear Taboo: The United States and the Non-Use of Nuclear Weapons Since 1945*. Cambridge: Cambridge University Press.
Taylor, Bryan C. 1998. Nuclear weapons and communication studies: a review essay. *Western Journal of Communication* 62 (3): 300–15.
Taylor, Bryan C. 2007. 'The means to match their hatred"': nuclear weapons, rhetorical democracy, and presidential discourse. *Presidential Studies Quarterly* 37 (4): 667–92.
Taylor, N. A. J. 2019. Manifesto for an archive of nuclear harm. *Resilience: A Journal of the Environmental Humanities* 7 (1): 65–7.
Teaiwa, Teresia K. 1994. Bikinis and other s/pacific n/oceans. *The Contemporary Pacific* 6 (1): 87–109.
Thompson, Edward Palmer. 1968. *The Making of the English Working Class*. Harmondsworth: Penguin.
Thompson, Edward Palmer. 1978. *The Poverty of Theory and Other Essays*. London: Merlin Press.
Thompson, Edward Palmer. 1982a. Notes on exterminism, the last stage of civilisation. In *Exterminism and Cold War*, ed. New Left Review. London: Verso.
Thompson, Edward Palmer. 1982b. *Zero Option*. London: Merlin Press.
Thompson, Edward Palmer. 1990. The ends of cold war. *New Left Review* 182: 139–46.
Toon, Owen B., Charles G. Bardeen, Alan Robock, Lili Xia, Hans Kristensen, Matthew McKinzie, Roy J. Peterson, Cheryl S. Harrison, Nicole S. Lovenduski, and Richard P. Turco. 2019. Rapidly expanding nuclear arsenals in Pakistan and India portend regional and global catastrophe. *Science Advances* 5 (10): eaay5478.
TPNW 1MSP. 2022a. Draft Vienna Action Plan. First Meeting of States Parties to the Treaty on the Prohibition of Nuclear Weapons. https://documents.unoda.org/wp-content/uploads/2022/06/TPNW.MSP_.2022.CRP_.7-Draft-Action-Plan-new.pdf (accessed 9 March 2023).

TPNW 1MSP. 2022b. Draft Vienna Declaration of the 1st Meeting of States Parties of the Treaty on the Prohibition of Nuclear Weapons: 'Our Commitment to a World Free of Nuclear Weapons'. First Meeting of States Parties to the Treaty on the Prohibition of Nuclear Weapons. https://documents.unoda.org/wp-content/uploads/2022/06/TPNW.MSP_.2022.CRP_.8-Draft-Declaration.pdf (accessed 9 March 2023).

Transparency International. 2021. Track and trace: identifying corruption risks in UK public procurement for the Covid-19 pandemic. https://www.transparency.org.uk/sites/default/files/pdf/publications/Track%20and%20Trace%20-%20Transparency%20International%20UK.pdf (accessed 15 February 2023).

Turco, Richard P., Owen B. Toon, Thomas P. Ackerman, James B. Pollack, and Carl Sagan. 1983. Nuclear winter: global consequences of multiple nuclear explosions. *Science* 222 (4630): 1283–92.

Turner, Katlyn M., Lauren J. Borja, Denia Djokić, Madicken Munk, and Aditi Verma. 2020. A call for antiracist action and accountability in the US nuclear community. *Bulletin of the Atomic Scientists*, 24 August. https://thebulletin.org/2020/08/a-call-for-antiracist-action-and-accountability-in-the-us-nuclear-community/ (accessed 15 February 2023).

United Nations. 1968. Treaty on the Non-Proliferation of Nuclear Weapons (NPT). https://www.un.org/disarmament/wmd/nuclear/npt/text/ (accessed 15 February 2023).

United States Government Accountability Office. 2020. Defense aquisitions annual assessment. United States Government Accountability Office. https://www.gao.gov/products/gao-20-439 (accessed 15 February 2023).

United States Strategic Command (@US_STRATCOM). 2022. Today, we pause to remember Dr. Martin Luther King Jr.'s enduring legacy of selfless service. Twitter, 17 January. https://twitter.com/us_stratcom/status/1483094747795263488?lang=en-GB (accessed 15 February 2023).

USA Today. 2021. Elon Musk's episode of 'SNL' was 3rd most-watched of the season, behind Dave Chappelle, Chris Rock. *USA Today*. https://eu.usatoday.com/story/entertainment/tv/2021/05/12/elon-musk-snl-dave-chappelle-chris-rock-saw-higher-ratings/5052352001/ (accessed 15 February 2023).

Van Munster, Rens, and Casper Sylvest. 2021. Nuclear weapons, extinction, and the Anthropocene: reappraising Jonathan Schell. *Review of International Studies*: 1–17. doi: 10.1017/s0260210521000061

Vitalis, Robert. 2015. *White World Order, Black Power Politics: The Birth of American International Relations*. Ithaca, NY: Cornell University Press.

Voyles, Traci Brynne. 2015. *Wastelanding: Legacies of Uranium Mining in Navajo Country*. Minneapolis: University of Minnesota Press.

Wagner, John, and Michelle Yee He Lee. 2020. Sen. Burr asks Senate Ethics Committee for review of his stock sales amid uproar over possible influence of coronavirus briefings. *Washington Post*, 20 March. www.washingtonpost.com/politics/sen-richard-burr-r-nc-says-he-has-asked-senate-ethics-committee-for-review-of-his-stock-sales/2020/03/20/43861396-6ab8-11ea-b313-df458622c2cc_story.html (accessed 15 February 2023).

Walker, R. B. J. 1986. Culture, discourse, insecurity. *Alternatives: Global, Local, Political* 11 (4): 485–504. doi: 10.1177/030437548601100403

Walker, R. B. J. 1990. Security, sovereignty, and the challenge of world politics. *Alternatives* 15 (1): 3–27.

Wallace-Wells, David. 2020. We had the vaccine the whole time. *New York Magazine*, 7 December.

Wallace-Wells, D. 2021. Ten million a year. *London Review of Books* 43 (23).

Walter, Barbara F. 2022. *How Civil Wars Start: And How to Stop Them*. London: Viking.

Waltz, Kenneth N. 2003. More may be better. In *The Spread of Nuclear Weapons: A Debate Renewed*, ed. Scott D. Sagan and Kenneth N. Waltz, pp. 3–45. New York: W. W. Norton.

Warrick, Joby, and Walter Pincus. 2007. Missteps in the bunker. *Washington Post*, 23 September. https://rec.aviation.military.narkive.com/fZzg6ecv/missteps-in-the-bunker (accessed 15 February 2023).

Weart, Spencer R., and Gertrud Weiss Szilard. 1978. *Leo Szilard: His Version of the Facts, Selected Recollections and Correspondence*. Cambridge, MA: MIT Press.

Weldes, Jutta. 2014. High politics and low data. In *Interpretation and Method: Empirical Research Methods and the Interpretive Turn*, ed. Dvora Yanow and Peregrine Schwartz-Shea, pp. 228–38. New York: M. E. Sharpe.

Wellerstein, Alex. 2021. *Restricted Data: The History of Nuclear Secrecy in the United States*. Chicago: University of Chicago Press.

Wellerstein, Alex. 2022. NUKEMAP. https://alexwellerstein.com/projects/nukemap/ (accessed 15 February 2023).

Wells, Herbert George. 2009 [1914] *The World Set Free*. London: The Floating Press.

Wendt, Alexander. 1992. Anarchy is what states make of it: the social construction of power politics. *International Organization* 46 (2): 391–425.

Wheeler, Nicholas J. 2018. *Trusting Enemies: Interpersonal Relationships In International Conflict*. Oxford: Oxford University Press.

White House. 2022. Joint Statement of the Leaders of the Five Nuclear-Weapon States on Preventing Nuclear War and Avoiding Arms Races. https://www.whitehouse.gov/briefing-room/statements-releases/2022/01/03/p5-statement-on-preventing-nuclear-war-and-avoiding-arms-races/ (accessed 15 February 2023).

Whyman, Tom. 2019. Want to be prime minister? Hope you're ready to nuke millions. *VICE Magazine*, 13 November.

Williams, Heather. 2018. A nuclear babel: narratives around the Treaty on the Prohibition of Nuclear Weapons. *The Nonproliferation Review* 25 (1–2): 51–63. doi: 10.1080/10736700.2018.1477453

Williams, Heather. 2019. Asymmetric arms control and strategic stability: scenarios for limiting hypersonic glide vehicles. *Journal of Strategic Studies* 42 (6): 789–813. doi: 10.1080/01402390.2019.1627521

Williams, Jenessa. 2021. The Phoebe phenomenon: a year on from 'Punisher's sad girl summer. *The Forty Five Magazine*, 25 June.

Williams, Paul. 2009. Nuclear criticism. In *The Routledge Companion to Science Fiction*, ed. Andrew M., Butler Mark Bould, Adam Roberts, and Sheryl Vint, pp. 246–55. London: Routledge.

Williams, Paul. 2011. *Race, Ethnicity and Nuclear War: Representations of Nuclear Weapons and Post-Apocalyptic Worlds*. Liverpool: Liverpool University Press.

Wilson, George. 1978. Missile hole plan seen as curb to Soviet buildup. *Washington Post*, 13 July. www.washingtonpost.com/archive/politics/1978/07/13/missile-hole-plan-seen-as-curb-to-soviet-buildup/05b2c060-86a0-4689-afbf-30f5b950a0f9/ (accessed 15 February 2023).

Wintour, Patrick. 2021. UK's Trident plan incompatible with non-proliferation treaty, peers told. *The Guardian*, 18 May. www.theguardian.com/world/2021/may/18/uk-trident-plan-incompatible-with-non-proliferation-treaty-peers-told (accessed 15 February 2023).

Wirtz, James J. 2018. Nuclear weapons in the information age. *The Nonproliferation Review* 25 (3–4): 333–5.

Witze, Alexandra. 2020. How a small nuclear war would transform the entire planet. *Nature* 579 (7797): 485–8.

Woodward, Bob. 2020. *Rage*. Simon & Schuster.

Woodward, Bob, and Robert Costa. 2021. *Peril*. Simon & Schuster.

World Meteorological Organization. 25 August 2020. *United in Science 2020: A Multi-Organization High-Level Compilation of the Latest Climate Science Information*. World Meteorological Organization. https://trello-attachments.s3.amazonaws.com/5f560af19197118edf74cf93/5f59f8b11a9063544de4bf39/cdb10977949b38128408f5322f9f676d/United_In_Science_2020_8_Sep_FINAL_LowResBetterQuality.pdf (accessed 15 February 2023).

World Meteorological Organization. 2021. Climate change indicators and impacts worsened in 2020. World Meteorological Organization, 19 April. https://public.wmo.int/en/media/press-release/climate-change-indicators-and-impacts-worsened-2020 (accessed 15 February 2023).

Xia, Lili, Alan Robock, Kim Scherrer, Cheryl S. Harrison, Benjamin Leon Bodirsky, Isabelle Weindl, Jonas Jägermeyr, Charles G Bardeen, Owen B. Toon, and Ryan Heneghan. 2022. Global food insecurity and famine from reduced crop, marine fishery and livestock production due to climate disruption from nuclear war soot injection. *Nature Food* 3: 1–11.

Zeleney, Jeff, Dan Merica, and Kevin Liptak. 2017. Trump's 'fire and fury' remark was improvised but familiar. *CNN*, 9 August. https://edition.cnn.com/2017/08/09/politics/trump-fire-fury-improvise-north-korea/index.html (accessed 15 February 2023).

Zvobgo, Kelebogile, and Meredith Loken. 2020. Why race matters in international relations. *Foreign Policy* 237: 11–13.

Index

1975, The (rock band) 84
24 (TV series) 3, 35

Acton, James 110
Adger, W. Neil 127
Afghanistan, NATO forces withdrawal 150
Agyapong, Mary 94
Ahmed, Sara 10
Alexis-Martin, Becky 7, 59
Alfaro, Mariana 42
Amadae, S. M. 67
Angeli, Jake ('QAnon Shaman') 131–2
Anti-Ballistic Missile Treaty 29
anti-nuclear protest movements 27, 28, 54, 105–7, 150
'apartheid,' nuclear 50–1, 101, 105, 108, 134, 137–8
Arbery, Ahmaud 108
Arbuthnott, George 87, 92
Ardern, Jacinda 155
arms control measures
  'arms control' concept 60–1
  of First Nuclear Age 25–7, 29–30, 63
  nuclear testing bans 26, 31–2, 72, 105, 110
  scholarship on 62–3, 71–2
  of Second Nuclear Age 31–3, 37
  specific Treaties *see* Treaty name
  of Third Nuclear Age 12–13, 18, 33, 45–6, 143, 147, 151, 160
Aukus nuclear submarine deal 150
authoritarianism, populist *see* democratic deficit in nuclear politics

Bacevich, Andrew J. 117
BAE Systems 115, 116
Baker, John Carl 9
Bangkok Treaty 33
Ban Treaty (Treaty on Prohibition of Nuclear Weapons) 18, 46, 143, 147, 154, 155, 160
Bell, Duncan 104
Benedict, Kennette 137
Bevin, Ernest 135
Biden, Joe (and Biden administration)
  arms control measures 12–13, 33, 45, 147, 151
  inauguration (2021) 17, 130, 131, 133, 138
  Iran, negotiations with 148, 151
  nuclear weapons, views and rhetoric on 145, 155
  nuclear weapons development 155
  Open Skies Treaty, re-entry ruled out 66
  overseas nuclear facilities upgraded 153
  Presidential election victory (2020) 131, 159
  Xi Jinping, meeting with 156
bikinis 104–5
Billingslea, Marshall 111, 112
Birks, John W. 120
Biswas, Shampa 50, 55, 105, 137
Black Lives Matter movement 101, 108, 113
Black Panther Party 106–7
Bon Iver 84
Booth, Ken 48, 136, 137
Borger, Julian 133
Boyd, Matt 156

Braut-Hegghammer, Målfrid 44
Brezhnev, Leonid 29
Bridgers, Phoebe 83–4, 85
Brodie, Bernard 22–3, 46
Brooks, Rayshard 107, 113
Bull, Hedley 61
Bulletin of the Atomic Scientists 84–5
Burke, Anthony 48, 53
Burns, William 152
Bush, George H.W. 30, 31
Bush, George W. 31, 34, 35
Bush, Kate 28
Butler, George Lee 29

Callamard, Agnès 68
Calvert, Jonathan 87, 92
Campaign for Nuclear Disarmament (CND) 27, 81
Campbell, Andrew 132
Canticle For Leibowitz, A (Miller, 1959) 27
Capitol building attack (6 January 2021) 17, 49, 129–30, 131–3, 138, 139, 142, 143
Carter, Jimmy 29
Chauvin, Derek 99, 100
Chernobyl (TV miniseries, 2019) 5–6, 11
Chernobyl nuclear power plant disaster (1986) 6, 11, 28
Chinese nuclear policy
  'no-first-use' policy 45
  nuclear testing 151, 157
  nuclear weapons development 46, 111–12, 149
  trilateral treaty demands rejected 60, 66, 67, 110
Churchill, Winston 23–4
Chyba, Christopher 44, 45
Cirincione, Joe 33
civil wars 141–2, 147
Clark, Brett 118–19
climate change
  as crisis interlinked to others 48, 84, 110
  harms of 128–9
  militarism and exterminism contributing to 17, 118, 119–21, 122, 127–8, 147, 158–9
  see also environmental harms

Clinton, Bill 32
Clinton, Hillary 39–40, 132
CND (Campaign for Nuclear Disarmament) 27, 81
Cohn, Carol 49–50
Cold War *see* First Nuclear Age
Collina, Tom 110, 133
colonialism *see* nuclear imperialism
Comprehensive Nuclear Test Ban Treaty (CTBT) 31–2, 110
Cooke, Steve 137
Cooper, Neil 63
Corbyn, Jeremy 81, 85
Corker, Bob 78
Coupe, Joshua 122
COVID-19 pandemic
  defence spending during 89–90, 116–17, 123–4
  'money meant for face masks' scandal 123, 124–5
  nuclear security lessons 16, 48–9, 89, 90–2, 95–8
  outbreak 87
  state responses 11–12, 87, 89, 94–5, 97, 115
  state unpreparedness 87–8, 93, 94, 146, 158–9
Cox, Robert W. 46, 47
Craig, Campbell 67
Crenshaw, Kimberlé 49
critical analysis of Third Nuclear Age
  critical nuclear studies 46–9, 62–3
  discourse analysis 5, 43, 51–2
  intersectional approach 40, 49, 113–14, 159
  nuclear culture 3–6, 13, 16, 52–3, 85–6
  nuclear exterminism 8–10, 14, 38, 53–5, 118
  nuclear harms *see* nuclear harms
  nuclear imperialism *see* nuclear imperialism
  nuclear masculinity 13, 48, 49–50, 157, 158
  research resources and methods 4–5, 15–16, 56–7
Croft, Stuart 61, 62
Crutzen, Paul J. 120
CTBT (Comprehensive Nuclear Test Ban Treaty) 31–2, 110

Cuban missile crisis 25, 28
cultural representations *see* popular culture

Dahl, Robert 134
Daniel, J. Furman 4
'Davy Crockett' tactical weapon 24
Day After, The (Meyer, 1983) 4 28
decolonial nuclear studies *see* nuclear imperialism
defence spending data 76, 89–90, 91, 116–17, 122–4
democratic deficit in nuclear politics
  authoritarian populism and democratic backsliding 17, 121, 130, 133, 138–43, 147, 159–60
  nuclear 'apartheid' 50–1, 101, 105, 108, 134, 137–8
  outlined 55–6, 134, 138
  policy decisions, opacity and lack of oversight 97, 135, 136–7, 140
  sole authority over launch decisions 56, 90–1, 132–3, 135–6, 146, 147
Derrida, Jacques 5, 43
deterrence theories
  of First Nuclear Age 20–1, 22–4, 35, 45, 67
  low-yield warheads, deterrence justification 77–8
  nuclear 'sponge' idea 17, 126–7, 129
  nuclear taboo *see* nuclear taboo
Deudney, Daniel 67, 136
disarmament measures *see* arms control measures
discourse analysis 5, 43, 51–2
disinformation 25, 82, 89, 94–5, 140, 141
Doomsday Clock 84–5, 151, 156
Dowd, Maureen 79
Downman, Maxwell 43
Driver, Christopher 27
drone strikes 78–9
Dr Strangelove (Kubrik, 1964) 3, 4, 27, 52

ecological harms *see* environmental harms
Egeland, Kjølv 69, 72

Einstein, Albert 8, 19–20, 21, 22, 37, 103
Eisenhower, Dwight D. 117–18
Engel, Eliot 66
Enloe, Cynthia 117
Enola Gay B-29 bomber 7, 144, 145
environmental harms
  indigenous communities, disproportionate impact 10, 13–14, 50, 51, 55, 103–5, 108
  militarism and exterminism contributing to 17, 118, 119–21, 122, 127–8, 147, 158–9
  'nuclear winter' 53, 96, 120–2, 156
  see also climate change; nuclear harms
Eschle, Catherine 52
Esper, Mark 60, 65
exterminism, nuclear 8–10, 14, 38, 53–5, 118

Fail Safe (Lumet, 1964) 3
fake news 25, 82, 89, 94–5, 140, 141
feminist theory 13, 49–50, 52
Fender, Sam 74–5, 81, 83, 84, 85, 86
Fihn, Beatrice 91
First Nuclear Age
  arms control measures 25–7, 29–30, 63
  commencement 19–21, 37, 102–3
  deterrence theories 20–1, 22–4, 35, 45, 67
  general characteristics 2, 8, 22, 30–1, 37–8
  Japanese atomic bombings *see* Hiroshima and Nagasaki bombings
  'near-miss' incidents 28–9, 126
  nuclear weapons arsenals 1, 21, 24, 25, 30, 64
  nuclear weapons development 24–5
  nuclear weapons testing 21, 22, 103–5, 148
  peace movements 27, 28, 54, 105–7, 150
  popular culture of 3, 4, 27–8, 104
Floyd, George 16, 99, 100–1, 107, 108, 112–13, 114, 146
Freedman, Lawrence 62

French nuclear policy 21, 22, 26, 96, 123, 136, 148
Frisch, Otto 20–1
Fu Cong 66
Futter, Andrew 1–2, 92, 137

Gaddafi, Muammar 34
Gardner, John W. 60
gendered language (nuclear masculinity) 13, 48, 49–50, 157, 158
Gerstein, Daniel M. 88
'Global War on Terror' 2, 8, 34–5, 38
Godzilla (Honda, 1954) 28
Goldsboro B-52 crash (1961) 28
Gorbachev, Mikhail 1, 29, 30, 63, 64, 154–5
Gordon, Philip H. 79
Gorman, Amanda 17, 130, 131, 133
Gould, Kenneth A. 119
Gove, Michael 90
Graham, Shirley 106
Greenham Common protests 27, 150
Gregg, Aaron 115, 123, 124
Grenfell Tower fire disaster (2017) 115
Grove, Jairus 48
Groves, Leslie 24, 79–80
Gusterson, Hugh 112, 118
Guterres, António 2, 60, 129, 152, 154

Habiger, Eugene E. 36
hacking of nuclear weapons 36
Hahn, Otto 19
Hall, Stuart 52
Halperin, Morton 61
Hancock, Matt 93
Hanson, Marianne 135, 136
harms, nuclear *see* environmental harms; nuclear harms
Hecht, Gabrielle 34
Herbert, Jon 41
Hershey, John 81
hibakusha (victims of Hiroshima and Nagasaki bombings) 6–7, 111
Hiroshima and Nagasaki bombings
 background to 19–21, 37, 102–3
 casualties and other harms 6–7, 21, 116
 Enola Gay B-29 bomber involved in 7, 144, 145
 investigative journalism on 7–8, 81
 launch decision 135
 nuclear testing to mark 75th anniversary 17, 111
 racism factor 102–3, 105, 147
Hogg, Jonathan 53, 81
Hohmann, James 42
Hooks, Gregory 119–20
Horton, Richard 94–5
Hughes, R. Gerald 28
humour 71, 72–3
Hurston, Zora Neale 106
Hussein, Saddam 34, 35
hypermasculinity, nuclear 13, 48, 49–50, 157, 158
hypersonic missiles 45, 75–7, 80, 146, 151
'Hypersonic Missiles' (Fender, 2019) 74–5, 81, 83, 85, 86

Ignatenko, Lyudmilla and Vasily 6–7
imperialism, nuclear *see* nuclear imperialism
Indian nuclear policy 22, 31, 33, 45, 46, 102
India-Pakistan nuclear warfare, predicted effects 121–2
indigenous communities, nuclear harms to 10, 13–14, 50, 51, 55, 103–5, 108
INF (Intermediate-Range Nuclear Forces) Treaty
 adoption 1, 4, 29–30, 63
 significance 61, 63–6, 72
 US withdrawal from 1, 16, 42, 44, 59, 60, 61, 64–5, 111, 146
Inglehart, Ronald 139
International Atomic Energy Agency 26, 34, 149, 150
international law *see* arms control measures
International Relations
 critical approaches *see* critical analysis of Third Nuclear Age
 institutional racism in 109–10
intersectionality 40, 49, 113–14, 159
Intondi, Vincent J. 105–7

Iran
  international nuclear inspections in 149, 150
  Joint Comprehensive Plan of Action 32, 44, 79, 80, 111, 112, 148, 151
  Natanz nuclear facility, Israeli cyber attack on 148–9
  US drone attacks on 78–80
Iraq War (2003–11) 34
Iron Maiden (rock band) 28
Israeli nuclear policy 22, 31, 123, 136, 148

Jackson, Susan T. 117
Jackson, Van 42
Jägermeyr, Jonas 121–2
Jantz, Eric 104
Japanese atomic bombings *see* Hiroshima and Nagasaki bombings
Johnson, Boris 82, 90, 93–4, 140, 146, 159
Joint Comprehensive Plan of Action (Iran deal) 32, 44, 79, 80, 111, 112, 148, 151
Jones, Alex 132
Jorgenson, Andrew K. 118–19

Kahn, Herman 46
Kaplan, Fred 135
Keating, Jeffrey 119
Kennedy, John F. 25–6, 28
Khan, Abdul Qadeer 33, 151
Khan, Imran 121, 151, 159
Khrushchev, Nikita 25, 28
Kimball, Daryl 110–11
Kim Jong-un 42, 48, 50, 110–11, 136, 153, 156, 159
Kim, Michelle Hyun 84
King, Martin Luther 106
Kissinger, Henry 46, 105, 149
Koch, Lisa Langdon 69
Korda, Matt 65, 111, 148
Kowalski, James 36
Kristensen, Hans 90–1
Kultez, Valerie 104

Latham, Rob 35
Leake, Jonathan 87

Legvold, Robert 44, 45
Lengefeld, Michael R. 120
Le Pen, Marine 140
Levin, Bess 90
Libyan nuclear policy 34
Limited Test Ban Treaty 26, 105
Loken, Meredith 109–10
Lord, Ellen 124, 125
low-yield warheads 45, 76, 77–8, 80, 111, 146, 155
Lucas, Edward 45
Lutz, Catherine 117

Mac, Annie 74, 75
McClain, Elijah 113
McCrisken, Trevor 41, 43
MacKenzie, Donald 80, 81
McNamara, Robert 28
Macron, Emmanuel 44, 159
MAD (mutually assured destruction) 23–4, 45, 67
Maddock, Shane J. 105
Mad Max (Miller, 1979) 27
Malcolm X 106
Manhattan Project 20, 21, 103
masculinity, nuclear 13, 48, 49–50, 157, 158
Mattis, James 42
media representations
  news media 81–3, 136
  popular culture *see* popular culture
Medvedev, Dmitry 32, 152
Meier, Oliver 139–40
memes 52, 56, 82, 83
Michaels, Jeffrey 41
militarism
  concept 8–9, 53–4, 117–18
  environmental harms of *see* environmental harms
  political economy of *see* political economy of nuclear weapons
Miller, Nicholas L. 44
Milley, Mark 133
Minihan, Mike 156
misinformation 25, 82, 89, 94–5, 140, 141
Modi, Narendra 121, 141, 159
Moniz, Ernest J. 65
Morgenthau, Hans 61
Moruroa Files 148

Müller, Harald 68
Musgrave, Paul 4
Musk, Elon 59, 69–70, 70–1
Mutimer, David 63
mutually assured destruction (MAD) 23–4, 45, 67

Nagasaki bombings *see* Hiroshima and Nagasaki bombings
Narang, Vipin 44
NATO (North Atlantic Treaty Organization) 23
Nena 28
neoliberal nuclear procurement *see* political economy of nuclear weapons
Netanyahu, Benjamin 159
news media 81–3, 136
New START (New Strategic Arms Reduction Treaty)
　renewal (2021) 12–13, 45, 147
　Russian participation suspended 2, 154, 156, 157
　significance 32–3
　US non-renewal threat 33, 42, 111
Non-Proliferation Treaty (NPT) 26, 31, 72, 96, 105, 108, 137, 157
non-use of nuclear weapons *see* nuclear taboo
Norris, Pippa 139
North Korean nuclear policy
　hostility with US over 42, 48, 50
　nuclear testing 31, 34, 110–11, 148, 150, 151, 153, 155
　nuclear weapons production 150, 156
Northrup Grumman ICBM contract 17, 125–7
NPT (Treaty on the Non-Proliferation of Nuclear Weapons) 26, 31, 72, 96, 105, 108, 137, 157
nuclear accidents and 'near-miss' incidents
　Chernobyl nuclear power plant disaster (1986) 6, 11, 28
　in First Nuclear Age 28–9, 126
　in Second Nuclear Age 35–6
　in Third Nuclear Age 42
'nuclear ages' concept 1–2
nuclear 'apartheid' 50–1, 101, 105, 108, 134, 137–8

nuclear culture 3–6, 13, 16, 52–3, 85–6
nuclear exterminism 8–10, 14, 38, 53–5, 118
nuclear harms
　environmental *see* environmental harms
　model predictions 92–3, 95–6, 121–2, 156
　radiation sickness effects 6–7, 104
nuclear imperialism
　critical nuclear race theory, need for 112–14, 159
　defined 13
　indigenous communities, nuclear harms to 10, 13–14, 50, 51, 55, 103–5, 108
　(institutional) racism 16–17, 49, 101–2, 107–12
　Japanese atomic bombings, racism factor 102–3, 105, 147
　nuclear 'apartheid' 50–1, 101, 105, 108, 134, 137–8
　orientalism 17, 35, 51, 111–12
　peace movements, African American activism 105–7
nuclear masculinity 13, 48, 49–50, 157, 158
nuclear 'sponge' idea 17, 126–7, 129
nuclear taboo
　erosion 16, 45, 58–9, 69–71, 72–3, 140, 160
　reinforcement need 158
　theory of 36–7, 67–9
nuclear testing
　bans 26, 31–2, 72, 105, 100
　by China 151, 157
　environmental harms of *see* environmental harms
　of first bombs 21, 28
　in First Nuclear Age 21, 22, 103–5, 148
　by France 148
　by India and Pakistan 22, 33, 102
　by North Korea 34, 148, 151, 153, 155
　Russian resumption 33, 65–6, 146, 153
　US resumption 17, 42, 60, 65–6, 110–11, 146

nuclear weapon-free zones 26–7, 33
nuclear weapons arsenals
   in First Nuclear Age 1, 21, 24, 25, 30, 64
   in Second Nuclear Age 31, 32
   in Third Nuclear Age 1, 41, 153–4
   see also political economy of nuclear weapons
nuclear weapons development
   first bombs 19–21
   hypersonic missiles 45, 75–7, 80, 146, 151
   by India and Pakistan 33
   by Iran 44
   low-yield warheads 45, 76, 77–8, 80, 111, 146, 155
   by North Korea 34, 42
   tactical weapons 24, 30, 45
   tests see nuclear testing
   see also political economy of nuclear weapons
NUKEMAP (online tool) 92
Nunn, Sam 65

Obama, Barack 32, 34, 41, 78
On the Beach (Shute, 1957) 27, 104
Open Skies Treaty 66, 111
Oppenheimer (Nolan, 2022) 156
orientalism 17, 35, 51, 111–12

Pakistan-India nuclear warfare, predicted effects 121–2
Pakistani nuclear policy 31, 33, 46
Pappalardo, Joe 89–90
Partial Test Ban Treaty 26, 105
Paul, Thazha V. 68
peace movements 27, 28, 54, 105–7, 150
Peierls, Rudolf 20–1
Pelindaba Treaty 33
Pelopidas, Benoît 69
Pence, Mike 49, 132–3
Petrov, Stanislav 29
Pifer, Steven 89
Planet of the Apes (Schaffner, 1968) 27
Pocan, Mark 123
political economy of nuclear weapons
   COVID-19 pandemic, lessons from 89, 95, 97
   defence spending data 76, 89–90, 91, 116–17, 122–4

   introduction to study 115–16
   lobbying and Pentagon 'revolving door' 49, 125, 129, 136
   militarisation of US economy 116–18, 123, 147, 148, 150–1, 159
   'money meant for face masks' scandal 123, 124–5
   Northrup Grumman ICBM contract 17, 125–7
Pompeo, Michael 1, 60
popular culture
   critical analysis of 3–4, 13, 16, 52–3, 85–6
   of First Nuclear Age 3, 4, 27–8, 104
   of Second Nuclear Age 35
   of Third Nuclear Age 5–6, 11, 74–5, 80–6, 157
populist authoritarianism see under democratic deficit in nuclear politics
postcolonial nuclear studies see nuclear imperialism
post-truth politics 82, 140
'prepper' movement 35
Press, Daryl G. 69
Procter, James 53
procurement, nuclear see political economy of nuclear weapons
Putin, Vladimir
   arms control measures adoption 31, 33, 147, 151
   on INF Treaty demise 60
   nuclear weapons, views and rhetoric on 2, 45, 65, 76, 144, 152, 153, 155, 156
   power to launch nuclear weapons 136
   see also Russian invasion of Ukraine (2022–)
Pym, Olivia 84

QAnon conspiracy theory 132

Raab, Dominic 90
racism see nuclear imperialism
radiation sickness 6–7, 104
Raisi, Ebrahim 149
Rarotonga Treaty 27
Reagan, Ronald 1, 4, 29, 63, 64, 107

realism 46–7
Reid, Jimmy 137
Rice, Condoleezza 34
Robock, Alan 121
Roosevelt, Franklin D. 18, 20, 21, 37, 135
Roy, Arundhati 101, 102
Russian invasion of Ukraine (2022–)
  casualties and other harms 158
  'dirty bomb' allegation against Ukraine 155
  Putin's nuclear threats 2, 45, 144, 152, 153, 155, 156, 160
  stability hopes shattered by 12–13, 85, 156
  Ukraine's call for nuclear defences 153
  US responses 145, 152
  Zaporizhzhia nuclear plant endangered 154
Russian nuclear policy see Second Nuclear Age; Third Nuclear Age

Sagan, Carl 53, 120
Sagan, Scott D. 69
Said, Edward 51
SALT I and II (Strategic Arms Limitation Talks) 29
Samuel, Olamide 109
Sanders, Bernie 123
Sanders-Zakre, Alicia 91
Sauer, Tom 63
Scarry, Elaine 56, 137, 138
Schelling, Thomas 61
Schwab, Gabriele 59, 103, 113–14
Scott, Len 28
Second Nuclear Age
  arms control measures 31–3, 37
  commencement 30–1
  deterrence theories 36–7
  general characteristics 2–3, 8, 38
  'near-miss' incidents 35–6
  nuclear terrorism fears 33–5, 142
  nuclear weapons arsenals 31, 32
  popular culture of 35
Semipalatinsk Treaty 33
Singer, J. David 119
Smetana, Michal 68
Smith, Chad L. 119–20
Smyth, Henry De Wolf 7
social media memes 52, 56, 82, 83

Soleimani, Qasem 78, 79, 80
Soros, George 132
SORT (Strategic Offensive Reductions Treaty) 31, 32, 64
Soviet nuclear policy see First Nuclear Age
START (Strategic Arms Reduction Talks) 29–30
START I Treaty 30, 31, 64
START II Treaty 31
Star Wars missile defence system 29
Stewart, Mallory 145
Stimson, Henry 7
Strassmann, Fritz 19
Strategic Arms Limitation Talks (SALT I and II) 29
Strategic Arms Reduction Talks (START) 29–30
Strategic Offensive Reductions Treaty (SORT) 31, 32, 64
Sturgeon, Nicola 82, 85
Swinson, Jo 81–3, 85
Szilard, Leo 19–20, 37, 103

Tabatabai, Ariane 79
taboo, nuclear see nuclear taboo
tactical nuclear weapons 24, 30
Takaki, Ronald 102–3
Tannenwald, Nina 36–7, 67–8
Tatenhove, Jason van 142
Taylor, Breonna 107–8, 113
Taylor, Bryan C. 136–7
Teaiwa, Teresia 104–5
Terminator, The (Cameron, 1984) 27–8
testing of nuclear weapons see nuclear testing
Third Nuclear Age
  arms control measures 12–13, 18, 33, 45–6, 143, 147, 151, 160
  commencement 1, 16, 40–4, 59, 60, 67
  concept 1–2
  democratic deficit see democratic deficit in nuclear politics
  general characteristics 2, 3, 8, 22, 44, 65–6
  'near-miss' incidents 42
  nuclear taboo erosion 16, 45, 58–9, 69–71, 72–3, 140, 160

nuclear weapons arsenals 1, 41, 153–4
nuclear weapons development *see* nuclear weapons development; political economy of nuclear weapons
nuclear weapons testing *see* nuclear testing
popular culture of 5–6, 11, 74–5, 80–6, 157
potential end of 157–60
see also critical analysis of Third Nuclear Age
Thompson, E.P. 8–9, 10, 38, 53–5, 118, 122
Threads (Jackson, 1984) 28
Tillerson, Rex 41
Tlatelolco Treaty 26–7
Tomero, Leonor 150–1
Toon, Owen B. 121
Top Gun: Maverick (Kosinski, 2022) 3, 153
Torbati, Yeganeh 115, 123, 124
Toro, Tom 97
TPNW (Treaty on Prohibition of Nuclear Weapons) 18, 46, 143, 147, 154, 155, 160
Treaties *see* treaty name
Truman, Harry S. 103, 105, 106, 135
Trump, Donald
  administration *see* Trump administration
  classified documents allegation 154
  COVID illness hospitalisation 90–1, 146
  defence procurement, views on 125
  immigrants, views and rhetoric on 112
  impeachments 159
  Iran, views and rhetoric on 79–80
  nuclear weapons, views and rhetoric on 40–3, 48, 50, 152
  'nuking' hurricanes proposal 16, 57, 58, 70, 71, 146
  Presidential election victory (2016) 39–40, 139
  Presidential election defeat (2020) and 'steal' claim 131, 132, 139
  re-election hopes 157

Trump administration
  COVID-19 pandemic unpreparedness 88
  immigration policies 112
  INF Treaty withdrawal 1, 16, 42, 44, 59, 60, 61, 64–5, 111, 146
  Iran, drone strikes on 78–80
  Joint Comprehensive Plan of Action (Iran deal) withdrawal 44, 79, 80, 111, 112
  New START, threatened non-renewal 33, 42, 111
  Nuclear Posture Review (2018) 41, 77–8, 111
  nuclear testing by 17, 42, 60, 65–6, 110–11
  nuclear weapons development *see* nuclear weapons development; political economy of nuclear weapons
  Open Skies Treaty withdrawal 66, 111
  US Capitol building attack by supporters *see* Capitol building attack
Truss, Liz 155, 157, 159
Turco, Richard P. 120
Turner, Kaitlyn M. 108–9, 113

UK nuclear policy 14–15, 46, 81–3, 97, 135–6, 148, 149
Ukraine, Russian invasion of *see* Russian invasion of Ukraine (2022–)
uranium mining 13–14, 50, 55, 103, 119
US nuclear policy *see* First Nuclear Age; Second Nuclear Age; Third Nuclear Age

Valentino, Benjamin A. 69
videogames 35, 52
Vieluf, Maren 139–40
Vigil (TV series) 150

Walker, R. B. J. 47
Wallace-Wells, David 128
Walter, Barbara F. 141–2
Waltz, Kenneth 46
'War on Terror' 2, 8, 34–5, 38

Wellerstein, Alex 92
Wells, H. G. 19
Wells, Matthew 69
Wendt, Alexander 47
When the Wind Blows (Murakami, 1986) 28
Williams, Heather 41, 76
Williams, Jenessa 84
Williams, Paul 102, 104, 107
Wilson, Nick 156
Wirtz, James J. 40

Wroe, Andrew 41
Wunderlich, Carmen 68

Xi Jinping 110, 136, 156, 159

Yeltsin, Boris 31, 32, 36

Zala, Benjamin 1–2
Zarif, Javad 79
Zelensky, Volodymyr 153
Zvobgo, Kelebogile 109–10

EU authorised representative for GPSR:
Easy Access System Europe, Mustamäe tee 50,
10621 Tallinn, Estonia
gpsr.requests@easproject.com

www.ingramcontent.com/pod-product-compliance
Lightning Source LLC
Chambersburg PA
CBHW051612230426
43668CB00013B/2082